SECOND THOUGHTS

SECOND THOUGHTS

Former Radicals Look Back At The Sixties

Edited by
PETER COLLIER and DAVID HOROWITZ

973.92
S445

MADISON BOOKS
Lanham • New York • London

Library of Congress Cataloging-in-Publication Data

Second thoughts : former radicals back at the sixties / edited by
Peter Collier and David Horowitz.
p.   cm.
1. Radicalism--United States--History--20th century. 2. United
States--History--1961–1969. 3. United States--Social
conditions--1960–1980. 4. Counter culture. I. Collier, Peter.
II. Horowitz, David, 1939–   .
E841.S4   1988   88–13427 CIP
973.92--dc19
ISBN 0–8191–7147–6 (alk. paper)
ISBN 0–8191–7148–4 (pbk. : alk. paper)

All Madison Books are produced on acid-free paper.
The paper used in this publication meets the minimum requirements of American
National Standard for Information Sciences—Permanence of Paper for Printed Library
Materials, ANSI Z39.48–1984.   ∞

There is one thing alone
that stands the brunt of life throughout
    its course;
a quiet conscience . . .
In this world second thoughts, it seems,
    are best.

—Euripides

CONTENTS

ACKNOWLEDGMENTS

The Second Thoughts Conference was made possible by grants from the Lynde and Harry Bradley Foundation and the John M. Olin Foundation, and by technical assistance provided by James S. Denton and the National Forum Foundation.

FOREWORD

WHY SECOND THOUGHTS?

Peter Collier

On the weekend of October 17–18, 1987, a group of former New Leftists met in Washington to talk about the '60s and the years since then. Some were activists who had worked to reform the system. The Rev. Richard Neuhaus, for instance, had founded Clergymen and Laity Concerned about the War, and David Hawk, of the Cambodian Relief Program, had been deeply involved in events surrounding the Khmer Ruge Genocide; Other participants, part of the heavy infantry of the Movement, had yielded to the temptation to spell America with a "k." Ronald Radosh, once a member of the Young Communist League, had as a Marxist historian helped develop the intellectual assault on "corporate liberalism." Jeff Herf had been a member of the Revolutionary Youth Movement faction of SDS when the Weatherman sect went underground and began its campaign of terrorism.

But if the experience of the people who came to the Conference was varied, there was a common theme in the conclusions they had drawn from it: the '60s left had failed them personally and been a disaster for the country. And so they came to Washington to bury the New Left rather than to praise it.

In this they were going against the grain. It is no coincidence that the Second Thoughts Conference, as this meeting was called, occurred at almost the exact moment that books such as James Miller's *Democracy Is In The Streets,* Maurice Isserman's *If I Had A Hammer,* and Todd Gitlin's *The Sixties*—all of them affirmative, indeed euphoric, views of the New Left experience—were being published. The Second Thoughts Conference was the equal and opposite reaction to these celebrations of SDS and the Movement, a voice of experience challenging the voice of innocence these authors adopted in talking about an era they insist was motivated primarily by an earnest idealism and moral passion they seem to believe is sadly lacking in the present day.

The participants at the Second Thoughts Conference gave testimony that serves as an antidote to any simplistic, monochromatic view of the "lessons" of the '60s. Others might try to manipulate the truth of the era into an exhilarating lesson for a new generation of activists, but those who came to Washington to tell about their second thoughts had a different curriculum in mind. For them the history of the Movement was a cautionary tale that should not inspire but rather give pause to the huddled millenarians awaiting the advent of the Next Left. For participants at this Conference, the leftism in which they had once believed was an infantile disorder. They felt that it was time to grow up and understand the past rather than condemn another generation to repeat it.

At one point in the proceedings I was talking to one of the dozens of left journalists who came to the Conference initially to jeer and ultimately to fret over whether or not it portended the advent of a movement of domestic contras. "Why Second Thoughts?" he asked me. I thought of the famous story of Emerson visiting Thoreau in jail when he was protesting the Mexican-American War. "Henry, why are you in here?" he asked. Thoreau replied, "Waldo, why are you out there?" It turned out, however, that the journalist was asking not about ultimate causes, but what had led to this particular meeting at this particular time and place.

The answer has to do with an article my friend and collaborator David Horowitz and I wrote for the *Washington Post* in 1985. Entitled "Lefties for Reagan," it laid out the reasons why the two of us weren't marching anymore, at least not to the drumbeat of the left; and why we had voted for a man whom, when he was governor of California in the '60s, we had denounced as a fascist and whose troopers we had fought in the streets. The article told why two people who had been present at the creation of the New Left in Berkeley in the late 1950s, who had later been civil rights and anti-war activists and editors for the New Left magazine *Ramparts* (in which capacity they were under surveillance by the CIA and FBI according to files obtained under the Freedom of Information Act), were, by the late '70s, feeling bruised by their convictions. The article discussed how what had happened in Southeast Asia, Africa, and Central America had led us to rethink our former commitments to charismatic Third World redeemers like Ho, Mao, and Fidel;

how we had been chastened by the new and brutal imperialism of the
Soviet Union; and how we had come to see democracy as precious and
perishable, imperilled by exactly those hostile ideologies we and other
New Leftists had once embraced with such enthusiasm.

Needless to say, we were denounced for our heresies by our old
friends; words like "traitor" and "turncoat" were murmured in our
presence, and we scented the unmistakable odor of the *auto da fe* when
we entered certain rooms. But there were also affirmations which convinced us that there were intelligent political life forms out there. One of
them came from Jim Denton, Director of the National Forum Foundation, who helped us put together the Second Thoughts Project whose
centerpiece would be a conference involving people like ourselves whose
gods had failed. We began contacting others we knew or were told had
gone through a process of reappraisal something like our own. Each of
them was an individual with an interesting curriculum vitae, but as we
talked with them, a profile of the second thoughter (as one journalist
called us during the Conference) began to emerge.

The second thoughter was different from his political ancestor in the
'30s whose retreat from leftism was caused by great Rubicons like the
Hitler-Stalin Pact which he refused to cross. For us there was no single
conversion experience; no epiphany on the road to Damascus. Rather
there was a slow glacial action of doubt whose cumulative effect was to
alter the personal political landscape, subtly at first and then decisively.
For many the trigger for reevaluation had been what happened in
Southeast Asia in the aftermath of the U.S. defeat in Vietnam, when the
bloodbath we all said would never happen did in fact occur. For others
the summary moment was the realization that the change in what we
had once called "the objective conditions" had accelerated the slow
motion imperialism of the USSR and made the Soviets dangerously
aggressive outside what had been their "sphere of influence." Whatever
the initial event, however, all of us began by making an attempt, often a
desperate one, to keep the faith; to make the left live up to our aspirations
for it. This is, of course, a syndrome Arthur Koestler identified more
than a quarter of a century ago when he wrote, "After the lost weekend
in Utopia, the temptation is strong to have one last drop." But once
under way, the process of transformation takes on a velocity of its own.
In the case of second thoughts, this transformation was hastened by the
way the true believers on the left treated our doubts; by the painful
discovery that our comrades much preferred the useful lie (such as the
one which held that Hanoi was not instituting a reign of terror in the
South in 1975, for instance, or that Castro had not created a vast gulag

in Cuba by the '80s) to the difficult but potentially cleansing truth. In the last analysis, second thoughters found, it was impossible not to feel, once again in Koestler's words, that "clinging to the last shred of the torn illusion is typical of the intellectual cowardice that prevails on the left."

Almost all of those who participated in the Conference had experienced a crystalline moment which embodied the new and disturbing insight they had had into the nature of the left, an insight which would ultimately cause them to turn their back on its smelly little orthodoxies. The experience black civil rights activist and journalist Julius Lester recounted is in this sense an epitome. It came in 1969 during the New Haven trial of seven Black Panther Party members accused of murdering another Party member named Alex Rackley, a time when Lester was writing for the radical publication *Liberation:*

> "Three Party members admitted their active participation. Yet black and white radicals were demonstrating in the New Haven Green and many articles were published in the radical press demanding that the New Haven Seven be freed. The rationale? It was impossible for blacks to receive justice in America. White sycophancy toward the black movement had set a new standard for madness, I sat down to the typewriter. . . . The editors of *Liberation* held the article for three months. Finally I had a tense meeting with them again in which they argued that the prosecution could use my article against the Panthers. Did I want that? How many times during my years in the Movement had someone tried to control my thoughts, my words, or my deeds by saying that such-and-such would not be in the interest of The People; that such-and-such would merely play into the hands of The Enemy; that I was being 'individualistic' and that people in the Movement had to 'submit to discipline'. . . ."

The conference provided many dramatic moments such as Lester's look back at the emotional self-brutalization demanded by the '60s left. There were also solemn moments such as theologian Michael Novak's description of how he came to reject the left because of its cynical insertion of Marxism and other temporal ideas into the spiritual realm. And Robert Leiken describing the McCarthyite attacks he had suffered at the hands of the left as a reprisal for criticizing the way the Sandinistas had stolen a democratic revolution from the Nicaraguan people. There were moments of humor such as P.J. O'Rourke's description of how a leftist gang called the Balto Cong had stolen his girlfriend and thus caused his second thoughts; or film critic and former Yale University activist Michael Medved talking about the radical chic in Hollywood which makes "airhead activists" out of brat pack stars and starlets. There were moments of passion such as the appearance of Fanor Avendano, a young Nicaraguan who had been jailed in 1979 for protesting the Somoza regime and by the Sandinistas 8 years later for organizing draft resistance against a rule he felt was far more tyrannical. Or a speech by Fausto Fonseca Amador, brother of FSLN founder Carlos Fonseca, who left the Sandinistas because of the ties with Moscow and Havana his brother helped forge and who now leads a non-violent self help organization of some 30,000 poor people in Costa Rica.

There were also moments of controversy. One of them occurred during an evening panel in which Hilton Kramer, Norman Podhoretz, William Phillips and others of an earlier generation turned an historical perspective on second thoughts into an attack on the "cultural barbarism" and "political illiteracy" of the '60s generation. This moment, one of the most interesting of the Conference, would be used by Sidney Blumenthal, a leftist partisan whose work appears in the lifestyle section of the *Washington Post,* as an example of how an attempt by David and me to transform disaffected former leftists into right-wingers had been de-railed. Of course we intended no such thing, and in fact this moment provided a good opportunity for second thoughters to understand that they could never be fully neo-cons or neo-libs, but were condemned by their experience in the '60s always to be *sui generis.*

Usually books comprised of conference proceedings merely put into print that which was dull enough when it was spoken aloud. *Second Thoughts* is, I think, quite another species of work. Some of the pieces included here were written as position papers; some are transcribed from oral presentations. All were of uniformly high quality. They allow this book, like the Conference itself, to offer a rare insight into the intersection between the personal and the political. They also capture a unique moment when members of a radical generation talk about finally coming home again. The imaginative reader will perhaps be able to look between the lines and see the earnest discussions in the corridor of the hotel where the Conference was held and even look in on the shouting matches in some of the rooms. It was almost like old times in the vigor of the debate, except that this time, of course, we were interested in preserving American values rather than trying to bring them low.

INTRODUCTION

A REVOLUTIONARY PARABLE

David Horowitz

It seems appropriate to begin this inquiry into Second Thoughts with a story which is a paradigm for the whole process of the political look backward, a story which comes to us through one of the participants at this conference, Doan Van Toai. Twenty years ago, Doan Van Toai was a supporter of the National Liberation Front in South Vietnam. During the Vietnam War, he led student strikes against the Saigon regime. And at the end of the War, he rejoiced when the North Vietnamese Army liberated South Vietnam. But after liberation, Doan Van Toai, along with hundreds of thousands of other South Vietnamese, was arrested by the liberators and put into prison. Emblazoned over the entrance to the prison where Toai was incarcerated was a slogan of Ho Chi Minh's which said: "Nothing is more precious than liberty or independence."

Doan Van Toai had been arrested more than once by the Thieu regime before the North Vietnamese victory, but this time it was different. Before he had been tried in a court of law, but now when he asked his captors what his crime was they said: "That is for you to work out." When he was arrested by the old regime, Doan Van Toai had never felt alone. His friends and supporters knew where he was and what he had done. But now, not even he was told what he had done, or when he might be released. Not even his wife was told where he was.

Thrown into the new Communist prison in a state of fear and uncertainty, Doan Van Toai met an old South Vietnamese Communist named Tang. Tang had been imprisoned 15 years under the French; he had been imprisoned 8 years under Diem; he had been imprisoned 6 years under Thieu. Now he was imprisoned by the guardians of the future about which he had dreamed all those years. And now Tang had a new dream.

1

In their Communist jail cell, Tang confided his new dream to Doan Van Toai. "My dream," he said, "is not that I will be released. My dream is not that I will see my family again. My dream is to be back in a French prison 30 years ago."

Tang's impossible dream was to restore his lost innocence and faith, to have his youthful vision of a revolutionary future back. Tang's dream tells us why second thoughts are so difficult to have, why first thoughts are so difficult to give up.

Because the dream of revolution gives meaning to an individual life, a sense of identity and power. The dream of revolution is also what gives power to the Left. It is the seductive illusion that allows the Left to recruit soldiers to its ranks and to neutralize its enemies. The Left celebrates murderers like George Jackson, and mass murderers like Pol Pot. The Left rationalizes genocide in places like Cambodia and Afghanistan and Tibet. The Left defends police states in countries like Vietnam and Cuba and, in fact, in all revolutionary societies. The Left supports imperialist interventions in Africa and Asia—socialist imperialism.

For 70 years the Left has created national gulags and has promoted an economic panacea, Marxism, which has impoverished hundreds of millions of the world's poorest inhabitants, and which today threatens millions of people in countries like Ethiopia with imminent starvation. Yet this Left is called "compassionate" and "idealistic" and "progressive," not only by its own propagandists, but by the representatives of the very liberalism it intends to destroy. To make cynicism and nihilism appear compassionate and idealistic—this is the power of the Left's seductive illusion. The illusion of a revolutionary redemption about which Tang dreamed in a French prison nearly half a century ago, while waiting for the liberation that never came.

The Czech novelist Milan Kundera has a name for this illusion. He calls it "totalitarian poetry." To explain this phrase, Kundera invokes the image of the French surrealist poet, Paul Eluard, who became a Communist and wrote hymns of praise to the Socialist future, who sang of peace, brotherhood and justice, while his own friends perished in the gulag he praised. Here is the way Kundera explains this secret power of the Left. "People like to say: revolution is beautiful. It is only the terror arising from it which is evil. But this is not true. The evil is already present in the beautiful; hell is already contained in the dream of paradise. It is extremely easy to condemn gulags, but to reject the totalitarian poetry which leads to the gulag by way of paradise is as difficult as ever. Nowadays people all over the world unequivocally reject the idea of gulags.Yet they are still willing to let themselves be hypnotized by totalitarian poetry, and to march to new gulags to the tune of the same lyrical song."

Second thoughts are thoughts which reject not just the gulags created by the Left, but the totalitarian poetry itself—the destructive and seductive illusion of a revolutionary future which makes the gulags possible in the first place.

That is why second thoughts are so dangerous to the Left. Because they expose the destructive illusion—the "totalitarian poetry"—that gives the Left its power. That is why Tang is erased in his own country, why we only know of his existence through Doan Van Toai. That is why the Left denounces all of those who have second thoughts as sellouts and renegades and seeks to erase them as individuals and discredit their truth. And that is why second thoughts need to be heard.

PART I

SECOND THOUGHTS ON A POLITICAL DECADE

Rev. Richard Neuhaus
Ronald Radosh
Michael Medved
Robert Leiken
Sam Leiken
Jeff Herf
Barry Rubin
David Horowitz
Peter Collier

CHAPTER 1

SECOND THOUGHTS

Rev. Richard Neuhaus

Second Thoughts are not about Damascus Road experiences, or about conversions. In fact, I think very much at the heart of the Second, Third, and Thousandth Thoughts that many of us have had is that language about conversion ought to be reserved for things more important than politics.

Second Thoughts are about incremental growth and prudential wisdom. They are about stumbling and trying to find your feet again. Twenty-two years ago (this week actually), we founded what was then called "Clergymen Concerned About Vietnam," which today lives on in a kind of shadowed afterlife as "Clergy and Laity Concerned." Along with Father Dan Berrigan and the late Rabbi Abraham Joshua Heschel, I was the first co-chairman of Clergy Concerned.

Just this past week I was talking at some length with the person who I guess will be writing the definitive biography of Heschel, and he was particularly interested in where I thought Heschel would be today. I think Heschel would be here today, among the Second Thoughters. I can't prove that. But over these years and especially in the years since his death in 1972, I have done my thinking and praying and speaking very much in the spiritual presence of Heschel. And I am confident that we would be in as wholehearted agreement today as we were so many years ago.

It is common in discussions when people ask "how did you get from there to here," for the response to be, "well, the world has changed; I haven't changed that much." And of course, there is some truth but also some self-deception in that. John Henry Cardinal Newman famously said "to live is to change and to be perfect is to have changed often." So I feel I have given strong evidence of being on my way to perfection.

And yet if I look back, the continuities strike me much more strongly than the discontinuities. In the early 1960s, I said that I hoped to be always religiously orthodox and culturally conservative and politically liberal and economically pragmatic. And 25 years later I still wish to be exactly that.

The great thing that has changed, of course, more than any change in me, it seems, is what has been meant by "politically liberal" over the last two decades. I should say that I am still a Democrat and a very loyal member of the party, except in recent years when it comes to voting. Well, you can't go along with the party on everything, you know.

But if I look back on those times on what some have called "that slum of a decade" of the 1960s, and the confusion and the chaos and the brutality of it, all that seems very clear. And yet also to be lifted up is the more difficult to remember and the wondrous moral coherence of it—for those of us who were there. In the civil rights movement in the late 1950s and early 1960s as a pastor in the Williamsburg Bedford-Stuyvesant section of Brooklyn, in a black parish, there the very air you breathed was hope. And it all made a great deal of sense. Not a utopian vision, but just a solidity of moral rightness, such as perhaps one could only experience when one is much younger. A kind of exaltation, and I am not embarrassed about that.

The stirring sense of a shared moral purpose that was once evoked for a brief time by the term "the Movement" must be understood. It was to be a band of happy warriors, to believe that somehow your contribution to fulfilling the American experiment—and it was to fulfill the American experiment and not to undo it or to oppose it—to believe that your contribution was to go up against what were then viewed as the secure and smug establishments.

Yet I also remember in the mobilization, I think it was in 1969 or maybe 1968, being on a platform with Norman Thomas. And it was one of those events in which the American flag was burned by a number of people. And Norman, with tears really in his eyes, said "Richard, don't they understand that our purpose is not to burn the flag, but to cleanse the flag?" And of course, the answer is that they did not understand. Or if they understood, they did not share that purpose.

There are dramatic breaks along the way to "second thoughts." For me in 1967, it was publishing an article in a national magazine questioning the logic of what was then called the "liberalized abortion movement," in which I made the argument, an argument I would still make today, that liberals planted their flag on the wrong side of that debate, and ought to have been on the side of compassion and caring and extending the community for which we accept shared responsibility. But it was with that article that for the first time in my life, I experienced what many others had experienced earlier, and that is the profound bigotry and anti-intellectualism and intolerance and illiberality of liberalism. And I confess that it came to me as something of a shock. It was my one deviation up to that point. But it was to be followed by many others.

Perhaps most dramatically in 1976 when Jim Forest of the Fellowship of Reconciliation still a pacifist and still very much on the left, when Jim and I after in vain trying to reach the representatives of Hanoi at the UN and elsewhere, drew up a petition to place in a number of newspapers and we decided that we would ask all the nationally prominent leaders in the anti-war movement to join us in protesting the massive, systematic, brutal violations of human rights by Hanoi after the fall of Saigon. And we wrote to 104 whom we and others identified as believable national leaders of the anti-war movement. And the division was just about 50–50, it was something like 51–53 on our side, with the others making very clear, in a way that shocked me, that there was no criticism of the left, regardless of what Hanoi had done, or any of the others who were on "the right side" of the revolution. That was a moment of truth produced by a moment of such massive mendacity.

There are many lessons that I have tried to draw, and one could go on and on and write books about this, and given my proclivities I probably will. But one was a dawning realization that America is a rather fragile and audacious experiment, and that the ideas upon which it is premised have enemies—not just accidental enemies, but enemies "in principle." It sounds like an obvious thing, but there you are. That America is an experiment that must be nourished and renewed. That it is not a natural way for a society to be ordered, this way of liberal democracy. It is a most unnatural thing in terms of the broad and brutal span of human history. And therefore it is not enough to contribute to it by going up against the assumed defenders of it. Because you discover at a certain point in your life that there are very few intelligent, principled, reflective, courageous defenders of it. And then you know that you have to join that small band which is the band in defense of the audacity of the American experiment.

Another lesson that one learns is that, as Richard Weaver said, ideas have consequences. Especially in the religious community it began to dawn on me more and more how there had developed a pattern of what could best be described as "no-fault prophecy," just like no-fault insurance and no-fault divorce. That people could get up and make prophetic pronouncements about this, that and the other thing, and then when things turned out to be quite the opposite of what they declared them to be, despite the rivers of blood and the piles of corpses, they would simply walk away from it and go on making their prophetic pronouncements somewhere else. And it was this profound and pervasive moral frivolity in the religious communities, but not only there, that began to impress itself upon me very deeply indeed. Prophetic posturing for which the poor pay the price. The poor in the Third World, and, I must say autobiographically for me, very powerfully, the poor in black Brooklyn, the community all-too-well described by the word "underclass" today.

Other lessons: never to form common fronts and coalitions, except with great care. A coalition without consensus on democratic values is corrupted from the start, and it will inevitably undermine whatever purpose for which it is formed, no matter how noble that purpose may be. And a test of such commitment to democratic values, not a sufficient test but a necessary test, is a considered and uncompromising anti-Communism. People who cannot say that they are anti-Communist without adding a dozen qualifications are doubtfully anti-Communist. Those who have read the history of this century must be able to say that they are anti-Communist with the same unqualified self-evident taken-for-granted character of saying that we are anti-Nazi—and yet that is a rare thing in our political and intellectual culture today.

Another lesson learned is that in international politics especially, one should never say what many of us said in the late 1960s, and that is that things could not get worse. It was said then that maybe all the talk about a bloodbath and what Hanoi would do afterwards, maybe there is some truth to that, we would say—I would say—but when you look at what is already happening, it could not get worse. That was a terrible, terrible self-delusion. It got worse, much, much, much worse.

Finally, I am asked, by some of my friends, a few with whom in the bond if not of political stability at least of religious commitment, I still maintain conversation—I am asked if it doesn't bother me to be found in the company of the conservatives? And I say "not at all, really; I haven't signed up with any faction or caucus, aside from that small band that understands the constituting beliefs and truths that must be defended and nurtured and transmitted to another generation." But among neo-conservatives and most conservatives, I have found in recent years a freedom of expression, for the most part, an intellectual curiosity and a moral seriousness that oddly enough I once associated with liberalism.

And so to live is to change and to be perfect is to have changed often, and to change is to acknowledge error and even moral culpability. We shouldn't find that process as difficult as some of us do. For, after all, there is forgiveness and there is tomorrow, and it begins today, and it is beginning right here.

CHAPTER 2

HANGING UP THE OLD RED FLAG

Ronald Radosh

Twenty years ago—indeed, even five years ago—I held firmly to most of the loyalties favored by those who see themselves as part of the American Left. In the 1960s I considered myself to be a revolutionary socialist, and I looked upon the emerging New Left movement as a group of spirited young people who would eventually see the need to develop a socialist ideology and would hopefully turn to Marxism as their guide. I did not predict, as some did, that when this New Left discovered Marxism, it would become the vehicle that would turn them towards nihilistic fantasies of violence that would culminate in the antics of the Weather Underground and the Brinks' murderers.

Like many others in the New Left, my political roots were in the radicalism of an earlier era—the pro-Communist milieu of the New York immigrant radicals of the '20s and '30s. As a youngster, along with other "red-diaper babies," I attended the Left-wing Camp Woodland, and the "progressive" Elizabeth Irwin High School, whose illustrious alumni included Weatherwoman Kathy Boudin, Communist leader Angela Davis, the Rosenberg children Michael and Robert Meeropol, the present editor of the fellow-travelling *Nation,* Victor Navasky, and Mary Travers of the folk-pop group Peter, Paul and Mary, who now sing the praises of the Communist regime in Nicaragua.

Working for my Ph.D. in history at the University of Wisconsin with William Appleman Williams, the dean of the "cold-war revisionists," I wrote for the new radical journal *Studies on the Left* in the early 1960s, and helped develop the concept of "corporate liberalism," an ideology that according to people like myself was responsible for the onset of the Cold War. Many of the radical theories that later led the Students for a Democratic Society into precipitous action against America came from

13

the political analysis we developed and were epitomized by the New Left slogan "liberals are the enemy." When the Vietnam War began to escalate, we invoked it as evidence of the validity of our theoretical exercises. When democratic socialists like Irving Howe condemned the New Left for "harsh criticism of Saigon and either silence about or approval of Hanoi," my comrades and I retorted that the enemy of our enemy was our friend. We regarded the Vietnamese war as a simple liberation struggle against the American aggressor. Therefore we responded with hostility to the suggestion that Communists might be enemies of freedom, or that a Communist victory in Vietnam might be worse for the Vietnamese themselves. To us, the Vietcong were progressive allies, and all anti-Communists our reactionary enemies. We held that anti-Communism was simply a mask for counter-revolution, and we sided with the anti-imperialist revolutionaries of the Third World.

It was a long and often jagged trajectory that led to my break with these assumptions. Of the episodes that hurried my progress, perhaps the most important was my direct experience with the Cuban Revolution. For those of us whose hopes for revolution lay in the Third World, Cuba was a beacon. Fidel Castro was a 20th Century Bolivar, a man who had succeeded in "liberating" his small island even though it lay in the direct path of the monster colossus to the North. During the summer of 1973, I was given the chance to travel to Cuba for a month with a small group put together by Sandra Levinson, Fidel's longtime cheerleader and one of New York's most prominent radical chic personalities. As I left for Cuba, I held to the sentiment expressed in 1960 by C. Wright Mills: "I am for the Cuban revolution. I do not worry about it. I worry for it and with it."

Instead, what I saw shocked me. While the Cuban population was squeezed into overcrowded buses in the August heat to ride to 12 hour a day jobs, we sat at lobster lunch at the *Habana Libre* nee Hilton, chatting with Regis Debray and members of Che Guevara's family, indulging ourselves in revolutionary political chit-chat. When we got to travel around the island, we were confronted by a sobering reality: horrible working conditions in factories, brute exploitation of the labor force, the lack of free trade unions, and constant exhortation to fulfill the Plan imposed from above. We also toured Havana's famed psychiatric hospital, where we found zombie-like political patients who had been heavily drugged. In answer to our concerned queries, the medical staff bragged about the many lobotomies they had performed. When one of our tour group expressed dismay at this, another who was to become a future founder of the Committee in Solidarity with the People of El Salvador

(CISPES) responded with a classic line: "We have to understand there are differences between capitalist lobotomies and socialist lobotomies."

It was moments like this that forced me to begin to confront the totalitarian cliches of the Left, which I had previously shared. During these discussions I found myself condemned by my comrades for opposing the Soviet invasion of Czechoslovakia in 1968; anything that undermined support for the USSR hurt Cuban socialism, I was told; our struggle was only against the United States. I was accused of arrogance by my fellow travellers for daring to criticize the Cuban Revolution. For "all its flaws," they said, the revolution was "a beautiful and profound reality."

When the Nicaraguan Revolution took place in 1979 my experience with Cuba made me cautious and then skeptical, especially as I saw the same unmistakable deceptions and betrayals of the revolutionary hopes. Yet, as if the past had never occurred, my comrades on the Left now proclaimed the Sandinistas to be the paladins of a new socialist order. Ten years after travelling to Cuba, I went to Nicaragua to report for *The New Republic* and observed with sadness the evolving totalitarian agenda of the Leninist *comandantes*. The criticisms I made of their agenda for Nicaragua from the perspective of democratic socialism resulted in further rupture of old friendships. Former comrades told me that I should be only "constructively sympathetic," and that I should write only about what was positive in the revolution. If I felt it necessary to report anything negative, it had to be attributed to the U.S. opposition to the revolutionary advance. As a former Marxist and pioneer of the New Left, Leszek Kolakowski had once observed: "[to the man of the Left] all negative facts to be found in the non–socialist world . . . are to be imputed to 'the [capitalist] system,' while similar facts occurring within the socialist world have to be accounted for by . . . the same capitalist system."

The third critical episode in my political evolution was the result of my historical research into the Rosenberg case, which was published in 1983 as *The Rosenberg File: A Search for the Truth*. As a high school student immersed in the culture of Communism, I had been initiated into the world of political activism in the campaign to save the Rosenbergs from execution as atomic spies. I was a member of the Youth Committee to Secure Justice for the Rosenbergs. Later, as an adult, I had continued to believe that the Rosenbergs were innocent, and that evidence would eventually come to light to prove that the U.S. government had conspired to frame and murder them.

When new evidence did become available in the form of the massive

FBI files opened to the public under the Freedom of Information Act, I decided to apply my training as a historian to a reconsideration of the case. But after securing the release of the previously closed FBI files on the case, I saw that rather than leading to the Rosenbergs' vindication, the new documents actually provided persuasive evidence that Julius Rosenberg was involved in spying activities on behalf of the Soviet Union and was in fact the central figure in an espionage ring. In an article written with Sol Stern in 1979 for *The New Republic,* and later in the book, I drew these conclusions, but also argued that the same documents revealed that the government had no legal case against his wife, Ethel, who had been prosecuted solely in the expectation that the pressure might induce her to turn state's evidence against her husband.

Once again, the response of the Left when confronted with the truth was that politics came first: Even if my conclusions were correct, my old political friends let me know I should have kept them to myself. Since I had not kept them to myself, I had betrayed the Left. People I had known for years stopped talking to me and no longer wanted to be seen associating with me; others said I had become a traitor to the Left and its heritage. As far as the Left was concerned, it was much better to perpetuate a lie, if the lie was "politically correct," than to tell the truth and let the chips fall where they may. Even some comrades in the democratic Left told me that although they always knew the Rosenbergs were guilty, I was wrong to have written my book. "This isn't a matter of history," one of them said to me, "but current politics." Even though I had clearly stated my opinion that the death sentences the Rosenbergs were given were unwarranted and therefore a "crime," the editor of the *Nation,* Victor Navasky, cynically spread the lie that I had "posthumously endorsed" those very sentences and thus provided ammunition for the "fascist" arsenal of the Reagan Administration. One former political friend and neighbor of mine—now a functionary at the "Center for Constitutional Rights" even wrote in a review that the book had "all the earmarks and objective consequences of an FBI cointelpro operation."

By this time I was ready to give up my hopes for a new anti-totalitarian Left and to agree with Kolakowski's wry conclusion that Communism was a "skull that will never smile again." The Left still believes, against all available evidence, that the "enemy of my enemy is my friend." When Leftists like Jesse Jackson defend Yassar Arafat, Fidel Castro and Daniel Ortega, it is because these terrorists and dictators are "on the side of the Left." But in 1987 I can no longer support the opponents and enemies of America's democracy, which, unlike the corrupt and dictatorial socialist states of the world, incorporates the very values—equality, liberty, justice—the Left claims to defend.

Looking back now, it is clear to me that that early "defector" from the Left, Sidney Hook, courageously understood the real struggle of our time when the rest of us were blind. Hook was right in defining the struggle as that of democracy versus totalitarianism and in arguing that despite all of its "failings, drawbacks and limitations, the defense and survival of the West was the first priority" for true socialists and humanitarians. In 1987, Hook's words seem especially prophetic, as does Dwight Macdonald's wise counsel from an earlier epoch to "choose the West." To make such a choice does not mean to abandon one's opposition to incorrect, unwise and even immoral policies, but rather in opposing such policies to honor the standards of our own democracy and strengthen its defense. America's enemies hold to no such standards. Hook and Macdonald knew what my generation of the Left has refused to recognize—that the Western democracies are living, developing societies open to change and responsive to popular pressures. The governments of our real enemies are not. By its very *raison d'etre*, the Left defines itself as standing on the other side of the barricades in the great battle of our time. Realizing this at last, I have said goodbye to the Left and hung up the old Red flag for good.

CHAPTER 3

IRONIES OF A POLITICAL DECADE

Michael Medved

During the Sixties it never occurred to me that I might be considered a radical. I functioned within an environment so isolated from the American mainstream that my left-wing political activism seemed normal, conventional, even moderate.

I began participating in demonstrations against the Vietnam war during my sophomore year at Yale in the fall of 1966, and my involvement in the Movement intensified as the war escalated. I led the drive to terminate ROTC at Yale and organized the well-publicized walkout from our senior class dinner to protest "war criminal" McGeorge Bundy's selection as guest speaker. During my first year at Yale Law School I became local chairman of the Vietnam Moratorium and helped to lure 50,000 protesters to the New Haven green in what the press described as the largest demonstration in Connecticut history.

My motivations in all this stemmed from a visceral distaste for the war rather than a coherent political critique. There was also the matter of self interest (and I was typical rather than exceptional in this). The idea that our government might ask me to sacrifice my one precious life in order to defend the regime in Saigon seemed to me an outrage, an obscenity. Like most other students at elite universities, I had little trouble developing schemes for avoiding the draft, and these personal strategies created what I perceived to be a moral imperative for political action.

In my role as an anti-war crusader I quickly learned all the soothing cliches so characteristic of the Movement. These cliches were woven into a liturgy which, endlessly chanted, became a matter of unquestioned faith. Our enemies in Vietnam were motivated by nationalism, not Communism; warnings of a "blood bath" following an American withdrawal from Southeast Asia were groundless McCarthyite scare tactics; if only we halted the bombing and came to the negotiating table, we could arrange for a coalition government that would provide a secure and peaceful future for all people in both North and South Vietnam. And so on.

My fervent belief in such propositions, combined with my discomfort with the more confrontational leaders of anti-war protest, led me into the "political process," as we somewhat defensively called it, rather than toward street violence. I volunteered in Eugene McCarthy's presidential campaign early in 1968, and then went to work full-time for Robert Kennedy once he entered the race. RFK's assassination in Los Angeles, just a few yards away from where I stood during the victory celebration at the Ambassador Hotel, seemed to place some sort of fateful, holy seal on my political commitment. Two years later I dropped out of Yale Law School to take a job as head speechwriter for Joe Duffey, Connecticut's anti-war candidate for the U.S. Senate. We won an upset victory in the Democratic primary, then lost to the Republicans in the general election. I went on to three more years of professional campaigning, working for the re-election of Representatives Al Lowenstein and Ronald V. Dellums, for George McGovern's '72 presidential race, and many other "crucial" contests. To me, and to many of my friends and acquaintances in the cause, these campaigns transcended mere politics. They were part of the eternal struggle between good and evil, desperate skirmishes in what we proclaimed to be the "battle for America's soul."

This lofty conception of my own political calling could not, of course, survive everyday encounters with reality. The first major blow to my youthful certainty came when I discovered that some of the enlightened office-holders whose "progressive" positions I most admired were actually quite loathsome human beings: cruel to their families, abusive of their assistants, ruthlessly exploitive of women, thoroughly manipulative of the public. In fact, by the time I walked out of my job with the Ron Dellums re-election drive (my last campaign), I began to suspect that there was an inverse connection between messianic rhetoric about the welfare of humanity, and ordinary decency to specific human beings.

I was "burned out" on politics by age 24, and full of skepticism about my leftwing heroes, but I continued for more than a year to accept their political ideas as revealed truth. Then in October of 1973 the Yom Kippur War shook my life with the force of a philosophical earthquake.

Up to that time, I had never taken a role in Jewish communal affairs or felt a particular concern for the fate of Israel. I had two first cousins who had chosen to make their life in Jerusalem, but they seemed to me no more at risk than other cousins living in Philadelphia. Along with most other Americans, I took Israel's security for granted and made jokes about the hopeless incompetence of the poor dumb Egyptians.

The Yom Kippur War instantly shattered these smug illusions. In the first days of the war, Soviet-supplied SAM missiles shot scores of Israeli planes out of the sky, while the Arabs advanced into the Sinai and on the Golan, inflicting heavy casualties. Despite confusing reports from the media, it became clear that Israel faced a far more desperate and threatening situation than it ever had in 1967.

This situation forced me to confront a fact that I had never before been willing to accept: that freedom, security and ultimately survival itself depend on military power.

This notion should have been painfully obvious to anyone familiar with the history of the twentieth century, but because of my long, desensitizing experience with the doublespeak of the peace movement it struck me with the force of a revelation. For years, we'd all been talking about the "uselessness" of planes and tanks and missiles, and condemning the folly of wasting money on "outmoded machines of death" that could otherwise have been spent on school lunches for hungry children. But suddenly, the survival of the Jewish state—and the lives of my own flesh and blood, serving on the front lines, as well as their wives and children at home—depended on precisely the sort of weapons that we had always derided.

I followed the progress of the war with a painful sense of irony. One of the military expenditures that I had energetically opposed during my political days and condemned as a flagrant waste of taxpayers' money, for instance, was the giant C–5A transport plane. In October of '73 this turned out to be the only plane capable of resupplying Israel with the tanks and jet fighter parts that it needed so desperately. I noted too that in those nightmarish, bloody days, all of our enlightened democratic European allies refused to grant the US landing rights for the crucial resupply of Israel, and we were forced to turn finally to Portugal, which I had always considered an evil, fascist state. Without refueling stops at the Portuguese Azores, the emergency resupply of the Israeli Army would not have been possible.

Domestic reaction to the war offered additional enlightenment. My former employer, George McGovern, in his capacity as chairman of the Senate subcommittee on the Middle East, urged the administration to take a cautious, "even-handed" policy toward the combatants. Fortunately, the President disregarded this advice. Richard Nixon—who'd always functioned as the devil himself in my anti-war theology—rushed to provide the massive and timely resupply that allowed Israel to defend itself successfully.

Before the Yom Kippur War my membership in that loosely defined family of liberal activists and peace crusaders seemed far more important to me than any atavistic ethnic identity as a Jew; after the war, when so many of those ostentatiously "good people" had turned their backs on Israel, my role as a Jew became more and more significant to me.

I began participating in the Soviet Jewry movement and became far more sophisticated concerning current realities in Russia. For the first time, I read Solzhenitsyn, devouring both volumes of *The Gulag Archipelago*. Though I had completed three courses in Russian history at Yale I had learned next to nothing about Stalin's genocide. (To this day, it is still possible for students to make their way through our finest secondary schools and colleges while remaining shockingly ignorant of the record of Communist oppression. Everyone is painfully aware of Hitler's murder of the six million, but we seldom encounter discussion of the even more prolific slaughter by Stalin and Mao).

In 1975, I found myself working for an advertising and public relations firm in San Francisco that specialized in ultra-liberal causes and candidates. I had begun annoying my associates by insisting that they listen while I read aloud selected passages from Solzhenitsyn during lunch hour. At one memorable party in Berkeley, I made myself a pariah and offended the hostess by suggesting that Scoop Jackson might have a better understanding of the Soviet Union than George McGovern.

But my final and emotional break with my remaining Left-wing friends didn't come until the fall of Saigon and the bloody denouement in Cambodia. Watching the eloquent news footage of the millions of peasants who fled before the Communist onslaught, I couldn't accept the notion that they were all guilty pro-western collaborators, or foolish victims of CIA propaganda. As events unfolded, and reports of widespread suffering and bloodshed became harder and harder to deny, I felt that those of us who had participated in the anti-war movement had a moral obligation to admit that we had been profoundly wrong concerning the postwar future of Southeast Asia and the nature of the Vietnamese and Cambodian Communists. When the Movement's mouthpieces not only refused to confront these errors, but sought instead to continue to blame the United States for the mounting horror, I lost my last remaining shreds of sympathy for the organized Left and its leaders.

After that, it was as though a spell had been broken. I began to view things in a wholly different light. Developments on both the global and the personal dimension conspired to push me light years away from my old orthodoxy.

When a burglar ransacked my Berkeley apartment, for instance, I spent weeks following up the case and trying to prod the police into action. They eventually apprehended the criminal but as I pursued the matter through the judicial process I found myself utterly shocked by the pointless leniency of the system. The 23–year-old black career thief had a record of seven prior convictions for burglary; this time around, the police managed to connect him to 11 different break-ins, including the one in my home. The public defender—an impassioned liberal—pleaded for mercy, citing his client's deprived childhood and his victimization by an unjust and racist economic system. To my absolute horror, this defense resulted in a suspended sentence.

After the trial I began to fear for my own safety—the defendant's murderous stares in my direction during the time his attorney was convincing the jury that he had been put upon by a malign "system" conveyed a clear threat and contributed to my decision to move from Berkeley to Los Angeles. The old saw declares that "a neo-conservative is a liberal who's been mugged by reality." In my case, I'd already begun moving to the right before becoming the victim of a crime, but that experience certainly helped to accelerate the process.

Research for my first book, *What Really Happened to the Class of '65?*, also played a role in my political education. Working with David Wallechinsky, one of my friends from high school, I set out to explore the lives of members of our own class in the ten years since graduation. We initially expected to focus on a series of colorful and exhilarating stories showing how a group of privileged, upper-middle class kids made the most of all the varied options available to them in a turbulent but exciting era. As we traveled the country and conducted our interviews, however, we discovered one depressing account after another—showing lives blighted by drug use, self-indulgence, dime-store spiritualism, arrogance, and ingratitude toward the previous generation. In short, our research, and the book that resulted from it, stood as an indictment of the so-called counter-culture and the fashionable ideas with which I had at one time identified.

Finally, most importantly, my growing commitment to Jewish study and observance helped me achieve a new political and cultural orientation. Unfortunately, American Jews have been so prominently identified with Left-wing causes that most people remain unaware of the profoundly conservative thrust of our religious tradition. The essence of traditional Judaism involves a reverence for the past and a distrust of human nature unrestrained by law—values that are difficult to square with the faddish liberalism of today.

For the past decade I've been trying to live my life as an observant Jew and to play a role in the current Jewish revival in America. I'm the president of a traditional congregation and educational center, a husband of two-and-a-half years, and the father of a ten-month-old daughter. I manage to combine this cautious, bourgeois personal life with a rather risky approach toward earning a living. Since 1976, I've pursued a career as author and critic—my seventh book appeared in 1986—and for the last three years I've co-hosted the national television movie review show called "Sneak Previews."

When I run into old friends from the '60s, they are not at all surprised at my professional focus, and only mildly shocked that I've become religious. What disturbs them far more is the change in my political outlook; they can scarcely accept the fact that I am now one of those who unequivocally prefers Calero to Ortega, Will to Wicker, and Bork to Brennan.

For my part, however, I recognize that my passage from the Left to a vigorous anti-Communist and pro-American position is neither unique nor exotic. Many others have made—and are making—similar journeys. The great value of the "Second Thoughts" project comes in assembling these stories, and demonstrating that we are not isolated aberrations, but part of a considered, and inevitable response to the trauma of recent history.

CHAPTER 4

THE CHARMED CIRCLE

Robert S. Leiken

Though my revolutionary time has faded into a smog of stale slogans, boring meetings and forgotten pamphlets, I remember vividly the day I got "radicalized." Nixon had announced the incursion into Cambodia, touching off a national student strike. But it wasn't solely the war news that converted me into a leftist. Like many of my comrades I was pushed to rebellion by profound but imperceptible and causal changes in my surroundings as much as I was pulled by the exhilarating political events of our times.

On that sunny May Day, while bombs rained on Cambodia and students marched, a friend and I strolled through Harvard Square contemplating, not without twinges of self-reproach, how to spend the holiday our pupils had presented us. My colleague Jack and I were out of step and out of sorts. We regarded demonstrating futile, dreary and pretentious. But partying was unseemly and studying unthinkable. Nothing seized us. One of those esoteric words I collected flapped inside my paltry, pedantic Joycean interior monologue: "velleity" (a slight inclination).

We stopped at one of the "Parisian" coffee houses, but we didn't feel a bit like Sartre. Colleagues at the next table reminded us that a faculty meeting had been called for 4 p.m. for a strike vote. "Were we going?" Finnegan's "aginbite of inwit" throbbed.

Notwithstanding intermittent flings of activism and Marxism, I had kept the war and the movement at a gentlemanly distance, preoccupied by a faltering marriage and the graduate school grind, diverted by my bizarre friends and the distraction of teaching history and literature to Harvard undergraduates. A few classmates took freedom rides to the South, but I stayed home or in the library. Yet by the late '60s, as my students' raucous demos and "love-ins" re-educated dowager Cambridge, the elegance of the New Criticism was losing its charm. In 1968 I spurned a "tenure track" appointment at a prestigious English Department for a job in M.I.T.'s radical Humanities Department. There I joined my friend Jack to teach an introductory Humanities course he had titled "God and Logic."

Yet the unceasing war posed relentless questions, and the Movement supplied increasingly plausible answers. I began to jest miserably that my best pedagogic efforts served only to equip future defense technicians with small talk for nights out with the wife. I was "polishing the ornaments of the military-industrial complex."

Those languorous lamentations were routine in my circle, where only a few had evolved out of the existentialism of the fifties into the revolutionism of the '60s. Lacking a larger stage on which to act out our epic yearnings, we secretly identified with the heroes we taught in school. But craving to be Aeneas, we suspected we were only Mitties. Our paragons were artists—the beatniks on the road, the exiles, Henry Miller, Robert Graves, Kerouac, Joyce. Later, prompted by the plight and the revolt of Blacks, by the contrast between our own and the "other America," and, above all, by the war, some of us took to the Movement. Revolution, Marxism and the Left might provide the "coherent social faith and order which could perform the function of knowledge for the ardently willing soul." (George Eliot, *Middlemarch*)

Jack and I resumed our wanderings despondently. Our May Day largesse was drowning in that banal void so familiar to middle-class intellectuals in "advanced capitalist society." Some friends passed. They were on their way to a demonstration at the State House. We languidly turned down their invitation: "What difference would one more body make?" Jack groused after they'd left.

Like myself, Jack sympathized with the civil rights and anti-war movements, occasionally helped out when a more committed friend asked, but kept it all at arm's length, vastly preferring to spend entire days reading philosophy or history or poetry. He was more learned than I and more cautious which perhaps saved him from, or deprived him of, my fate.

Jack went home to read. At three in the afternoon, I found myself suntanning on a roof with a female friend. My inclination towards her was slight. The afternoon, the "holiday", had slipped away. Was this how I was going to spend my days? The void threatened to open beneath my feet. Wasn't there something else to do? Suddenly—another dispensation from the students—I remembered the strike meeting. Seized by an unfamiliar sense of resolve, I departed politely but purposefully.

Anti-war chants rose from the packed Kresge auditorium as I drew near. Half the faculty appeared cowed; the other half awed. An activist stood at the door dispensing red armbands like tickets of admission. I put one around the sleeve of my brown corduroy sports jacket. I did not remove my badge of rebellion for weeks. Without knowing it I had entered a charmed circle.

Within a week I had tasted the supreme experience of imprisonment— for speaking at a high-school strike protesting Kent State. Already, I was a hero. Two hours in jail earned me my 15 minutes of fame in Cambridge. Within a year I was addressing 100,000 demonstrators on the Boston Common.

My conversion was all the more thorough-going for being somewhat belated. After donning the red armband, I did not look back—at least not for a decade. I abandoned old friends and old career to become a full-time "movement person" and revolutionary. The rupture was to shape my outlook over the next decade. The Left, like Adam in the garden, imparted names and values. The Movement constituted its own world.

Though it was dedicated to changing the world, the Movement centered in the university. Its great impact, one that lasted for years, for lifetimes, was made on those within its walls. Teachers like myself, often "politicized" by their students, worked with other teachers preparing educational programs to politicize *other* students. Radicalized students joined SDS and engaged in its factional fights. Some tried to organize high school students. But except for an occasional demonstration, faculty and students rarely engaged the rest of the population directly. Those that did formed small collectives and went to live in working class communities. But they usually remained isolated groups for many years until, in most cases, they dissolved and their leaders returned to the university. We were all better at imagining vast social change than at entering into the lives of its proposed beneficiaries.

Conservative friends who have never been on the Left tell me that leftists are driven by personal resentment and envy. Those were not my motivations, nor those of most of my comrades in the anti-war movement and on the revolutionary Left here and in Latin America. Milan Kundera's representation of Czech Communists ("the best, the most intelligent, the most dynamic") is surer: he pictures them dancing in a circle, dreaming "an idyll of justice for all." That dream, those noble purposes, exacted sacrifices, passionate intensity, and a commitment of time and energy which mere resentment and envy could never rival. Later when that nobility and idealism had been exhausted in allegiance to a sect and the idyll given way to a noxious regime, the circle narrowed, the dance became a goose-step, and the dancers chanted self-righteous cant.

Nonetheless I cannot agree with those who would segregate the two phases of the Movement—its original good "participatory democratic" side and its bad totalitarian denouement. The Movement was a magic circle for those within because of the depravity of those without. Its purity of purpose justified and even demanded unsavory means. For most of us that meant only an occasional lie, though even those would sometimes exact severe bouts of self-recrimination. Our struggle meant renouncing personal pleasures and goals, but it also provided a handy excuse to neglect family, friends, neighbors and country. Lovers of kind but haters of kindred, the "struggle" exacted all our benevolence and leisure. Thus we grew insensible to and alien to the life around us. Workers who were not "advanced"—advanced meaning those who accepted our ideas—were regarded with condescension, though they made up the bulk of the class we were assaying to liberate. We disdained the institutions of representative government in favor of our allegedly more democratic (because "participatory") street demonstrations, strikes and riots. This elitism mated the "participatory democracy" of the early movement with the revolutionary vanguardism of its later days.

The exclusivity of our charmed circle and its condescension towards the masses presaged totalitarian societies in which the ruling elite is sustained by obliging the population to spy on neighbors and friends: "As citizens, . . . supposed to live in the perfect unity of goals desires and thought. . . . As individuals, . . . expected to hate each other . . ." (Leszek Kolakowski). At the same time our arrogance conspired with a raging innocence, an incapacity to conceive of evils greater than those done by our parents, our capitalists or our government. Together they smoothed the path from protest at home to apologetics for "socialist" dictatorships. Meanwhile the circle narrowed, many dropping away in disgust or "selling out" to job or family. Those that remained did not have to live under the regimes they celebrated, thus they could still strut as champions of the poor and oppressed well after making it in the academic or publishing world.

Is the totalitarian gulag contained in the original "idyll of justice"? Must those who seek to create an earthly paradise inevitably create its opposite? But what movement for social change does not rest on such dreams and illusions? We cannot afford to bolt the door against any such movement and all such dreams. Yet I have not discovered a way to protect the dream from the gulag.

But these were not my worries at that time. Then, frustrated solely with the narrowness of the movement, its inability to communicate its Marxist ideas to the working class, I left Cambridge bound for Cuba and Allende's Chile after fresh epic heroes: Che, Fidel, Camilo Torres and their like. I wanted to see how the real revolutionaries did their thing.

I got no farther than Mexico and Central America, but that was far enough. The revolutionary Left in Latin America was indeed more familiar with the working class than my American comrades. Some organizations even boasted mass followings and some even worker-members. I lived a double life—as visiting American professor and clandestine revolutionary. But though my life was now thoroughly alienated, I felt that for the first time the contradictions of my bourgeois existence had been resolved. Endeavor was justified now. I worked not for the egotistical fruits of my own career or a reputation, but for humanity. No longer a stranger in the universe, I had found the warm comradeship, ardor and self-sacrifice of revolutionary work. I lived almost exclusively on enthusiasm.

But inside the revolutionary organizations, I began to observe disturbing cracks under the surface harmony of our enchanted circle. Despite a formal commitment to group democracy, "revolutionary intellectuals"—usually university students and young professionals—came to determine policy. Our tasks gradually shifted from supporting and publicizing the demands of the workers to leading them—a task for which one qualified by virtue of a few months studying political pamphlets, above all Lenin's *What Is To Be Done.* Support for popular grievances yielded pride of place to Marxist-Leninist study circles and to the interests of the small group or "party." Alleging the requirements of clandestinity, most leaders would continue to lead their relatively privileged petty-bourgeois lives; a few would go "live among the masses" in shanty towns, slums or peasant villages. But the distinction between workers—no matter how "advanced"—and their intellectual leaders was obvious just as soon as serious discussions began. Moreover, the inevitable rivalry among intellectuals led to a proliferation of small self-righteous groups. Squabbles among sects and parties took pride of place while the workers' desire to improve immediate conditions got slighted as "economist." Groups split apart and the workers returned to their less "advanced" companions. At the time I deplored the deleterious consequences of "sectarianism" for the revolutionary movement. Only after the first years of the Sandinista regime, did it occur to me to be relieved at our failures, and that the cracks in our circle foretold relations in revolutionary society.

Contrary to my expectations, workers and peasants in Latin America had little of the anti-Americanism of their mentors. However such feelings among the intellectuals, along with Leninism's promotion of revolutionary vanguards, rendered these leaders susceptible to Soviet propaganda. The Cubans, and to a lesser extent the Vietnamese, were Moscow's catspaws in the revolutionary movement. Local Communist parties were usually in disrepute. Instead, popular leaders were invited to Havana where they were seduced, bribed and indoctrinated. Seeing the machinations of Moscow and Havana at first hand gradually aroused my suspicions.

I heard my first systematic critique of the Soviet Union not from Cold War anti-communists but from revolutionary communist dissidents. The problem was not communism and subversion, but the betrayal of the revolution and of socialism. What made the Soviet Union evil was its resemblance to America. The Chinese criticisms of the Soviet Union as "socialist in word but imperialist in deed" suited my prejudices by fencing off "revolutionary" Marxism-Leninism from the Soviet aberration.

North Vietnam's conquest of South Vietnam and destruction of the N.L.F., Soviet-backed coups in South Yemen, Ethiopia, and Angola, the boat people, Pol Pot's atrocities, Vietnam's invasion of Cambodia, and the Soviet invasion of Afghanistan were part of a sequence of events which fanned the struggle on the Left over Communism and the U.S.S.R. It soon became apparent that the Left's ruling circles would not tolerate a politics which regarded the United States as anything less than the main, if not the sole, source of evil in the world.

Whereas in the Sixties the Left had boldly pried into the secrets of American imperialism, now its intellectual shepherds concealed or excused Soviet imperialism and communist atrocities, assuring that their flock remained incapable of imagining any evil greater than Reagan. No longer iconoclastic and audacious, the Left had become conservative, obscurantist and frightened of the facts. In the face of complexity it had been overcome by fatigue. It seemed to imagine that a "progressive" program could be framed simply by inverting everything the Right said. In the face of adversity—the souring of revolutions, the crisis of socialism, the malaise of the Third World—it resorted to stereotypes, equivocation, and deceit. Cant became its *lingua franca*.

Just as I was coming to realize that the Left was no longer consistently anti-imperialist (if it ever had been) but merely anti-American, Soviet expansionism in the Third World was driving me to the conclusion that the United States could be a defender of national independence and a positive force in world politics. But I was still far more a socialist than a democrat; my idyll was still being built in non-aligned socialist regimes like China, Zimbabwe and, perhaps, Nicaragua. Democracy was necessary chiefly because it provided better conditions for the struggle for socialism. My evolution to a thorough-going anti-totalitarianism required the direct experience of Sandinista Nicaragua.

My decade among Mexican revolutionaries, workers, peasants and *"marginados"* proved an invaluable apprenticeship. As Nicaraguans warily disclosed their plight and as Nicaraguan friends, many of them former revolutionaries or supporters, poured out their hearts to me, shock and sadness gave way to outrage. Though I'd visited Russia and Eastern Europe and had had one lengthy stay in Cuba, it took this intense daily exposure for me to take in the full evil of totalitarianism, a term I did not thereafter shrink to utter. Walter Laqueur, I believe, has observed that with the exception of Orwell, only exiles, or those like Koestler who had experienced it directly, had been able to comprehend totalitarianism. The feeling of being watched, heard, reported on by invisible technical or intimate human means, the clamorous exhortations from loudspeaker, radio, block committee, school teacher, and supervisor, the helpless, muffled popular outcry of "hoax" against a cynical clique that went on impoverishing and oppressing even as it boasted of its generosity and sympathy, the sense of entrapment—all this hardly begins to convey the conviction that this was something infinitely worse than what I knew of the stupid, brutal authoritarian regimes of the region. The maddening, specious Party cant, echoed by American flunkies and even journalists, that these desperate Nicaraguans esteemed or even tolerated their new rulers, who were too busy enriching themselves to notice how despised they'd become, provoked me into print.

My critical report on the Sandinistas, printed in *The New Republic* was met with blind fury on the Left and by its orchestrated effort at defamation. The Sandinistas were as valuable to the American Left as it had been to them. Its ranks, frayed by Cambodia, Afghanistan, and Mariel, had to be hardened against any threat to the restorative powers of Sandinismo, especially a threat from within. Revolutionary tourists were deployed to bear witness against my "lies." With supreme confidence they recited the views of "the Nicaraguan people," failing to notice that the gulf between their Sandinista hosts and most Nicaraguans was as wide as that between Western leftists and their own "masses."

The Movement's invincible condescension resurfaced whenever Leftist tourists bore witness to "revolutionary Nicaragua."

I was declared anathema and cast out of the charmed circle. Like Kundera "I have been falling ever since." Previously the dance had fallen into a lock-step and the revelation into a dogma, and now the idyll was revealed as a hoax. It is a curious fact that leaving the Left demands greater sacrifices than joining it. It is no less true that my excommunication was a second liberation. My free fall makes it now possible to approach social and political phenomena without the exhilarating but deceiving habit of abstraction and sweeping generalization—to proceed "from the particular to the general" as Marx once recommended. Things once cast aside as dull, obsolete and irrelevant, like the American Constitution, have acquired a new luster.

I do not know where I shall land. Some of those who have departed the circle have gone no farther than to reject "Stalinism"; others renounce Lenin too; still others Marx. Many have become liberals and "cold war liberals" or conservatives and neo-conservatives. Perhaps because I am still re-evaluating my values and ideas, I have not settled down in any of these addresses. I believe it is the same for many others. Those labels seem residues of the fifties when the American political mainstream flowed within narrow boundaries. Those boundaries were eroded by, among other things, our movement, by the revival of the Left which proceeded to swallow a large section of traditional liberalism, and to fill the old political terminology with a new content. Though in a broad historical sense I still locate myself on the Left, I cannot do so in an ideological environment where grasping the danger of Soviet imperialism is considered "moving to the Right." I cannot forswear Marx's perception that capitalism is an internally contradictory, exploitative and transient system, but I also share his view that in most of the world— especially the Third World—what is needed is more not less of it. Though I now reject the destructive illusion of romantic revolutionary socialism, it is not to endorse Pinochet's Chile (nor Somoza's Nicaragua).

I no longer consider myself part of the advancing tide of socialism fighting a decaying capitalism. Perhaps I should call myself a democratic socialist, but the idyll has faded into the future and mine is now a defensive struggle in favor of the pretty good or rather bad against the infinitely worse.

Defending the underdog and building a fairer future were values that brought me into the movement. Defense of the weak and hope for the future means resisting, not abetting, Soviet imperialism. As a former participant, I feel a special obligation to join with those who, while preserving the movement's genuine contributions to civil and minority rights, cultural freedom and social enlightenment, wish to combat its baneful effects on our schools, our media, our politics, and our thinking. Our political differences and differing idylls must be seen in the light of our common danger. Like Sidney Hook a generation ago, I find that I have more in common with a democrat who differs with me on economic questions, but who also firmly believes in civil rights and a peaceful method of resolving our economic differences, than with any professed Socialist who would seize power by a minority coup, keep it by terror, and take orders from a foreign tyrant.

CHAPTER 5

POLITICAL FACTS/RADICAL FICTIONS

Samuel Leiken

I was not a red diaper baby—far from it. I grew up in the suburbs of New York City. My father was a prosperous clothing manufacturer and a Republican, my mother an FDR Democrat. The family was semi-lapsed reform Jews.

My radicalization began as a teenager when my father's business went under. I developed strong sympathy for the little guy and a dislike of monopolies.

Nonetheless politics was not a particularly important part of my life until I went to the Helsinki Youth Festival in August, 1962. Sponsored by the USSR, the festival brought together Communist and left-leaning youth from both the Eastern bloc and the West with anti-colonialist youth from the Third World. Two impressions stayed with me from the festival. First was the third world students I met, many of whom had to be smuggled out of their countries. They told stories of valiant independence struggles against colonial regimes and recounted incidents of torture, murder and other human rights violations that outraged me, especially since many were from colonies ruled by Britain and France, which were supposed to be democratic countries. There were also many Cubans at the festival who displayed unbridled enthusiasm for their revolution and their country.

My second lasting impression was of the Communist "youth." I remember my amazement that the head of the World Federation of Democratic Youth was 42! The Communists struck me as professional bureaucrats who wanted to control youth groups. This was certainly true of the American delegation.

I went to Helsinki as part of the American delegation. My trip was partially sponsored by the Independent Research Service, which, years later, I learned received some of its backing from the CIA. Its goal was to send non-Communist youth as part of the delegation. There was a lot of in-fighting within the delegation, which deepened my impression of the Communists as manipulators and bureaucrats.

Helsinki whetted my interest in politics, but it was the civil rights movement and the sit-ins that captured my imagination. After returning from Helsinki in the fall of 1962 I joined the Columbia University chapter of CORE.

The outrage I began to feel in Helsinki when talking with African students intensified as the sit-ins spread in the South. It was simply inconceivable to me that our country, which claimed to be the leader of the *Free* World, tolerated the denial of basic rights of citizenship to non-white citizens. For me the civil rights movement became a beacon of morality, fighting for what was good and just in America. The establishment, which countenanced and accommodated these violations of basic human rights, was the epitome of hypocrisy.

After serving as president of the CORE chapter, part-time work in the civil rights movement could no longer satisfy my growing commitment to right the wrongs of society. I dropped out of Columbia in 1963 and worked full-time for the Northern Student Movement (NSM).

Founded originally to support the Student Nonviolent Coordinating Committee (SNCC), NSM discovered that there was plenty of "institutionalized racism" in the North. Its leadership, white students from elite colleges, gave way to black, college-educated militants who felt more inclined to confront the problems of the black underclass than to militate on college campuses. The new leadership, much like SDS, sought to move from the campus to the community by setting up organizing projects in eight ghetto areas.

NSM's politics combined SDS' "participatory democracy" (in this case empowering the black masses) and black nationalism. Malcolm X was our inspiration and black power, once enunciated by SNCC, our rallying cry.

Comprised of students and ex-students, NSM had a theoretical bent. It regarded much of the civil rights leadership, as well as the Communist Party, as too accommodating and reformist and felt that integration presented a strong danger of coopting the movement into conventional politics.

While NSM shared many things with SDS including personnel, it was not a "left" organization. We did not think participatory democracy meant endless meetings leading to consensus. We were anti-establishment, even revolutionary, but took little interest in factional disputes or foreign policy. NSM began to disintegrate when many of our project leaders and community activists took full-time jobs in the poverty program.

Impatient with the pace of civil rights progress, NSM, like its counterpart the Student Non-Violent Coordinating Committee (SNCC), turned to black power. For NSM, black power meant that civil rights organizations must have black leadership and that coalitions with "white" organizations were only possible once black organizations achieved independence from whites. In practice, this policy meant that whites had to leave both NSM and SNCC. Although I left NSM in 1965, its radical politics remained mine.

My radicalism evolved into cynicism, however, as I watched my former comrades-in-arms use their civil rights contacts to get well-paying jobs in the federal anti-poverty program. Many became "poverty pimps" promoting their own careers by selling out the interests of the communities where they had been organizers. I lost faith in politics as a solution for social ills, turning instead to youth work in west Harlem where I could affect individual lives. As part of my NSM legacy, I still believed the black community had to solve its own problems. My role would be to help black youths acquire the skills and self-confidence they lacked.

Five years of youth work led to a severe case of burnout. The intractability of the problems I confronted daily—drug addiction, illiteracy, unemployment, illegitimacy, etc.—made me feel like I was putting a Band-Aid on cancer. It was clear that the entire system needed to be changed.

My burnout led me to leave New York and head south to Mexico to reflect and reconsider. I went partly at the urging of my brother, Bob, who had already spent some time there.

Our first day in Mexico was the beginning of my re-entry into politics. On our way south we went by way of the city of Chihuahua. The city walls carried revolutionary slogans and on its outskirts was a workers' community established by a land seizure. Peasants in the outlying areas had been inspired by the success of that *colonia* and land seizures were spreading. Local university students had taken to commandeering city buses, filling them with supporters, and heading for the countryside to protect the expropriators. On a tip from some students we set out to investigate a recent seizure. My job was to hold the tape recorder. When we arrived we met the leadership and learned of their grievances. What we did not find out until the last minute was that at any moment they expected the military to expel them from the land. They were prepared to resist with small arms. We were not. We packed up the tape recorder and headed south. I spent almost two years in Mexico. My initial acquaintance with the revolutionary movement deepened once I had learned to speak Spanish. In addition to taking courses in Marxism at the National University I participated in workers' study circles organized by a small, Marxist revolutionary group that my brother introduced me to.

I worked on a translation of a manual on Marxism used in the study circles and wrote a critique of the Chilean left under the Popular Unity government for the group. It was that analysis that first opened my eyes to ultra-leftism, albeit not far enough.

Since my outlook was revolutionary, I was prepared to orient my analysis around a view that the Chilean Communist Party's influence was too reformist and thus the Popular Unity government was unprepared to defend itself against the counter-revolution. Instead it became apparent that the fault lay with the left socialists and the MIR (a *Fidelista,* clandestine group) which sought to advance their program without winning mass support and were not prepared to compromise with moderates. Because of its ultra-left and sectarian policies, the Allende government by 1973 had polarized rather than unified the popular classes. What could have and should have been natural support for the Allende government by the moderate political parties became instead organized opposition. With the masses divided, a military coup became far more feasible.

Despite my critique of ultra-leftism, I returned to the US brimming with revolutionary enthusiasm, feeling I had at last found a solid intellectual footing on which to base my activism: scientific socialism. Determined to put my socialist principles to the test, I spent the next nine years as a welder, machinist, and union activist.

My time in the union movement, working in shops and shipyards, disabused me of some of my more extreme notions. You could not shun union elections as "bourgeois, sham democracy," and expect to have any influence with union members. Fighting the company over grievances makes you conscious of the importance of incremental gains and defending what you already have.

For seven years I worked in a large defense plant where dissident workers and college educated leftists built a reform movement in our local. Our biggest internal problem was keeping the fervor of the leftists from destroying the carefully built ties to working class activists.

One May Day one of the more outlandish "revolutionary parties" held a rally at our plant gate. A dozen militants unfurled red banners urging the workers of the world to unite against US imperialism only to be greeted by 200 angry workers wielding, among other things, small American flags taped to baseball bats!

Foreign policy was rarely an issue in my union work, but my time in Mexico had given me an international perspective. The boat people fleeing from Indochina, the North Vietnamese takeover of the NLF and the Soviet occupation of Afghanistan confirmed my view that the Soviets and their allies used socialism to commit imperialism.

My union work and my interest in international politics coincided when the Solidarity movement arose in Poland. It was during the struggle to build labor support for Solidarity that I began to sour on the left. *Solidarnosc* embodied the values that had caused me to join the labor movement. It was a democratic, socialist, anti-totalitarian mass workers movement led by workers and intellectuals.

Yet the leftists at my plant were unwilling to join the local's Solidarity support committee for fear that criticisms of the Soviet Union would stir up red-baiting. How trade unionists, and trade union dissidents at that, could refuse to support a genuine mass workers movement whose goals were identical to their own was incomprehensible. Part of the explanation was their ultra-leftism. They simply could not conceive of allying with any political force that was also supported by Ronald Reagan.

Another part of the explanation was that they could only identify with struggles against the US and its allies. They believed that their internationalist duty meant undermining the American imperialist Goliath. They felt that opposing Soviet human rights violations (if any) was someone else's business. That is not internationalism but inverted nationalism. Nationalism means automatically putting your own country's interests first, while this perverse view always puts opposition to US interests first. Like nationalism, it exaggerates the importance of one's own nation and sees events from that distorted perspective. Real internationalism means adopting the interests of all mankind, speaking out against oppression no matter whose ox is gored.

Its one-sided stance on foreign policy, as well as the dogmatism and ultra-leftism it exhibited on domestic issues, made me re-think my view of the left. I began to question the left position on issues like reflexive support for welfare programs that fail to cope with the problems of the black underclass; the knee-jerk, no compromise stance of labor's left and its inability to produce a viable program to deal with harsh economic realities; and the double standard of liberals and the left who, for example, criticize Pinochet's human rights violations in Chile and ignore the death of hundreds of thousands of black peasants in Ethiopia at the hands of a Marxist dictatorship. My left-wing friends warned me against turning into a right-wing, anti-Communist.

Apart from the self-serving notion that you are automatically a rightist if you disagree with the left, my friends proved prescient. I have become an anti-Communist, but not because I no longer think that it would be better to live in a world of consistent political and economic democracy. No, I am an anti-Communist because I prefer imperfect democracy to no democracy.

The historical experience of the socialist countries has convinced me that Marxist single party states, however well-intentioned at their creation, have led to the rise of new elites who rule to perpetuate their existence. You cannot have socialism without democracy, and without democracy the process of fighting for socialism leads to totalitarianism.

My values haven't changed as much as my politics have since the '60s. While I prefer living in this country to any other, I believe there is still a great deal wrong that must be changed. Where I am different from my younger self is that I no longer accept the notion that the left has a monopoly on truth or that its views are inevitably progressive. I am far more willing to re-examine my premises than I used to be. I am much more cautious about extreme positions and am less willing to label the good guys and bad guys too quickly. A visit to Nicaragua in 1984 made that clear to me. I spoke with independent trade unionists whom the Sandinistas labeled class enemies because they wanted the right to strike. I talked to graduates of the literacy program who couldn't read their diplomas. I met with political activists whom the Sandinistas called revolutionaries when they had opposed Somoza but were now branded as enemies for making the same democratic demands of the new government that they had made of the old.

I have had a great number of second thoughts about the left as a result of my political experience. Having just expressed a reluctance to label things precipitously I am not certain how to label myself. I prefer to let the facts speak for themselves.

CHAPTER 6

WHEN I HEAR THE WORD 'MOVEMENT'...

Jeffrey Herf

I was a member of SDS from 1965 to its end in 1969 while a student at the University of Wisconsin in Madison. In 1969 I fought in the faction fight of SDS, and decided despite the urging of some friends not to join the Weatherman faction of SDS. In 1970, I worked on the trial of the New York Black Panther 21. I returned to graduate school in 1973, wrestled with dilemmas of politics on the level of social theory, and by the time I completed my doctorate in sociology from Brandeis in 1980 was still torn between disillusionment and a desire to hold on to a vision of the good old days—and good old friends—of the 1960s. In the early eighties, I completed a book about how the Nazis viewed modern technology, and wrote several essays in support of the NATO "double track" decision of 1979 to deploy medium range nuclear missiles in Western Europe and to open negotiations with the Soviet Union over these weapons. A long process of many small steps, rather than a dramatic epiphany, characterized my second thoughts about my leftist days. When the euromissile controversy took place, I decided I did not want to make the same political misjudgments I felt I'd made in the past.

There was a great deal I relished about the New Left years: community, intellectual stimulation, friendship. It was then my intellectual inclinations took shape and led to a career in scholarship. I read widely in modern European intellectual and cultural history, and in social and critical theory. I made what I thought would be life-long friends, and read books that opened up the great traditions of Western history and thought. I still am proud of our efforts on behalf of civil rights, and recall the pain but also excitement of the early years of the women's movement.

But I have had second thoughts. They began in regard to the war in Vietnam. In the antiwar movement, we argued that the war was not only, or even primarily a "bad policy," or not in the "national interest." Rather, the war was first and foremost immoral. It was immoral, we thought, because both the ends and the means were wrong. We argued with growing boldness that the other side, the Communists, were the true representatives of the aspirations of "the Vietnamese people" rather than the South Vietnamese government. If the Communists won, that would be preferable to continuation of the war. Continuation of the war would mean continued use of napalm, cluster bombs, free fire zones, and B–52 strikes, all of which, we said, amounted to a war waged against the people of Vietnam. The war was a counterrevolution tending to genocide. How else, we asked, could a great power defeat a "people's war"?

The radical elements of SDS—the Weatherman faction and the Marxist-Leninist sectarians of 1969–1971, formed a fifth column on behalf of the Vietnamese Communists, a "front in the belly of the beast" of American imperialism. The importance of these numerically insignificant groups was amplified by the efforts of the broader popular front in which most of us moved and which "objectively" served the interests of the Vietnamese Communists without expressing enthusiasm for their cause. By the late '60s, I shared in the radical conviction that a Vietnamese Communist victory would be preferable to continuation of the war. Like most everyone I knew, I tired of political slogans, faction fights, and meetings and as the war wound down I turned back to a scholarly career.

After 1975, the boat people, Cambodian Holocaust, and creation of a Vietnamese Gulag shook most everyone I knew who had been in the New Left. All of what we had said would not happen did in fact occur. The Communists were every bit as bad as American supporters of the war said they would be. I think that if North Vietnamese domination had led to anything remotely approaching the "humane collectivism" we predicted, we would have sought to take credit for the great event. Instead there followed "post-Marxism" and "post-modernism," a kind of disillusioned and urbane mood of plague on both your houses. But while a previous generation of leftists had discussed "the god that failed," we who had been in the New Left said and wrote little of a critical nature about our own political judgments in the '60s.

Our greatest political misjudgment concerning the war was to believe that Vietnamese Communism would bring a better society to South Vietnam. Debate will continue about whether the United States should have been involved in the first place or, once involved, how it should have fought the war. But we in the radical Left had presented ourselves as occupiers of the moral high ground. After the catastrophes following the Communist victory in 1975, such claims no longer made sense to me. One way we have had of handling the issue is to suggest that we were not politically important in the face of the power of the American government. But clearly public opinion, which we influenced, did become an important political factor in the outcome of the war. While the great majority of Americans who opposed the war in Vietnam, never adopted a benign view of a Communist victory, there can be little doubt that the actions of the antiwar movement from the street demonstrations of the late '60s to the lobbying of Congress in the 1970s were intended to, and in fact did, place restrictions on the ability of the American government to support the government of South Vietnam. In this sense, dissent in the United States was an important factor in the strategic calculation of the North Vietnamese Communists. Just as it would be incorrect to suggest that the antiwar movement alone, irrespective of the progress or lack of progress in Vietnam, caused the American withdrawal from Indochina, it would be no less mistaken to argue that the New Left and antiwar movement had no impact on the outcome of the war. But even if we had been utterly irrelevant politically, the fact of our misjudgment would remain.

What sets those of us who are "second thoughters" apart from our contemporaries is, I think, less a disillusionment with the political views of the late '60s, than a decision to make public our willingness to support American and generally Western policy in contemporary conflicts with Communist states. The intellectual life of the 1970s was rife with disillusionment with past leftist utopias. The popularity of Foucault, the enduring influence of the Frankfurt School, the Marxism of the humanities and social sciences all indicated no great enthusiasm for "really existing socialism" but a plague on all houses, Communist and capitalist. I confess to a certain initial sympathy for this mood for, after burning my fingers with Commitment in the late '60s, I was not eager to leap again into any new promises of redemption through politics. In a sense, the '70s are reminiscent of the late 1950s, the archetypical era of the end of ideology.

This intellectual mood, while preferable to the Third Worldism and violence cults of the late '60s, loaded the intellectual dice in favor of withdrawal and selective political engagement. For me, these issues came to a head in the debates about medium range nuclear missiles in Western Europe. My father is a refugee from Nazi Germany. I've been engaged in a study of modern German history, society, and culture for some time, spent several years doing research there, and keep up with current developments in West Germany. At first, my reaction to the missile controversy was sympathy for the peace movements and opposition to the NATO decision. Indeed, I even wrote a letter to *The New York Times* in summer 1981 to protest what seemed to me then the epitome of instrumental rationality gone berserk: nuclear strategies of limited war. Initially, I found the arguments of the anti-missile opposition convincing.

But whereas in the '60s I dismissed all arguments in favor of American policy in Vietnam as propaganda, in the early '80s I was willing to consider the arguments for deployment of American medium range nuclear missiles in Western Europe. Perhaps Western claims about the Soviet military build-up were really true. Perhaps the NATO decision was a response to West European appeals for restoration of a balance of military forces in Europe. And perhaps the claims of the peace movement concerning the desire of the United States to limit nuclear war to Europe were not true. In this context, to throw up one's hands, announce a plague on both East and West, and join the anti-nuclear movement would objectively serve the interests of the Soviet Union which had already deployed its weapons and was continuing to deploy more with each passing week. I could not, in all good conscience, with the experience of the New Left behind me, act as if the desire for peace and the fear of nuclear war had not become potent tools in a Soviet diplomacy of intimidation directed at Western Europe.

I wrote several essays in *Telos,* a quarterly journal of leftist social and political theory which originated in the late '60s. Several contributors had raised questions about the nationalist and/or irrationalist currents in the peace movement. I challenged the political arguments of the peace movement directly and presented the rationale of western defense policy. While pointing to confusion and naivete in the peace movement was common enough, to make an argument in favor of the NATO decision was more than most of my left leaning friends—some going back to the '60s—could endure. Although the NATO decision originated in the initiatives of the German Social Democratic Party, by 1981 and 1982, the lay public associated it with the new cold war of the Reagan Administration. Thus, to support the NATO decision was to support the "right" and Reagan.

To take such a political position was considered by a number of old friends on the Left as going beyond the pale. At their initiative, old friendships ended or cooled. But I was convinced by the argument that further deterioration of the balance of forces in Europe would eventually lead to an American withdrawal and subsequent neutralization and/or Soviet hegemony over Western Europe. The governments of Western Europe were obviously worth defending. These were not the right wing dictatorships in the Third World it was so easy to dislike. With the memories of the exit from Vietnam still vivid, how could we fail to respond to pleas from the Western European governments to see that a balance of forces was preserved? In 1987, when Mikhail Gorbachev accepted the zero-option first proposed by President Reagan in November 1981 I felt that the firmness and determination of the Western governments had paid off. Had the peace movements had their way in 1983, Gorbachev would never have had to contemplate dismantling his SS–20 intermediate range missiles deployed at such great cost because there would have been no Western missiles to serve as levers compelling the Soviet leaders to reduce their own weapons arsenals. So far none of my old friends have called up to say I was right after all and the Western "zero-zero option" wasn't so bad. But I have the satisfaction of knowing that my political judgment concerning foreign affairs is better in 1987 than it was in 1967.

The Left today is more a mood than a program, more a set of impulses than a vision. Aside from the Sandinistas, there are no revolutionary governments that arouse any enthusiasm in Western Europe and the United States, and even the Nicaraguan Communists have nowhere near the appeal that the Cubans and Vietnamese Communists did twenty years ago. The days of Third Worldism are over, refuted by the outcome of the war in Vietnam, the brutal dictatorships that have followed colonialism, OPEC's wealth, and the stunning successes of Asian capitalism. Nor is there any significant radical left directed at dramatically changing Western capitalism. Where the Left does become a political force, its major accomplishment is to lose national elections. No one, or almost no one, argues that communism is a good idea in theory or practice anymore. And socialism has lost much of its luster as welfare state capitalism proves more just and more successful than its antagonists thought possible.

In foreign affairs, whenever the Left favors unilateral disarmament or adopts gimmicks about nuclear freezes and moratoria, it consistently loses national elections. Western electorates want both peace and freedom. I do not mean to minimize disturbing trends in the Labor Party in Great Britain, the West German Social Democrats or the Democratic Party in the United States. If Britain, West Germany or the United States would pursue the programs of the Left in all those parties, both peace and freedom, in my view, would be endangered. But the important point is that the intellectual and moral conviction in a political program directed at fundamentally different societies and economies than exist in the West is nowhere near as powerful as it was fifteen years ago, while defense of democracy and anti-Communism is no longer as much the intellectual and moral taboo it was for a while in the late '60s. For me, the existence of this Second Thoughts Conference indicates that there is again, in our generation, a thoughtful defense of liberal values and of opposition to Communism in American intellectual and political life.

In the midst of talk of second thoughts and changing views, it is important to stress that changing one's ideas about politics is not synonymous with religious conversion. I am not a born again anything. For me there was much in the spirit and culture of the '60s that I treasure. Our conformism is well known, but at our best we were independent minded non-conformists. Being on the Left was not always a matter of obeying a herd instinct. At times, we did swim against the current. We were right to participate in the struggles for civil rights and, despite some painful adjustments, we are all better off for having lived through the revival and persistence of feminism. I really have no idea why those of us at this conference learned the lesson we've learned while so many of our peers stuck to the old time religion or just stopped thinking about politics at all. Absent the moral certainties that I had when I was an undergraduate, my second thoughts in the last decade have led me to a mixture of conservative, centrist and liberal views. They rest on the same iconoclasm and non-conformism that first drew me to the Left in the 1960s. Today, when I hear the word "Movement," I reach for my books and my word processor.

CHAPTER 7

LEARNING FROM EXPERIENCE

Barry Rubin

I grew up in Washington in the 1950s and 1960s having a great interest in politics and holding the characteristic liberal Democratic view of that era. Franklin Roosevelt, Harry Truman, John Kennedy and Hubert Humphrey (and, locally, Joe Rauh) were great heroes. My ideas have gone through something of a full circle, prompted by my experiences.

Those of us growing up in the innocent Fifties were taught that America was the closest thing possible to a perfect society. It was a land of affluence and justice. The main political and social questions had all been settled; ideology was outdated. Internationally, the United States was leader of the Free World against monolithic Communism.

Ironically, however, this relatively monolithic worldview invited its own antithesis. The new generation's discovery that there were serious political and cultural shortcomings was a natural one, but the excessive expectations made this experience far more traumatic than it should have been. Moreover, the symmetry of the belief system made it easier to conclude that to challenge it in part was to challenge it in whole.

There were four such findings that were central to my life in this regard. First was seeing the deep, comprehensive racism that blighted American life. Someone older might have noted that this very era of protest was also one of long-awaited progress and change. Someone younger would not have noticed at all. But for those whose formative teenage experiences included seeing the Poor People's Campaign, hearing the speeches of Martin Luther King, reading about or witnessing conditions in the South, and watching plumes of smoke rise from the Washington riots, the situation seemed something else entirely. And this last impression was reinforced by the dominant voices among black leaders—or at least those which were most often and directly heard in the period after King's assassination—that suggested more structural causes and revolutionary prescriptions for this problem.

The second destabilizing issue was the Vietnam war. However one looks at that conflict in hindsight, it then seemed to me at first a foolish and finally a criminal undertaking. The American media provided one with accounts and pictures of civilian suffering at U.S. hands, of our support for an unpopular dictatorship, of massive bombing, of limited success, and of an ordeal that would apparently never end unless protests prevailed. Contrary to later accounts, I clearly remember that the concern in the antiwar movement was as much for the American soldiers being killed and wounded as it was for the Vietnamese civilians.

Given these daily horrors, going on year after year, it was not so difficult to accept the idea, articulated by columnist Anthony Lewis, that no outcome in Indochina could be worse than the status quo. As one pondered why the United States was in Vietnam, such responses as idealism (defending democracy) or realism (blocking a Soviet or Chinese advance) seemed increasingly hollow. Other, less charitable explanations involving words like imperialism, aggressiveness, and arrogance, began to appear more likely.

As with the issue of racism, the incipient "movement" followed a set of evolving interpretations. These involved changing perceptions of the enemy: from non-people, to nationalist, to national liberationist (involving social transformation as part of self-determination), to accepting them as a Communist-led united front. The argument was that such an ideology was the only one capable of organizing and achieving such objectives.

In some of its conclusions, the Left (and, of course, hundreds of thousands of people participated in the antiwar movement without ever having been Leftists) was mirroring some traditional characteristics of their fellow Americans. After all, Americans were then (and in no small part are still) citizens of a reluctant great power who view overseas intervention with a great deal of suspicion. And the Left as much as other Americans seemed under the spell of that seductive idea that only we are real, that the rest of the world merely reflected our virtues or vices. Suddenly it seemed that the United States was waging the same kind of colonial war as the British fought in the 19th century against the Zulus or Mahdists.

In 1968, I worked in the headquarters of Eugene McCarthy's presidential campaign, which challenged the Administration's Vietnam war policy. President Lyndon Johnson's decision to drop out of the race seemed a great victory and the successes of McCarthy and Robert

Kennedy in the primaries were encouraging. We experienced a wave of hope and encouragement that was followed by devastating disappointments: the murder of Kennedy and the apparent theft of the Democratic convention by Johnson's stand-in, Vice-President Hubert Humphrey.

Humphrey's support for the war and the handling of the Chicago protestors seemed a terrible betrayal by the symbol of liberalism itself. (Walking to the office, I saw headlines about the Soviet invasion of Czechoslovakia which added to our despair, although the lesson it presented was overwhelmed by our own experiences during those days). I also saw demonstrators being beaten by the Chicago police and Mayor Richard Daley screaming anti-Semitic insults at Senator Abraham Ribicoff from the convention's floor. The police even invaded one of McCarthy's offices and harassed the campaign workers.

The conclusions were apparent: the nomination had been stolen, the democratic system had failed, and the "people's will" had no effect on the ruler's decisions. Something was seriously wrong. How could one understand and explain these mystifying developments?

I began college in September 1968, a time of uncertainty and upheaval in America that was unparalleled during the second half of our century. The university was supposed to be a center for intellectual debate and tireless investigation, yet instead it was a rather deadened place. In stark contrast to colleges undergoing drastic change or challenge, it was a particularly conservative place lacking that kind of energetic coexistence of alternatives. And if it was not a faceless "multiversity" along the lines of Berkeley, the quality of teachers and intellectual level of students did not provide many answers.

During my years as an undergraduate student and while working toward my master's degree, most of the inspiring teachers who showed particular concern for the students or who had something new to say were radicals. The students who were most interested in debating or doing something about them had similar beliefs. Radicalism, then, seemed not to be an anti-intellectual pursuit but rather appeared to embody the best kind of inquiry contained in that tradition.

For someone young in comparison to the formulators of the Port Huron statement—and much less cognizant of the sad lessons from the previous wave of radicalism in the 1930s—this was heady stuff indeed. After the 1968 convention, I became active in SDS for its remaining 15 months or so of its life and then worked as "foreign editor" for the radical *Guardian* newspaper.

At first, the experience of the movement itself was a positive one, providing a community for those who had been alienated, a sense of purpose, a body of opinions and knowledge, a perception of one's own importance, and even a whole set of cultural determinants.

In many ways, Marxism or radicalism is the opiate of the intellectuals. It provides them with structured answers to vexing questions, far simpler and more systematic than liberalism's essentially empirical/pragmatic view. It reinforces their isolation in like-minded communities prone to fads and insulated from many outside influences. It exhorts them to play a vanguard role in society, in sharp contrast to their usual place of neglect or even ridicule in American life. Finally, it offers them a way to be (at least in their own thoughts) integrated into the masses with whom they have a love/hate affair.

The problem in all this, of course, is that the movement and its members are increasingly forced to betray the very purposes or virtues that led them into battle in the first place. There is a stifling conformism, a growing willingness to distort truth in the service of ideology, and a whopping double standard applied internationally. Although periodically one would hear statements about a native American radicalism, the movement was incapable of avoiding apologetics for foreign dictatorships. I thought of this last-mentioned problem as "flunkeyism" or becoming a "Third World groupie." Why, I thought, were these people so willing to defend the national interests of other states without acknowledging America's right to act similarly.

One also became aware of the limitations of the intellectuals involved in all these exercises. Trafficking in ideas, they became increasingly isolated from reality. My Washington perspective led me to understand that individuals and political process were central in national decision-making, that debate was always going on even within the government, and that the economic determinist or ruling class concepts of the Left were simple, inaccurate cartoons.

Perhaps the most vicious component of the Left was its hysterical denunciations and slanders against anyone who disagreed with it. People also turned hatred on themselves, believing—as is common in many cults—that their doubts or deviations were only signs of individual weaknesses. And those who left were portrayed as opportunists. One talked less and less to anyone not sharing the faith. Again, the analogies to religious cults are compelling.

My personal experience with the radical newspaper where I worked (while also finishing my master's degree in history), brought home all these problems. I began to think of it as a miniaturized version of an Eastern European state, with the requisite fear, conformity, hypocrisy, distortions, and even anti-Semitism. Having begun with a determination to follow truth wherever it led, I now either had to abandon my political positions or my integrity.

During this whole period, I read deeply in the literature of Leftist disillusion from the 1930s and again found striking parallels. My colleagues were outraged that I would even read Solzhenitsyn, which, I thought, partly revealed the nature of the problem. But the 1960's movement was more complex and pluralistic than its predecessor, which had been largely devoted to a single party and foreign state. The attitude to the USSR was, if anything, negative, but the Soviets were more ignored than seen as an indicator of where Marxism led or as a factor conditioning legitimate U.S. responses in defense.

My trips to Cuba and China, in 1972 and 1973 respectively, were central factors in determining my decision to make a break. In China, a young man leaned over when the translator was otherwise occupied and told me about the bloodiness of the Cultural Revolution. The indifference to workers' interests, the lack of any form of democracy, and the pervasive militarism, among other negative characteristics, were quite visible. Even though China was a developing country—and enjoyed some real successes—it seemed a most unadmirable model. Glowing, uncritical reports from other visitors filled me with disgust.

Similar things could be seen in Cuba. There I even had the privilege of a short conversation with an official who had been a hero in the revolution and who told me how the regime was betraying the people and the country's independence. Whatever positive things existed during earlier days, Cuba was now well on the way to becoming a clone of the East European autocracies.

So I began a break with the Left in late 1973 that resulted in the loss of all of my friends and the whole intellectual and personal framework that had been built up over the previous five years. My life continued along lines fairly close to what would probably have happened without that detour. Experience in writing, speaking, and researching gained during that period served me well in later years.

But these experiences also showed me the detrimental nature of the Left; the danger posed by foreign dictatorships—first and foremost the USSR; the ways in which totalitarian control is camouflaged (often with remarkable ease) from those who do not want to perceive its underlying realities, and how well-intentioned people become manipulated or voluntarily turn into apologists for those who fundamentally oppose their own values.

Finally, it has made me particularly sensitive about how the questionable premises of the Left have infiltrated themselves into liberal thinking. Yet for me the conclusion is not that democratic liberalism be abandoned but rather that it be reinforced as the best weapon for preserving liberty and combatting the forces that would extinguish it.

CHAPTER 8

WHY I AM NO LONGER A LEFTIST

David Horowitz

My life as a leftist began with a May Day Parade in 1948, when I was nine years old, and lasted for more than twenty-five years until December 1974, when a murder committed by my political comrades brought my radical career to an end. My parents had joined the Communist Party along with many other idealistic Americans in the 1930's, before I was born. Just as today's leftists believe the seeds of justice have been planted by the Marxist Sandinistas in Nicaragua, my parents and their radical friends saw them blooming in Soviet Russia, which many of them visited during Stalin's purges. Not even the testimony of a Bolshevik legend like the exiled Trotsky could persuade them that they were deceived about the "new society" they thought they saw under construction in the socialist state. Confident that their own ideals were pure, my parents and their political friends dismissed Trotsky and all those whose experience had caused them to know better, smearing them as "counter-revolutionaries," and "anti-Soviets," and "renegades."

Twenty years later, when my parents reached middle-age, their arrogance betrayed them and took away their self-respect. In 1956 a power shifted in the Kremlin walls, and my parents along with the rest of the "progressive left" discovered that the socialist future they had served all their lives was nothing but a monstrous lie. They had thought they were fighting for social justice for the powerless and the poor. But in reality they had served a gang of cynical despots who had slaughtered more peasants, caused more hunger and human misery, and killed more leftists like themselves than all the capitalist governments since the beginning of time.

After Stalin's death, it was the confrontation with this reality, and not the famous Senator McCarthy's crusade, that demoralized and destroyed the old Communist guard in America. I was seventeen at the time, and at the funeral of the Old Left I swore to myself I would not repeat my parents' fate: I would never be loyal to a movement based on a lie or be complicit in political crimes; I would never support a cause that required the suppression of its own truths, whether by self-censorship or firing squads or political smears. But my youth still prevented me from truly comprehending what the catastrophe had revealed and I continued to believe in the fantasy of the "socialist future." When a New Left began to emerge a few years later, I was ready to believe that it was a fresh beginning and eager to assist at its birth.

For a long time, I was able to keep the promises I had made. As an activist and writer in the movement of the Sixties, I never endorsed what I knew to be a lie or concealed what I knew to be a crime, and I never stigmatized a dissenting view as morally beyond the pale. At the same time, however, I closed my eyes to evidence that would have shown me the Left had not really changed at all. Like the rest of my radical comrades, I welcomed Castro's triumph in Cuba which he proclaimed a revolution of "bread without terror" and "neither red nor black but Cuban olive green." And when Castro established his own dictatorship and gulag, and joined the Soviet axis, I too blamed his dereliction on the anti-Communist phobia of the United States, and averted my eyes from the truth.

A decade later, when the Vietnam War came to an end, there was a massive exodus from the New Left by those who had joined its ranks to avoid military service. I stayed. I had never been eligible for the draft and had joined the movement in order to serve the progressive ideal.

In 1974 I began a new project with the Black Panther Party, which the New Left had identified in the Sixties as the "vanguard of the revolution." I raised the funds to create a "Community Learning Center" for the Panthers in the heart of the East Oakland ghetto. The Center provided schooling and free meals to 150 children, and community services to an even larger number of adults. The following year the woman I had hired as a bookkeeper for the Center was kidnapped, and sexually tormented, and then brutally murdered by my Black Panther comrades.

When I first discovered what had happened, I was paralyzed with fear, a fear that grew as I learned about other murders and violent crimes the Panthers had committed—all without retribution from the law. In the eyes of the Left, at the time, the Panthers were still a persecuted "vanguard," victimized by racist police because of their role in the liberation struggle. The Panthers' leader had found refuge from several criminal indictments in Castro's Cuba; the Party's spokesmen appeared regularly at progressive rallies to agitate against the capitalist "repression" at home. In the eyes of the Left the Panthers were what they always had been: an embodiment of the progressive idea. To defend them against the "fascist" attacks of the police was a radical's first responsibility and task.

In reality the Panthers were a criminal gang that preyed on the black ghetto itself. With the weapons they had justified as necessary for "self-defense" against "racist authority," they pursued various avenues of criminal violence which included extortion, drug trafficking and murder. Not all of the murders they committed had a monetary rationale. Some were merely gratuitous, as when they killed a leader of the Black Students Union at Grove Street College in Oakland because he had inadvertently "insulted" one of their enforcers. The Oakland police were aware of the Panthers' criminal activities, but were rendered powerless to stop them by the nationwide network of liberal and radical Panther supporters who sprang to their defense. With community "fronts" like the school I had created, political lobbyists in the state house and political activists in the streets, with million dollar defense funds and high-powered attorneys, with civil liberties organizations ready with lawsuits and witnesses willing to perjure themselves, the New Left provided the Panthers with an Achilles Shield that protected them from the law. All the celebrated "Cointelpro" programs of the Nixon White House and the anti-subversive campaigns of the FBI, all the alleged wiretaps and infiltrations of the Panther organization, could not provide the means to sustain a single legal conviction of the Panthers for their crimes, or prevent the twenty or more murders they committed, including that of the woman I had hired. During a decade of radical protest as reckless in its charges as it was indiscriminate in its targets, the Left had made civil authority in America so weak that the law could not punish ordinary criminal acts when committed by its progressive vanguard.

Because of what I knew, I myself now lived in fear of the Panther terror. In my fear it became impossible for me not to connect these events with the nightmares of the radical past. Just as Stalin had used the idealism and loyalty of my parents' generation to commit his crimes in the '30s, so the Panthers had used my generation's idealism in the '60s. My political odyssey had come full circle. When I began, I had promised myself that I would never be silent when confronted by such misdeeds; that I would fight within the Left for the same justice as the Left demanded of the world outside. But I discovered now that I could not keep my promise and remain a part of the movement I had served.

Because a progressive vanguard had committed the crime, the duty of progressives was to defend the criminal. As a result, the Left suddenly became a hostile terrain. I had already been warned by the Panthers themselves to keep silent about what I knew. The facts I knew would not be conclusive evidence in a court of law, but they posed a threat to the Panthers' political shield. If the Panthers' criminal acts were exposed to the Left, they might lose their protection and support.

Of course, even if I told what I knew, the Panthers had little to fear. The whole history of the radical past, from Trotsky on, warned that my individual truth would have little effect on the attitude of the Left. Confronted by such a truth the Left would seek first to ignore and then to discredit it. Because it was damaging to the progressive cause.

At the murdered woman's funeral, I had approached her daughter, who was twenty-two and a radical like me. On the way to the graveside, I told her that I was convinced the Panthers had killed her mother. The daughter's grief for her mother was great, but so was the solidarity she felt for black people who were oppressed and for their "revolutionary vanguard." When, later, she was asked publicly what she thought about the tragedy, she said that as far as she was concerned the Panthers were above suspicion. To suggest the contrary was "racist."

What the daughter of the murdered woman did was "politically correct." I knew at the time that if I were to step forward and publicly accuse the Panthers of the crime, I would be denounced by my own community in the name of the values we shared. All my previous life of dedication and commitment to the radical cause overnight would count for nothing. My own comrades would stigmatize me as a "racist" and shun me as a "renegade," and expel me from their ranks.

My dedication to the progressive cause had made me self-righteous and arrogant and blind. Now a cruel and irreversible crime had humbled me and restored my sight. I had started out with others of my generation confident that we were wiser than our parents and would avoid their radical fate. But all our wisdom had been vanity. I could no longer feel superior to the generation that had been silent during the years of Stalin's slaughters. The Stalinists and the Panthers may have operated on stages vastly different in scale, but ultimately their achievements were the same: Stalin and the Panthers were ruthless exploiters of the radical dream; just like our forbears, my comrades and I were credulous idealists who had served a criminal lie.

Through this microcosm I saw what I had failed to see 18 years before at the time of "de-Stalinization," when the New Left was born. The problem of the Left was not Stalin or "Stalinism." The problem was the Left itself.

Although the Panther vanguard was isolated and small, its leaders were able to rob and kill without incurring the penalty of law. They were able to do so, because the Left had made the Panthers a law unto themselves. The same way the Left had made Stalin a law unto himself. The same way the Left makes Fidel Castro and the Sandinista *comandantes* laws unto themselves.

By crowning the criminals with the halo of humanity's hope, the Left shields them from judgement for their criminal deeds. Thus in the name of revolutionary justice, the Left defends revolutionary injustice; in the name of human liberation, the Left creates a new world of oppression.

The lesson I had learned for my pain turned out to be modest and simple: the best intentions can lead to the worst ends. I had believed in the Left because of the good it had promised; I had learned to judge it by the evil it had done.

CHAPTER 9

COMING HOME

Peter Collier

I first became politically "conscious," as we used to call it, in Berkeley in 1959. Long before the Port Huron Statement, some of my friends and I (we thought of ourselves as "beatniks" more than anything else) were already feeling the first faint tremors of the eruption to come, although it hadn't yet been named the New Left. There were vigils to protest against the execution of "red light bandit" Caryl Chessman, and sit-ins against racial discrimination in San Francisco. Demonstrations against HUAC in which the police washed students and other protestors down the steps of the City Hall with fire hoses became a national event. Joe McCarthy was dead and we had insulted his corpse just as Khruschev had insulted Stalin's.

As I look back on it now, it seems to me that the first couple of years of JFK's presidency was our equivalent of the phony war. Everything was ready; we were geared up for something, even if we weren't quite sure what it was. There was an inarticulate sense of imminence: our chrysalis was about to open.

I was working on a graduate degree in English at the time that the Free Speech Movement began. As the protest ripened, I was intrigued by the proposition that the university—the phenomenal world as I then knew it—was actually only a symbol for society at large in which power worked secretly to crush personal freedom just as the Chancellor crushed our student rights. As we slowly paralyzed the campus, it occurred to me that my generation was coming of age in a glorious rush. We had entered a new era in which, as Wordsworth had said, to be alive was bliss, and to be young was very heaven; an era when it was impossible to trust anyone over 30.

I found it impossible to pick up my dissertation after the FSM was over. It was no longer possible to conceive of life as a methodical march through a career. There was something more exciting, more "relevant" to do: CORE marches against employment discrimination in the restaurant row of Oakland's Jack London Square; pickets of William Knowland's dread Oakland *Tribune*. In the spring of 1965, Berkeley had its Vietnam Day, one of the first major teach-ins against the war. Previously Saigon had been a fantasy name for me—like Katmandu or Sri Lanka. Listening to Isaac Deutscher, I.F. Stone, and other speakers, I integrated it into my developing political geography. It was a place, as one speaker said, that was occupied by American soldiers just as the Alameda County Sheriffs had recently occupied our campus.

That summer I went to Birmingham to do voter registration work for SNCC, and to teach at Miles College. I was ready for a nonviolent martyrdom that never came. All the blacks I met that summer idolized Martin Luther King except for a short, coffee-colored SNCC worker named John Jefferson. A director of the voter registration project, he ridiculed King as "Gee-zuz" and "De Lawd." He surprised me by saying during one of our discussions, "It's not important who's got the Bible. It's important who's got the power, who's got the guns." It was the first time I had heard this kind of talk, but instead of being put off by it, I felt that I was hearing the sounds of the future.

By the time I got back to Berkeley I had already made a personal transition from civil rights to Vietnam. The question was not what to do. Like others, I passed through the early stages of the great foreign policy debate relatively painlessly, accepting as axiomatic the proposition that it was necessary to support the NLF and work against the U.S. involvement in Indochina. It was not a question of what to do, but only of how to do it; how to become an "organizer," and who to organize? These questions were answered for me when I became one of the coordinators of *Ramparts* editor Robert Scheer's bid for Congress.

Scheer had been an early critic of the war. He was articulate and outspoken, and, after interminable wrangling about whether or not to work within the electoral system, we decided to run him against incumbent Berkeley Congressman Jeffrey Cohelan, one of LBJ's favorite liberals. We came close to winning in a campaign that drew national attention, and softened Cohelan up so that another local radical named Ron Dellums was able to defeat him a couple of years later.

After the election Scheer got me a job at *Ramparts*. I came to the magazine just at that point in its history when it was readying its first expose of the CIA—in this case the Agency's infiltration of the National Student Association. Others followed. The magazine was soon making news as well as reporting it. Someone who worked there could keep one foot in journalism and the other in the Movement.

As the decade began to wind down, however, what some of us had considered the high moral seriousness of the Movement began to be overshadowed by countercultural hijinx and strange talk about "revolutionary violence." It was hard not to wonder if the New Left was degenerating into a self-dramatizing sham, a movement whose only truly necessary implements were the soapbox, the megaphone and the suppository. We were constantly told to give up the addiction to linear thought, to go with the flow. Cognitive dissonance was the order of the day.

We hated the war, but we loved it too. Vietnam justified every excess, every violent thought and deed. Heaving a rock at some corporation's window, we banished guilt by the thought, "This is for the Vietnamese." Trying to set fire to a university library, we said, "This is for the Vietnamese." The war gave us license; it also gave us an addictive sense of moral superiority. Vietnam was in our marrow. It was our war, the time of our lives. I remember one day in 1968 having a chilling thought after hearing that negotiations were possible: What if it ends? What will I do then?

We talked about the "revolution" constantly, domesticating the millennium. One day not long after Kent State my friend David Horowitz and I were sitting on the porch of the collective where Tom Hayden lived. "Well, fascism is here," Hayden said without apparent regret. "There will be civil war soon." On Hayden's advice, I bought a gun so I could be armed when the revolution arrived. I hid the loaded clip in one place and the gun itself in another so that my children could never find it. I always forgot where the hiding places were and went for months unable to put the whole gun together.

Soon all these histrionics made it clear that the Movement was nearing the end of a prolonged dry labor, and that the monstrous offspring we had been waiting for, the revolution, was going to be stillborn. People who had gathered for the apocalypse were dropping off into environmentalism and consumerism, and, in the sad case of Berkeley, into local politics. Some of my old comrades were going back to graduate school in the universities they had failed to burn down so that they could get advanced degrees and spread via "scholarship" the ideas that had already been discredited in the streets.

It was about this time that my daughter Caitlin was born and my father was diagnosed as having terminal cancer. Being sandwiched so suddenly in between life and death jolted me and made me feel that I had been living through a kind of rhetorical gauze for the past decade. I also felt guilty in the case of my father for not taking first things first. He and I had fought over politics for years. I would tell him some of the things I was doing; he would react as if I had slapped him. He couldn't master all of the facts about Vietnam beginning with French colonialism. ("I don't know Bao Dai from Bo Diddley," he once muttered during one of my harangues). After a while he stopped trying to argue with me about the war. Instead, he tried to talk about what this country had meant to him: how he had come to California during the Depression so poor that he and his mother and father had survived by eating "road meat," domestic and wild animals killed by passing cars; how he had worked two jobs during the war and gotten a citation signed by FDR for an improvement he'd designed on a certain power lathe. I had ridiculed him for seeing himself as a stick figure in the national melodrama. After a while we stopped talking about anything significant at all. We didn't see much of each other. When we did visit, they were times of long silences.

But once I found out he was sick, all this seemed irrelevant. He was dying and history was dying with him. Not the Hegelian claptrap radicals had in mind when they talked of History, but the trail an individual left after making his way through real obstacles, after making choices and accepting the consequences—a human record, in other words, a sense of *lived life*. He had created a world, I suddenly realized, that would vanish when he died; a world that had nothing to do with Vietnamese and Cubans, radicals and reactionaries. In thinking these things, I reproached myself for "bourgeois privatism," yet I knew that he was about to teach me a lesson about what really mattered.

My father's last summer we decided to go to South Dakota, where he'd been born. I watched him poke around in the crumbled foundations of the sod house where he'd lived his first years. We went to the Black Hills, where he'd hiked as a boy, and to the Pine Ridge Sioux reservation, where he'd watched warriors furtively perform the sundance in the days when it was still a forbidden ritual. We didn't talk much while we were there, but as we were returning home and his sickness was growing in him, he began to reminisce and talk about his life in a way he'd never done before. During one long stretch of Nevada highway, he said, "You know, I'm glad I was born a South Dakotan and an American. I'm glad I saw the beginning of the 20th century. I'm glad I lived through the Depression and the War. I think these things made me a stronger person. I'm glad I came to California because I met your mother there. I'm glad we had you for a son."

It was the longest speech I'd ever heard him make. It was also the most emotional. It may sound maudlin or smarmy as I write it down, but it wasn't when he spoke the words. It was a moment of acceptance and affirmation by someone whose life had often been disfigured by unremitting hard work and responsibility, and for whom words had never come easily. What he said and how he said it was so different from the chic bitterness and facile nihilism of my radical friends that I was shaken. It was like hearing speech, real and authentic speech, for the first time in years.

My father's death came at about the same time as the U.S. defeat in Vietnam. This was what we had worked for all those years, but when it came it gave little pleasure. My Movement friends seemed to feel that they had been cut adrift. I felt something like what Orwell must have felt after leaving Spain when he wrote "This war, in which I played so ineffectual a part, has left me with memories that are mostly evil."

As the Communists took over in Vietnam, Joan Baez and a few others tried to protest against their re-education camps and revolutionary tribunals. But what was left of the Left attacked the attempt to apply the standards of political morality we had claimed to believe in to the Hanoi regime. Tom Hayden and Jane Fonda, who were on their way to becoming the Mork and Mindy of California politics, led the charge on the west coast. Back east, it was the coalition of old line Communists and neo-fellow travelers that was forming into the present "solidarity Left." No matter that our old allies in the National Liberation Front were among the first to be crushed; no matter that South Vietnam was conquered by the North; no matter that the Khmer Rouge, which we had supported with great enthusiasm, had embarked on a policy of genocide. There were no enemies on the Left.

I believe that coming to terms with what was happening in Southeast Asia—the fact that there were more people killed there in the first two years of the Communist peace than had been killed in all of the anti-Communist war—would have been a cleansing experience for the Movement. It also might have allowed me to remain a Leftist, at least for the time being. But most of my old comrades preferred to avoid the reckoning. Like some sort of revolutionary cargo cult, they were ready to move on to the next cause—South Africa, Central America, wherever—ignoring the body count that piled up in the long totalitarian night they had left behind.

It was one thing to think such things as this, of course, and quite another to say them aloud. That would have meant stepping purposefully away from what I had been most of my adult life and leaving the community of the Left with its powerful vision of being a caretaker for the downtrodden. It was not the Left ideas I found hard to disentangle myself from, but the Left's sense of community with its beguiling conviction that it is on the side of history and morality. I could see saying goodbye to most of that, but not all. I entered a period of dormancy and political hibernation, hoping that events would take a turn that would confirm my old faith so that I would never have to admit how profoundly it had failed me and how I had failed myself by buying into it so uncritically.

Writing was a partial salvation. During the time that I had first been feeling traumatized by my leftwing commitments, I began a book with David Horowitz about the Rockefeller family. The project was actually an outgrowth of our success in fundraising the fourth Rockefeller generation, our contemporaries, in our efforts to keep *Ramparts* alive so that it could publish attacks on Nelson, David and the other Rockefeller family elders. We had started the book with the vulgar Marxist notion that the Rockefellers were a sort of executive committee of the ruling class, a Rosetta Stone by which we could understand American imperialism and power. The truth turned out to be quite different. They were a family not even in control of their own children, who were running away from the Rockefeller name, money and influence.

After the Rockefeller book, I began writing fiction—short stories for little magazines and then a novel, *Downriver,* which explored, under a sort of artistic grant of immunity, the issues I couldn't yet bring myself to confront in my nonfictional life—the way people got caught up in movements and in history; the effects of political belief on the affective life; the tension between political commitment and love.

David Horowitz and I began to test our growing disillusionment with the Left (which developed in symbiosis, with each of us playing Devil's advocate for the other) in a series of magazine articles. The first one was a piece on Fay Stender, the radical feminist lawyer who had been George Jackson's lover and attorney, and who had been paralyzed years after his death when she was shot by one of his former prison followers. We had of course supported Jackson when we were at *Ramparts,* proposing him as an innocent victim of a conspiracy of the criminal justice system. But as we began to reconstruct Fay's life and death (she had recently committed suicide), we discovered that Jackson had killed several people in prison, and that far from being a sensitive prisoner-poet, he had been a deranged con. The slogan he had inspired—"all prisoners are political prisoners"—seemed absurd to us in light of what we had found. We saw now what authorities close to the Jackson case had known all along: there are individuals who, for whatever reasons, are so flawed that they ought to be locked down as deeply as possible into the prison system.

We concluded this article by pointing out that the Left had honored Fay Stender as a fallen heroine but ignored her quintessential truth: that she had been taken advantage of and debased by her Left convictions. We were immediately attacked by people such as Jessica Mitford, the Bay Area's white glove Communist, and by former *Washington Post* editor Ben Bagdikian, who refused to accept a service award from a local media association because we were members. Previously such an attack against my standing as a radical would have been devastating. But this one gave me an odd sense of confirmation. It was not what we had said that was wrong, but the fact that we had said it at all. Instead of making me want to stop, the attempted excommunication made me want to push harder on doors I had before been afraid to open.

The next story we wrote was about what had actually happened to the Weather Underground. Among other things, we discovered in our chronicle of the rise and fall of this organization that the bomb that had blown up three of the Weatherpeople in the Manhattan townhouse had been intended for a dancehall full of Army enlisted men and their dates at Fort Dix. In the furor that accompanied the article's publication our old friends attacked us as turncoats. We told them that we felt that if someone had to die it was far better that it was the Weatherpeople than the innocent soldiers.

Late in 1980, I was asked by the USIA to lecture in Europe. The Soviets were already in Africa along with their Cuban lackeys, and had just invaded Afghanistan; the Iranians were holding U.S. citizens hostage. The Europeans I spoke to assumed I would join the parade of U.S. writers who had attacked America since the '60s. Earlier in my life I would have gladly done it. But I was revolted by events of the late Carter years and by the double standard Europeans used in judging the U.S. and the USSR, especially now that our defeat in Vietnam had so changed what we used to call the "objective conditions," creating a vacuum into which the Soviets had moved with typical brutality. I found myself defending America in my talks, at first somewhat timorously and then with growing aggressiveness. It was exhilarating.

This experience helped expel the last of the toxins that had accumulated over two decades. When I arrived back in this country I felt that I could finally tear up my political green card and discard the status as a legal alien under which I had lived for twenty-five years. I felt that I had finally come home.

PART II

SECOND THOUGHTS ON VIETNAM

Doan Van Toai
Scott McConnell
David Ifshin
David Hawk

CHAPTER 1

MY COUNTRY, VIETNAM

Doan Van Toai

I was born in 1945 in a small village 100 miles south of Saigon. Until I left Vietnam in 1978, I lived under one kind of repressive regime or another and never knew a time of peace.

When I was a child, my father was away from home fighting in a rural area as a Viet Minh cadre in the resistance struggle against the Japanese and then against the French. Because of his role, he was highly respected by the people in our village. When I was still very small, my mother began moving our family from one tiny hamlet to another to escape the French bombardments.

My parents and the majority of the Vietnamese people who supported the Viet Minh (and later joined the National Liberation Front to fight against the Americans) were not Communists. They did not even know what a Communist was. They were patriots who wanted Vietnam to be independent and at peace. The Communist leaders of the Viet Minh and the National Liberation Front hid their true faces and said they were nationalists. Their goal, they said, was national reconciliation for all Vietnamese and national liberation for Vietnam.

After our country was divided in 1954 between the Communist North and the non-Communist South, I would not listen to the stories about Communist repression. I refused to believe that a million Northerners had fled from the regime to find refuge in the undemocratic but (to them) less repressive South. Like many of my countrymen I didn't want to believe the reports of the bad that the Communists had done. I wanted to believe the good that they promised. To win over non-Communist Vietnamese like myself, the Communists cleverly recalled the patriotic struggle of the Viet Minh and created a new patriotic coalition in its image, which they called the National Liberation Front. Their goals, they said, were national reconciliation between Communists and non-Communists, North and South, and independence from all the great powers, Russia and China as well as the United States.

During the 1960s, I was a student leader at Saigon University. I organized sit-ins, strikes and demonstrations—all in support of the Revolution that I thought would free my country from domestic dictators and foreign aggression. These were the aspirations of my people. Most of us who took part in the struggle against the Saigon regime and their American supporters believed that they were fighting for peace and national independence for Vietnam. Most never gave any thought to whether they were for or against Communism. I never did.

In 1975 when the Communist armies of North Vietnam took control of the South I was eager to join in their plans to rebuild our country. Even when the Northerners took control of all the important government posts and institutions, I was not concerned. I was not afraid of the Communists of the North. I had never believed the refugees' stories of the Communist hell. But I also didn't share the partisans' dreams of a Communist paradise. I believed in the goals of the Revolution we all had fought for. I was confident that our Communist compatriots from the North would be as amenable to compromise as they had been in the past. And I was certain that they were more interested in our people's welfare than any foreign power or collaborator could be. I was the one who told all the relatives in our family that there was no reason to flee, who challenged my friends: "Why are you afraid of Communists? They have fought and died alongside us to achieve the goal of national reconciliation. That is the slogan they have shed their blood for. Isn't that proof enough of their sincerity and commitment?" For my part, I was ready to accept the personal sacrifices that the new Communist leaders would demand of me and that I knew would be required to rebuild our country and to make its hard won independence a success.

I had graduated Saigon University, and despite my political record, had been able to advance myself to the position of branch manager of a Saigon bank. In this post, I had continued my political activities but at higher level. My career as a student leader had earned me the trust of the revolutionary cadre, and for four years I wrote secret reports providing intelligence about South Vietnam's economic situation to the National Liberation Front. After the victory, when I was asked to take a 90% pay cut for the New Vietnam, I willingly did so. It was no different from the risks I had taken for the NLF in the revolutionary struggle. It was a personal price I was glad to pay for the sake of my country. But my attitude changed when the new regime turned its back on the promises of a national reconciliation and, taking off its patriotic mask, revealed its Marxist face.

When I was suddenly ordered to work on a plan to confiscate all private property and create a Communist state, I refused. The proposed scheme had nothing to do with the goals we had fought and died for, or with the aspirations of the South Vietnamese people, including the majority of those who had joined the struggle against the United States. My conscience would not permit me to cooperate in such a plan. I argued against it, but it was obvious that I was wasting my breath. It was not because of an oversight that there had been no prior discussion of this momentous change in the life of the nation. There was not going to be any discussion. It had already been decided in secret. And not even in South Vietnam. It had been decided in Hanoi. Perhaps even before the NLF was created, perhaps before I was born. The only thing I knew for certain was that suddenly what I thought or felt counted as nothing. I resigned from my post.

A few days later I was arrested as I was attending a public concert in the National Theater. I asked my captors "Why have you arrested me, what have I done?" They replied: "That is for you to work out."

During the War, I had been arrested several times by the Thieu regime. In all those times I had never felt lonely. Outside the walls of the jail I knew I had many supporters. We were all part of the same struggle and I felt like a hero. But when I was arrested this time, it was altogether different. I disappeared, completely cut off, totally isolated and terrifyingly alone. Every day I watched my fellow prisoners die beside me. No one was permitted to plead in their behalf, no one was allowed to know their fate. In the silence that surrounded us, I understood that the new Vietnam was a country without law. Lawyers had been abolished as capitalist parasites and all the law schools had been closed. The new Vietnam was a country in which people were put into prison without charges and kept there, even left to die there, without being given a trial. There was no institution the accused could appeal to. The Party controlled everything. There was no organization that could launch a protest. And if there had been such an organization it would not have mattered, because those who were arrested were simply cut off. In my own case, even my family was kept in the dark. My wife was not permitted to know why I was arrested, or where I was imprisoned or if I would ever be released.

Inside the prison, we were informed that our behavior, attitude and "good will" would be the keys to determining our release, whatever the crimes we might have committed. Our families were told the same thing:

their behavior would determine whether their loved ones were released. It was simple blackmail. In the first year of "liberation" more than a million individuals were imprisoned for political crimes. The new Vietnam was a society in which the people were ruled by political terror.

While I was in jail, Mai Chi Tho, a member of the central Committee of the Communist Party, addressed a selected group of political prisoners. He told us: *"Ho Chi Minh may have been an evil man; Nixon may have been a great man. The Americans may have had the just cause; we may not have had the just cause. But we won and the Americans were defeated because we convinced the people that Ho Chi Minh is a great man, that Nixon is a murderer and the Americans are invaders."* The lesson Mai drew was this: *"The key factor is how to control people and their opinions. Only Marxism-Leninism can do that. None of you ever see resistance to the Communist regime, so don't think about it. Forget it. Between you—the bright intellectuals—and me, I tell you the truth."*

Two and a half years after my arrest, my captors decided it was time to release me. As I stepped into the street I looked behind me at the prison I had left. In front of the building there were only a few policemen. There was no barbed wire, no watchtower, no forbidding wall. Over the entrance there was a large sign which said: "Nothing Is More Precious Than Liberty and Independence." It was Ho Chi Minh's best slogan, which the Communists used throughout the wars against the French and the Americans to woo the Vietnamese people and the rest of the world. Only those detained inside the prison and those guarding them knew what kind of place was hidden behind those words.

When I was still inside, I used to talk to one of the older prisoners who was a South Vietnamese Communist named Nguyen Van Tang. Tang had been imprisoned for 15 years by the French, for 8 years by Diem, for 6 years by Thieu and now for 2 years already by his own comrades, the Marxist rulers of the New Vietnam. While we were in prison together this old Communist said to me: "My dream is not that I will be released. My dream is not that I will see my family. My dream is to be back in a French prison 30 years ago."

Throughout the long years of war, even during the catastrophic famine of 1945 when two million people starved to death, Vietnamese people did not willingly leave their homeland. But with the Communist victory and the "liberation" that followed, hundreds of thousands of Vietnamese—liberals, anti-American activists, and even Communist dissidents—risked their lives, in boats on the high seas or on foot through dense jungles, to flee the terror of the Communist regime. Many fled to the United States. In 1978 I became one of them.

What I have found, since arriving in America, is a country where a person can do what he believes is right and fair—even if it means supporting his country's enemy in war—and still walk free. Jane Fonda visited Hanoi when it was being bombarded by her nation's air force. In the enemy's capital she said many things against her country and gave her support to the enemy side. But when she returned home, no one put her in jail for her crime. America is a place where people like Jane Fonda can do injustice to their country and still be honored and rewarded by the American people.

In the 1960s, many antiwar activists refused to believe that there were North Vietnamese troops in the South. Many antiwar protestors claimed that the NLF was really independent from the Communists in Hanoi, or that Ho Chi Minh and the Communists did not want to impose a Communist regime. Yet '60s activists and their followers are strangely silent about this Communist imperialism and Communist oppression. Even worse, they are once again raising their voices in defense of Communist revolutions pretending to be "nationalist" and "progressive" to the world at large.

Activists who protested against American intervention in South Vietnam in the 1960s should not be silent about human rights violations in Vietnam. They should not forget the people they once claimed to support. Their silence casts doubt on their sincerity. Their forgetfulness is a crime.

Most South Vietnamese like myself who fought against the Americans wanted independence and peace for Vietnam. We were not against America but against imperialism and war. With the help of Americans who were "anti-imperialists" too, we defeated America's armies and forced them to withdraw. Today South Vietnam is neither independent nor at peace. A new imperialism, more ruthless and brutal than any in the past, has conquered our land. In America, activists calling themselves "anti-imperialists" have come up with a new slogan: "No More Vietnams." If these words are sincere, those who invoke them will raise their voices against the Communist conquerors of Cambodia and Afghanistan, and they will support the national liberation movements that are fighting against the Communist imperialists in other nations as well.

C H A P T E R 2

THE THIRD FORCE: A VIETNAM FANTASY

Scott McConnell

As a teenager during the 1960s, I marched in anti-war demonstrations and rang doorbells for Gene McCarthy in New Hampshire; I also discussed the possibility of revolution with friends. By the end of the decade I was voicing a political line that sometimes echoed pronouncements from the Weather Underground—but only sometimes. Liberal and radical ideas blended together in a haze. Depending on my mood and company, I could sound like an admirer of Bobby Kennedy one moment and of Bernadine Dohrn the next.

In the summer of 1970 I put off going to college for a year, so I could go to work with a small anti-war "news agency" in South Vietnam. This trip was the result of a late night argument about the war with my father who challenged me to see Vietnam for myself before committing myself to draft resistance. I took the dare, and his offer of a ticket, and flew to Saigon.

The main task of the group of Americans I became involved with in Saigon was not simply gathering the news. We also gave tours to visiting American churchmen, political activists, and the occasional anti-war congressman. We sold American visitors on the viciousness and repression of the Thieu-Ky government. We argued that there was a democratic "third force"—spearheaded by Saigon's patriotic intellectuals, students, and Buddhist religious leaders—waiting in the wings to negotiate a settlement that would ensure self-determination and liberty for all Vietnamese if only the United States would withdraw its forces, cut its aid, and give peace a chance. All this was a fantasy, of course, and to this day I am unable to ascertain whether anyone in our group recognized the dishonesty involved in our enterprise.

If I had no coherent political ideology before going to Vietnam, I did assume that the United States was a malign and evil country, a sentiment I derived primarily from my sense of the Vietnam war, which had been established around 1966 when I was all of 14 and read several books about it. The one with the greatest impact on me was a skilled effort by Felix Greene, which had photographs and enough text to satisfy my need for the "facts." Greene's "analysis" promoted the notion that the National Liberation Front was essentially a movement of Jeffersonian democrats fighting for the national independence and the reunification of their country. He quoted the poems of Ho Chi Minh, and noted that crucial documents of the North Vietnamese and the NLF were derived from America's own Declaration of Independence while our own government, on the other hand, was propping up a dictatorship of corrupt landowners who were the antithesis of our own principles.

Once one embraced a view of Vietnam resembling Greene's, a long series of consequential beliefs concerning the United States fell smoothly into place. Whatever forces drove the U.S. to assault the Vietnamese with bombs and napalm, to crush their innocent aspirations for independence and democracy, and to support a clique of cruel autocrats must indeed have been powerful and aggressive and somewhat mysterious. It was said, in other books I encountered, that the U.S. was doing this kind of thing not only in Southeast Asia, but in Latin America and elsewhere in the world. By the late '60s it became apparent to me in a vague sort of way that U.S. corporations needed to crush indigenous democratic forces in these far away places so that their profits and markets could expand, and I was sure that if I read more I would eventually understand it all much better.

Needless to say, during the 1960s I did not meet much resistance to such views. On one side of my family there were Wall Street Republicans who were not much given to political argument, and who in any case were no match for my mastery of the terms of the 1954 Geneva Convention, say, or for the embarrassing quotations from former President Eisenhower I had memorized. On the other side of my family were independent radicals, one of them a beloved stepfather who had once been in the Communist Party and had retained many of the beliefs that had led him there. Nor did I encounter much opposition to my anti-Americanism in the culture at large. While it seemed prudent to wait until I had at least graduated from prep school before seizing buildings or anything like that, it was also clear that once one got into an Ivy League college, the way to get one's picture in *Life* magazine, or get a book contract, or to be praised as one of the best minds of one's generation, was to be as radical as possible.

My first sense that the views I had so glibly adopted were flawed came to me in Vietnam. Even though my days were spent in close contact with a coterie of left-liberal American activists in Saigon, I could not help but encounter many Vietnamese who did not share my view that the main interest of the National Liberation Front was rooting out corruption and establishing a democratic and unified Vietnam. Not only did I meet people who had previously fled the Communist North, often after they and their families had endured horrible suffering, but these Vietnamese seemed altogether decent and normal people with quite understandable hopes and fears and ambitions—and did not conform in the least to my image of the cruel and greedy bourgeoisie I assumed to be the main supporters of the "Thieu-Ky clique." Despite my ties with American activists in Saigon, after listening to these refugees from Ho Chi Minh's utopia, I began to wonder whether if I were Vietnamese I too might fear the Communists and not want to be ruled by them.

While thoughts like these were not enough to undermine my overall view of the war, they did raise subterranean doubts about the orthodox-ies I had so easily adopted. Such doubts were magnified a hundredfold by what I saw developing in neighboring Cambodia, a short plane ride away from bustling Saigon. Phnom Penh was an elegant city, just then starting to swell with refugees. Lacking the propagandistic guidance of a Felix Greene to shape my reactions, I found myself feeling an instinctive sympathy with the young and ill-equipped soldiers—often boys and girls with World War I vintage French rifles—who were every day struggling to keep open the waterways which fed the city.

These images of Southeast Asia were still with me a year later when I was in college, on the threshold of an education that would radically revise my sense of the Vietnam war and much else. I met professors of a generation now retiring from American universities, some of them refugees from Europe's great totalitarian experiments. With subtlety and passion and great learning, they opened up to me a perspective that was both completely fresh and yet, also jelled those doubts about the Left's virtue that had been raised by my own experience in Vietnam and Cambodia. Their point of view was, broadly speaking, that of anti-Communist social democracy; their message was, in barest essentials, that the United States had achieved something quite wonderful and relatively unique in our century by creating a society in which censor-ship, secret police, and concentration camps played no part. Further-more, American power—where it had been applied successfully—had played a decisive role in thwarting those who wanted to create more dictatorships in the world.

This perspective fit in with certain facts of the world's political geography, which I could not deny. In places where the United States was influential, there were elections, many newspapers, and few if any political prisoners. Of course there were exceptions—Greece and Spain and South Korea, although in time these situations too would change. On the other hand, in every country where the Soviet Union was the dominant super-power there were one party states, ration cards, block committees, arrests at dawn and the whole apparatus of coercion usually associated with fascism.

Obviously—and nothing could be more plain to anyone who had spent a year in Vietnam—it was impossible for Americans to make the world over in their own image; but it was just as obvious that in those parts of the world where American, rather than Soviet power, held sway, the democrats had a fighting chance of asserting a vision of society based on the primacy of political freedom and the rule of law.

This basic perspective was buttressed by considerable reading about the history of the Communist movement—certainly not enough to make me an expert in that vast and depressing subject—but enough so that when the North Vietnamese and Khmer Rouge marched into Saigon and Phnom Penh in 1975, I could sense that the pain for the people there was just beginning. The suffering, needless to say, was not visited only on the members of the "Thieu-Ky clique;" nor was it limited to the hundreds of thousands of average Vietnamese who worked and fought for the survival of an independent South Vietnam. After their conquest, the Communists were particularly quick to root out and imprison the leading members of the so-called "Third Force"—the non-Communist Vietnamese whom I and my colleagues had so admired because of their willingness to put their lives on the line in opposing the Saigon regime and supporting the liberation goals of peace and national reconciliation between all of Vietnam's political factions.

To people who have tried to keep informed of events in Vietnam since 1975, the reports from the overflowing Communist prison have been staggering. Though Party cadres often repeat that "the revolution does not wish to kill but to re-educate," the two fates have actually gone hand in hand. One victim who died under torture was Buddhist leader Thich Thien Minh—the chief strategist of the wartime religious opposition to Thieu and Ky—who in 1978 had the temerity to express doubts about the revolution's course to Buddhist worshippers. His fate may have been shocking for those who knew his role in wartime Vietnam, but such methods of imposing the Party's power over a newly "liberated" society have been a part of every Communist victory since 1917.

My first political thoughts were derived from my fantasies about Vietnam in the late '60s. My second thoughts began soon after seeing Vietnam for myself and were reinforced by what happened after the Communists won in 1975. I think that democracy—invariably associated with some form of capitalist mixed economy—provides a better life than does dictatorship based on the Marxist model. This is the case for both ordinary and exceptional people, and if one takes the pattern of emigration and immigration between the capitalist and Communist worlds as an indicator (what better one could there be?), the comparison is not even close.

And yet history is not a moral olympiad where virtue finds its own reward. The competition between the systems is not only about which one attracts more immigrants. It also concerns power. Thus I think the present struggles in the Third World between Communists and their varied opponents are profoundly important. Several of them—Central America, the Philippines, and indeed Afghanistan—have a clear bearing on the global military balance.

These battles have a further, somewhat psychological meaning as well. They are, in effect, the shadow indicators about the direction of political movement, about who owns the future. They are monitored throughout the world as signs of whether the tide is moving with democracy or with Soviet-inspired dictatorship. In this sense, the political infighting within the democracies over whether Third World Communist advances should be accommodated (and even welcomed) or combatted seems to me a variation on a question first posed to the West in 1917. This is whether capitalism—"late capitalism" in Marxian parlance—and its baggage of "bourgeois" democracy amount to nothing more than way stations along the road to a more "progressive" system of socialist dictatorship. It is a question which brings with it a corollary: whether the Communist Party dictators, who profess to rule in the name of the people, are themselves agents of an historical atavism which will eventually go the way of the despotisms of the past.

CHAPTER 3

A POLITICAL JOURNEY

David Ifshin

A conference entitled Second Thoughts sounds temptingly like an invitation to reinvent history one's own way. When the period in question is the end of the '60s, there is a particular temptation to see those events through the prism of what has occurred since, and to refashion events to better suit our own current views and self-images. In addition, the notion of "second thoughts" seems a bit understated for my own experience and, I sense, for that of many others.

I entered adolesence and adulthood with the Vietnam War. President Kennedy sent American advisers to Vietnam when I was in grammar school; the Tonkin Gulf resolution passed when I was beginning high school; the war did not end until I had gone through college, spent four years engaged in various activities and completed a semester of law school. During that time I had friends who were killed in the war, friends who became draft dodgers and draft resisters, friends who fled to Canada and, still other friends who concocted a bizzare variety of survival strategies. I cannot reinvent that time, therefore, as a coherent whole in which choices were always clear. Nonetheless, a day has not gone by in the last twenty years that I have not thought about that era in all of its agony and intensity.

My participation in the 1960s was not particularly ideological. In that regard, my story is more typical than atypical. When I finished high school in 1966, I supported the war in Vietnam, and I responded with considerable hostility to friends returning from their first and second years at college who challenged it. My opinions were generally consistent with the mainstream of that time: the United States represented a force of enlightenment and good in the world. The struggle in Vietnam was an extension of our broader role and responsibilities both to help the Vietnamese and to halt the spread of Communism.

When I entered Syracuse University in the fall of 1966, campus activism was almost unknown. Yet the earlier veterans of the civil rights marches in the South had a powerful presence, and the stirrings of discontent were already present. College offered a cosmopolitanism and a sophistication that had thus far eluded me. Yet, for me, the debate at that time had little to do with personal commitments. The first day of college I joined Army R.O.T.C. and when I later turned eighteen that fall, I gladly registered for the draft as another sign of approaching adulthood.

My support for the war was not something I cavalierly discarded one day out of convenience. Arguments about the war filled our classrooms and our evenings, and those discussions continued for years. At first, the majority supported the government's policy and often prevailed by utilizing the arguments of the Johnson Administration against the few that had come to oppose it. Yet inexorably, painfully, individual by individual, the dynamics of the discussion shifted to where the defenders had fewer and fewer arguments that were able to withstand the scrutiny of events.

In the spring of 1968, I was asked by the newly elected student body president to attend the congress that summer of the U.S. National Student Association in Manhattan, Kansas. At the congress, I was for the first time exposed directly to the torrent of passions and emotion as articulated by some of the most prominent anti-war leaders of the day, including Tom Hayden, David Dellinger, Dick Gregory, Rennie Davis, Michael Ferber and a host of others. While the confluence of passions and ideas was intense and fascinating, the underlying message was clear: in a time of great political and moral crisis, one could not afford the luxury of sitting on the sidelines. Once it was clear that U.S. foreign policy was misdirected, the only remaining question was the action one was prepared to take to stop it.

As an earlier supporter of Robert Kennedy and later Eugene McCarthy, I had already decided to work for Hubert Humphrey, by then the inevitable nominee in the general election. Nonetheless, I went to the 1968 Democratic Convention in Chicago in the belief that a peaceful demonstration there might strengthen the beginning of the Democratic Party's commitment to change our Vietnam policy. It was to be my first demonstration against the war.

I arrived on the Sunday before the convention and proceeded to Lincoln Park in the expectation that there would be a peaceful demonstration. I was in the Park no longer than twenty minutes with several thousand other people, mostly young, when an enormous number of riot police first surrounded the Park and then entered from every direction and began to swing at everything in sight. I remember backing away from a police officer at that moment who, unable to reach me, turned and split open the head of a young girl who could not have been older than 18. As her boyfriend tried to return to help her, he received even more brutal treatment. There may have been some provocation to cause that reaction, but I did not see it.

For the next several days, any attempts to demonstrate against the war were met with equal force. The experience was enormously disorienting; my reaction was disbelief. Surely the right to peacefully protest against a government policy was still guaranteed. Nonetheless, the culmination on Wednesday evening of an enormous force of police and national guardsmen arrayed against a relatively small number of would-be peaceful demonstrators throughout the night was disillusioning. I returned home an embittered and disillusioned opponent, not only of the Administration's policy, but now of the manner in which the government apparently intended to maintain support for it.

Late in the spring of the following year, I was elected student government president by appealing to the sense of growing alienation and frustration on the campus. A few months later, as president of the student government, I helped organize the Vietnam moratorium on campus. Over ten thousand participants peacefully marched, the largest demonstration in the history of the city. I became more involved in the National Student Association that year and attended several of the meetings of the anti-war coalition organizing the national protests. When, in the spring of 1970, there was a military invasion into Cambodia, Syracuse was one of the first colleges to go on strike following a meeting I helped organize on the quadrangle, after returning from an NSA press conference at which I, along with a number of other student body presidents, had called for such demonstrations.

Upon graduation, I went to the National Student Association Congress in Minnesota. There, I was elected president of USNSA and returned to Washington that fall. My predecessor had been in direct contact with NSA's counterpart organization in South Vietnam, an important element of the "Third Force," that opposed both the Communists and the Saigon regime. The South Vietnamese Student Association led by Huyen Tan Mam, had invited my predecessor to South Vietnam earlier that year along with other anti-war leaders. At that time, there had been demonstrations against the war, which had led to the imprisonment of many of the students. This relationship was transferred to me upon assuming office as one of the key elements of our policy. It was consistent not only with my own views, but with the policy the National Student Congress had adopted at the same meeting in which I was elected. The two student organizations had had the notion during the earlier meeting in South Vietnam, that support for the concept of a coalition government—including elements of the Third Force, the existing government of South Vietnam and the Communists—would be promoted by the concept of a "Peoples Peace Treaty." Prior to my election, the NSA Congress voted almost unanimously to make pursuit of such a document a goal of its next administration. It was during this period and out of this relationship that I first met Doan Van Toai, the author of *The Vietnamese Gulag,* and a fellow participant in this conference.

Following further imprisonments of student leaders in South Vietnam, NSA organized a protest of student body presidents to demand release of the students who had been imprisoned in South Vietnam. Following notification of their release, we asked to go to South Vietnam to meet with them ourselves. Since the visit of the group that included my predecessor that previous spring had only led to further troubles, the government of South Vietnam refused to issue a visa to the group that wanted to go. I recall going to the Embassy with three others to request our visas. Two of us were 1A for the draft and two were Vietnam veterans who wanted to go back. We were denied admission. Frankly, it did not seem like a big deal at the time since, given my draft status, I was likely to be able to get a visit without a visa in the not-too-distant future.

Nonetheless, the press covered the incident, and it led to an inquiry whether I would be willing to visit North Vietnam. The invitation was straightforward and played directly into a preconception I was drifting toward: that it was the government of South Vietnam that was repressive and that North Vietnam had been misportrayed. My subsequent visit there, a trip made by many other Americans, most more prominent than I (including a former Attorney General of the United States, Joan Baez, Dr. Spock, and others) reinforced my desire to believe that the other side was willing to end the war by forming a coalition government with the government of South Vietnam and the Third Force following U.S. withdrawal. This was emphasized repeatedly, usually in the form of support for the proposal offered by the Communist side at the Peace Talks through the Provisional Revolutionary Government, the political arm of the National Liberation Front. The reality that neither of these organizations was more than a Communist front was obvious even to us.

The most compelling parts of the trip, however, were not such discussions. Our hosts lost no opportunity to show us the physical and human toll of the war. Given our own sentiments and feelings in that regard, it could not fail to have the intended effect. We were shown exhibitions of so-called "American war crimes," always stressing that they were angry at the American government, not at individual Americans like us. I recall, in particular, one session in which a succession of individuals were brought in who had been wounded by American bombing: a man whose face had been melted by white phosphorous and who was breathing through two straws where his nose and been; a young teenage girl who could sit down only with great pain and difficulty because of fiberglass cluster bomb pellets still lodged in her body that could not be removed because the pellets were invisible to x-ray (a casing from a Honeywell anti-personnel bomb was laid on the table with the Honeywell name visible for us to see as we talked to them); a woman with a deformed infant who could not sit up in her hospital bed due to her constant nausea because she allegedly had drunk water polluted with defoliants.

In retrospect, the use of civilian casualties is obviously an enormously powerful force to influence untrained civilians who have arrived with preconceptions such as ours. Our reaction was predictable. Nonetheless, the Vietnamese continued to say to us that it was our government and not we who were responsible. Later that evening, however, I ran into some European visitors, who stated they were doctors investigating American war crimes. They were not so charitable. On hearing that I was an American, their comments were blunt, including direct comparisons to the Second World War and "crimes of silence." When I responded that as a Jew I found Holocaust comparisons from a European to be obscene, one inquired acidly whether I would consider a wartime German guiltless because he had visited a gas chamber and registered his disapproval. What had I *really* done, he asked, to distinguish myself from my countrymen who were waging, in his words, a war of genocide. After enduring their comments for a short time, one of the Vietnamese with me suggested there was a more personal statement I could make by being interviewed for the radio.

One of the great misfortunes that can befall someone who is twenty is to have someone put a microphone in front of them to record or broadcast his sophomoric statements. As president of NSA, I was frequently accorded that opportunity. On countless occasions, I had been interviewed by the broadcast and print media at a ridiculously young age. This was an opportunity, however, I would not soon forget. The statement I made was later broadcast by the North Vietnamese over the radio to my continuing embarrassment and shame.

It is too easy, however, to focus on that single event as an isolated error. In fact, it was simply an extension of a more fundamental error that I shared with too many others: a willful disregard of what was to happen not only to the people who worked with our government during the war, but to the Third Force itself under Communist rule. The story does not need repeating here; we all know it too well. The imprisonments, torture and petty brutalities of the Communists' relentless drive to convert the country into their own image of "social equality" is an evil that cannot be exaggerated. It is too easy for us to ignore both the results and the reasons.

It is not, however, as simple a matter as saying that had the war continued there might have been a happier ending. The policy itself of our government was so fundamentally flawed from the beginning that it is doubtful—regardless of what happened in the way of domestic support—that it could have succeeded. The war was lost long before domestic opposition reached significant proportions. Moreover, to blame failure of the war on lack of domestic support is to confuse cause and effect. It is the responsibility of the leadership of the government to develop and adopt policies that can be supported by the people at a cost whose toll is reasonable. When there is a failure of the leadership to meet that standard, domestic discontent is to be expected.

Later that following year, I set off for South America to attend a meeting in Salvador Allende's Chile. It is there that I began to see the struggle in a different context. A vibrant and historic democracy, Chile had just elected Salvador Allende by a small plurality as its President. The country was in turmoil, and the Communists decided to hold a meeting of their student organization there to express solidarity. It was in those debates and discussions that I began to understand more directly the reality of the threat. It was clear to any honest observer that the Communists were not going to promote a change in Chile peacefully. The Cubans were helping to arm them in the *barrios,* and we could feel an impending civil war in the air.

I returned to the United States where I worked first for the National Welfare Rights Organization and later for the Democratic National Committee in support of George McGovern's 1972 election. It was there that I began to become deeply disillusioned with the Democratic Party's foreign policy. Rather than directly engage the issues, there was a persistent superficiality about foreign policy, an analysis that could go no further than withdrawal of U.S. troops from Vietnam. While it was an end I still eagerly sought and was prepared to work for, its intellectual emptiness was manifest to anyone who cared to explore it.

At the end of the campaign, I decided to go to Israel to live and work for a while to get a different perspective on the world. I wound up on a kibbutz on the border, a kibbutz which had suffered heavily in the struggle with the PLO before Hussein dislodged them. After returning home following the end of the Yom Kippur War, my appreciation of America's place in the world had been deepened in a manner that can only occur in an environment where one sees it threatened directly and tangibly. One cannot be that close to confrontation with countries so heavily armed with Soviet weaponry without a dramatic impact on one's views. As C5A cargo planes landed every few moments to replenish an ally whose resources were almost exhausted during a time of enormous costs in human life, it made the earlier opposition to those aircraft that I had voiced ring hollow and bitter. Although details of that resupply and the internal politics of Washington later became apparent to me, the impact at the moment will never be lost.

After returning home and working construction for a while, I headed off to law school. I had decided that I would put political involvement behind me given how profoundly my views had evolved, when I was contacted by Scoop Jackson's presidential campaign manager. At his request, I agreed to help during the summer of 1975 as the campaign sought to make its peace with elements of the McGovern wing of the Party. I arranged several meetings with them and Senator Jackson; they accomplished little. They did, however, lead to an invitation to me to travel with him in San Diego for a few days. It was during that trip that I told Senator Jackson that I was probably not going to get involved in any more campaigns because of a difficulty of reconciling my current views with my past positions. His reaction was intense and unforgetta- ble. He upbraided me for believing that the United States could have C5A's for Israel alone and said whether I worked in his campaign or not, I had an obligation to turn my experiences into action for the things I had learned the hard way.

In many ways, it was that meeting that set me on the path to this Conference. But conferences and seminars are not enough. While we should not become so obsessed with the past that it paralyzes us, we need to do more than just learn from our mistakes. The people of Vietnam live under a brutal and repressive regime. It is wrong for people who opposed or supported American involvement in Vietnam out of a desire to help the people of that country to ignore the present reality. In my own case, I have co-founded with Doan Van Toai the Institute for Democracy in Vietnam. Its purpose is to help support pro-democratic forces in Vietnam, including the publication of a Vietnamese *samizdat*. It is a tribute to Toai's perseverance and courage that in addition to publishing *The Vietnamese Gulag* in Vietnamese and distributing it in Vietnam, the Institute will soon resume publishing his magazine of political commentary that he edited as a student leader of the Third Force.

C H A P T E R 4

THE CAMBODIAN TRAGEDY

David Hawk

The horrible fate of Cambodia under Communist rule has allowed many in both the anti-war Left and the pro-war Right to simply reinforce their prejudice saying, in effect, "If only the U.S. had never intervened . . . ," or, "If only the U.S. had not turned tail and bugged out. . . ."

Perhaps it is possible to get beyond this stale and unedifying approach. In any event I would like to offer two considerations based on developments in Cambodia in the 1970s and 1980s as they reflect on the inadequacy of attitudes and policy dispositions shared by some of the ideological tendencies in the political movement in which I was associated in the mid-to-late 1960s and early 1970s—the opposition to U.S. intervention in Indochina.

The first reflection on developments in Cambodia between 1975 and 1979 is obvious—the inability or unwillingness of some parts of the former anti-war movement to recognize the genocidal human rights violations in Cambodia under Khmer Rouge rule, and the attempt by some anti-war intellectuals and activists to minimize, obfuscate, cover-up, and deny the scale and scope of Khmer Rouge atrocities. A second reflection which derives from developments in and over Cambodia after 1979 is perhaps less obvious—the role for judicious and considered projection of U.S. power and influence in Southeast Asia.

FACING UP TO THE WORST

People opposed the U.S. war in Vietnam and U.S. policy toward Cambodia for a wide variety of reasons, many of which, in my opinion, remain entirely valid. But some parts of the anti-war opposition went on

89

to romanticize "the other side" and adopt a stance of "solidarity" with the Indochinese Revolution.

The New-Left wing of the anti-war movement posited faith and hope in third world socialism in the way that earlier generations of Leftists had posited faith and hope in the European proletariat (until the First World War) or the Soviet Union (until the Stalin show trials, the Hitler-Stalin pact, Hungary, or Khrushchev's secret speech or whatever). There was an even more widespread tendency among parts of the opposition to American interventionism to confer virtue on the victims of U.S. foreign policy.

For Cambodia this was clearly evidenced in a Preface, written by a prominent anti-war intellectual, to a book on the spread of the Second Indochina war into the Cambodian heartland, which heralded the inevitable victory of "liberation" as preparing the ground for a "new era of economic development and social justice" for Cambodia.

These words were written in 1972, and it should be noted that the Khmer Rouge did not begin the viciously repressive policies applied to the entire country after 1975 until 1973 in those zones then under their control. In 1972, as the extreme corruption and venality of the Lon Nol regime manifested itself, there were many Cambodians and westerners who believed that Prince Sihanouk's restoration (Sihanouk, then in exile in China was the nominal leader of the "United Front" against Lon Nol's Khmer Republic) would lead to the return of the easy-going Cambodian style "Buddhist Socialism" Sihanouk had long espoused.

Cheering on the Cambodian revolutionaries as portending economic development and social justice could be regarded as a very bad call but an honest mistake—a well-meant but entirely misplaced conferring of a wholly unmerited virtue on a radical nationalist movement in a country that was indeed being brutally victimized by more powerful neighbors and the world's greatest power. However, for some former opponents to the U.S. war policies in Indochina, as the nature of the Cambodian revolution manifested itself, after 1973 in some areas (which were almost entirely inaccessible to foreigners,) but far more clearly after 1975 with the cruelty of the extraordinary forced evacuation of the cities, this led not to a sadder but wiser re-evaluation of misplaced hopes but to a willful obfuscation and denial that amounted not only to a profound mis-interpretation of the nature of Marxist-Leninist rule in Cambodia but to nothing less than a determined cover-up of genocide.

In the face of abundant refugee accounts to the contrary and several serious analyses of the body of testimony this denial took numerous forms: confident assertions that the reports of atrocities were exaggerated propaganda; letters of protest to human rights groups that sought to mobilize opinion against the atrocities. The most disingenuous and guileful obfuscation was a footnote studded book co-authored by the Preface writer cited above, published in 1979, devoted largely to attacking the reliability of the refugee accounts and the honesty and credibility of the journalists and publications that gathered, reported, and printed the terrible atrocities recounted by the refugees lucky enough to survive escape attempts from the Khmer Rouge.

Ostensibly an analysis of how the establishment media was using the refugee accounts of Khmer Rouge atrocities to reconstruct the imperial ideology of cold war anti-Communism, the primary result of this and earlier formulations was to sow doubt about the reliability of those refugee reports. And so it did, at least in so far as some (though only some) circles of the former anti-war opposition were concerned. That some of the "New Left" were as blind or indifferent to the crimes of Pol Pot as some in the "Old Left" were to the crimes of Stalin is not the least of it. The alacrity and persistence of Pol Pot's defenders diverted attention and refocused discussion from "how should Khmer Rouge bloodlust best be exposed and protested" to "whether or not the refugee accounts exaggerated and were the reports of largely politically motivated propaganda."

Even if taken at face value, in light of the one to two million Cambodians (out of a population of six to seven million) who died at the hands of Pol Pot's fanatical Marxist regime in less than four years, a minutely footnoted exegesis demonstrating that there were a few and really quite minor and unimportant exaggerations among the refugee accounts, or really quite minor mistakes in the reportage of those accounts, or even that ideological opponents scored political points by citing Khmer Rouge atrocities is at best an absurd quibble. Yet this grotesque thesis had a chilling effect on the mobilization of opinion against the Cambodian genocide.

It took three years to even get the extreme Khmer Rouge violations onto the agenda of the U.N. (where, even after the U.N.'s own experts determined that the situation in Cambodia was genocidal and the worst to have occurred since Nazism, a coalition of Soviet bloc and third world countries succeeded in blocking consideration of the most thorough report of human rights violations the U.N. system had produced up to that time). The international community has yet to consider let alone condemn the extreme Khmer Rouge violations.

The reasons for the gross inadequacy of the laws, institutions and organizations envisioned and established after World War II to prevent, retard or at least protest and decry extreme violations of human rights to cope with the terrible crimes perpetrated by the Communist Party of Kampuchea are varied and complex.★ It is a complicated sad story and there are lessons aplenty for all. One of the sorriest parts of the story is the ideologically motivated willful disbelief. And even worse is the pseudo-agnostic position on the atrocities that aggressively sought to discredit the methodology and integrity of those who bore the unwelcome news of the horrors of "class struggle and proletarian dictatorship" in liberated Cambodia.

Minimally, it could be concluded that opponents of U.S. intervention ought to be more careful not to confer virtue on the victims of U.S. policy. At least U.S. intervention ought to be opposed, when it ought to be opposed, without extending sympathy or becoming self-deluded about the nature of the regimes American power would seek to subvert or destroy.

A ROLE FOR U.S. POWER AND INFLUENCE

A second reflection stemming from developments in and over Cambodia after 1979 relates to the role and propriety of U.S. power and influence as a contributory factor toward a more stable balance of power in Southeast Asia.

The ignominious American exit from Indochina led not to peace and stability in southeast Asia but to a power vacuum and regional disequilibrium. The Sino-Soviet struggle for power and influence in Asia spilled over or down into Southeast Asia as China and the Soviet Union engaged in mutually encircling or outflanking actions and the victorious Asian Communist revolutions—China, Vietnam and Cambodia—took to fighting each other and, in consequence, threatening Thailand.

★To name but a few: the most egregious violations are in fact the hardest to deal with; the atrocity stories of the refugees were so horrendous as to boggle the imagination in the sense that the extrajudicial execution of one Polish priest or four religious workers in El Salvador is an outrage while the deaths of millions is an abstraction; while the Khmer Rouge violations were reasonably well covered on the inside pages of the few newspapers that devote much space to international news, the virtual lack of television news coverage meant the stories never reached a critical mass in public consciousness; by 1975 the western, and particularly American, public was saturated with news of bloodshed in Indochina; the flaws in the U.N. definition of genocide; the ponderous nature of the U.N. human rights machinery; the relative weakness of the human rights movement which was just getting off the ground in the mid-seventies; etc.

The long overdue end of European colonialism, Japanese occupation and U.S. intervention led to the stunningly rapid reemergence of traditional pre-colonial patterns of interstate conflict in Southeast Asia. Vietnam and Thailand vie for power and influence, if not also territory, in Cambodia. China seeks weak and divided, if not also obeisant, neighboring states on its southern periphery.

With the clarity of hindsight it can now be seen that not only did America walk into Indochina backwards, get in far too deeply, and stay far too long—the U.S. also left far too completely. In short, the U.S. role and U.S. policy went from one extreme to the other. There are still former leaders of the anti-war movement who think that the main source of the Third Indochina War is the United States. To the contrary, the United States is fixated on the residual legacies of the Second Indochina War. American diplomacy toward the Third Indochina War is mostly a study in policy abdication. What is now desirable is for the U.S. to use its influence to promote a solution, and help provide the necessary great power guarantees for a settlement worked out between the primary parties and powers to the dispute. Yet currently, the only superpower diplomacy toward the Third Indochina War is that conducted by the Soviet Union.

An end of the Vietnamese occupation of Cambodia will require compromise between the Cambodian parties and a working out of tensions between Vietnam and China. But in all probability, a resolution to the Third Indochina conflict will require an influence capable of balancing and countervailing that of China and the Soviet Union. For obvious reasons that's not going to be Japan or Western Europe, which by default leaves the United States. The balance of forces that results in the stalemate that U.S. policy nominally opposes gives the U.S. considerable leverage were the U.S. to overcome its policy of non-influence.

Virtually all the parties and powers to the conflict—except perhaps the Soviet Union—want an increased U.S. role in the region: China to counter-balance the weight of Russia; Japan to counter-balance the weight of both China and the Soviet Union, ASEAN to counter-balance the weight of Russia, China, and Japan; the non-Communist Cambodian parties to counter-balance the vastly larger support given by the Soviet Union and China to their respective Cambodian Communist client parties. Even Vietnam realizes that barring a complete Sino-Soviet entente which would probably come about at their expense, a renewed U.S. influence is required in order to end its unhealthy over-reliance on its Soviet ally.

What is at issue here is not only an abstract notion of a stable balance of power in the region, although that would serve the interests of America's friends and allies in Southeast Asia. Also at stake is how long the present debilitating and stalemated war over Cambodia will go on. Lastly, for those who think that U.S. power and influence can be used to enlarge the scope for democracy, in the face of certain massive Chinese and Soviet support for the pro-Chinese and pro-Soviet Cambodian Communist parties, what is at issue is whether there will be much, if any, role in a possible post-Vietnamese occupied Cambodia for non-Communist politics. Yet, the U.S., having tried obsessively and vainly to do in Indochina what it could not, now largely resists doing what it could.

As noted at the outset, these observations and reflections based on the Cambodian tragedy after the U.S. defeat in Indochina pertain to the perspective and politics of the anti-war opposition in which I was active. Perhaps it ought to be at least noted that Cambodia is or ought to be no less difficult an issue for the former pro-war Right. The Communist Party of Kampuchea, still led by those most responsible for the genocidal policies of Khmer Rouge rule, are now allied with and partially supported by the Western democracies. The notion that the Western democracies might condition their diplomatic and material support for the Khmer Rouge State upon the removal of those who committed genocide has received scant consideration. The democratic powers have no operational policy or plan to prevent the return to power by the Khmer Rouge (their multilateral aid helped rebuild) in the event that Vietnam would adhere to U.N. resolutions and withdraw. The Department of State seems no less content than the isolationist Left to consign Cambodia to someone else's sphere of influence.

PART III

SECOND THOUGHTS ON NICARAGUA

Fanor Avendano
Arturo Cruz, Jr.
Fausto Amador
Xavier Arguello
Bruce Cameron
Robert Leiken
Ronald Radosh

CHAPTER 1

MY NAME IS FANOR

Fanor Avendano

My name is Fanor Avendano and I live in Managua, which they call the "City of Chaos" these days. I am from a laboring family and I have ten brothers and sisters. My father was a peasant who began to study how to read and write at age thirty. He is today a lawyer and he is vice president of the Social Christian Party. I started fighting against Somoza when I was 14 years old. I got involved in the fight against the Somoza regime because it genuinely denied human freedom; because very small groups dominated the economic resources of the country; because people lived in tremendous material and cultural deprivation; and because I had a very independent political point of view.

Many workers, students and young peasants supported the Sandinista front, not because they were Marxist but because they wanted to get rid of Somoza. In August 1978, when I was 16 years old, I engaged in battles with the National Guard. They arrested various of us leaders at the university and in the neighborhoods and in secondary schools. Somoza security police levied ten charges against us. We were tortured, usually in dark rooms, naked and without air conditioning, at the command of General Somoza.

Fortunately, we were released as a result of the seizing of the National Palace by *"Comandante Zero"*—Eden Pastora—who gave up the Palace on the condition of the release of the political prisoners. I was surprised to be free. We were all given the opportunity of staying in Nicaragua or going to Panama or Cuba. I was one of those who chose to remain in Nicaragua and continue the struggle.

After my imprisonment, I entered into the organizational structure of the guerilla movement. I couldn't participate in the final offensive against Somoza because I was ill as a result of the torture I had experienced in my final incarceration. A revolutionary triumph took place.

We all supported the original plan of the revolutionary government. We had the romantic illusion that everything that had been said during the war against Somoza would become a reality. We really thought that the larger estates of the great landowners were going to be divided up into small parcels for the peasants; that people weren't going to have to live in cardboard boxes anymore, but were going to live in houses worthy of human beings; that there would be an adequate budget for education and genuine university autonomy, that workers in the banana fields would work 8 hours a day instead of 12; that miners weren't going to have to destroy their lungs in those tunnels. We also believed that there would be a true cultural development.

Little by little in the first months, we began to realize that the nationalism which the Sandinista front had united behind was being discarded. The FSLN leadership attacked North American imperialism at the exact moment that Soviet imperialism began to penetrate our country. We got rid of the weapons and the militarism of the Somoza dictatorship, but a Sandinista Party army began to grow in its place. During the struggle, we had said that there would be more hospitals and schools, instead of army installations, and so it was a shock when, after the triumph of the revolution, the few schools that did exist were turned into Sandinista barracks for the Sandinista Army. It was also painful to see churches turned into Sandinista headquarters.

In the first months of the revolution, I began to see the growing Cuban influence. It even got to the point where people were saying that one Cuban had more power than a Supreme Court Justice. Eight months after the victory, most of the young people and many of the other members of the Social Christian Party ceased to support the government. The Sandinistas accused me, in particular, of having "bourgeois complexes." I told them that I ceased to support them because I wasn't a Marxist-Leninist, I was just one more person in the mass—the mass of students, workers, others who had been deceived; that our principles of human dignity and of liberty and democracy continued to prevail as far as we were concerned; that they were the real traitors to the Nicaraguan people. We had fought so that the workers would work 8 hours and not 12. But now they asked workers to give their Sundays up and work 16 hours on Sunday "for the revolution." We criticized Somoza and capitalism for exploiting the workers, but today the workers are more exploited than ever. If under Somoza we had pseudo-autonomy in the high schools and the colleges, professors now came in green uniforms to teach us war, and often they were Cubans or Bulgarians or Soviets.

Since the revolution, public health has completely collapsed. The economy is more chaotic than ever. Education is now totally partisan, the product and instrument of one party. Somoza had in his National Guard 12,000 men. The FSLN party has an army of 300,000 men. Instead of sowing beans we are sowing bullets. This is why I am in the struggle once again. I believe that the ideals of human dignity and freedom are betrayed by Left-wing groups, like the Sandinistas. I believe, too, that these ideals will ultimately prevail.

We are dedicated to the struggle for freedom in Nicaragua. We are against a continuation of conscription for the Sandinista Party's partisan purposes, which is quite different from conscription for military service in a government under a state of law. We are fighting against the disappearances of young men from our streets engineered by the Sandinista military. I have here a picture of a young man who was opposed to conscription and has been taken away. Nobody knows where he is. His family can't locate him. We are launching a campaign that he be reappeared. His is one of thousands of cases. What we have now is not military service to defend the country, but to defend a party which happens to be in power, which is the party called Sandinista, that calls its army Sandinista, which also has a police by the same name.

A lot of you are probably wondering how I could be here in Washington. How could I even leave Nicaragua? I had to make gestures through the Latin American Trade Union Federation and pretend that I was being invited to a meeting in Costa Rica in order for the Sandinista government to give me permission to leave for one month. But the practical truth is that you can leave once but never leave again. I have in my hand a copy of my conscription booklet which we all have to carry. If it is not stamped, we can't study, we can't work, we can't leave the particular province where we happen to live. That is to say, in other words, that in Nicaragua there is no freedom of movement, there is no freedom to leave the country, there is no freedom to study, there is no freedom to work, but freedom only to be a prisoner of the Sandinistas, or to fight and die for the Sandinistas.

So we continue our struggle mindful of the 10,000 political prisoners that exist in Nicaragua, inspired by the need of the mothers of political prisoners, and encouraged by the support which you give us. We continue with the idea that it is possible to defeat international Communism. We are not against Communists as people, as individual people, but as a system. We are not against capitalism either, as far as people are concerned, but as a system. We want democracy as much in Chile as in Cuba. I am convinced that if we prevail, Nicaragua will again be a free republic among free peoples.

CHAPTER 2

WHY I LEFT MY COUNTRY

Arturo Cruz, Jr.

I grew up in two Nicaraguan cities, Jinotepe, my father's town, and Granada, my mother's. Among my friends to be anti-Somoza was as natural as breathing. But my friends were the so-called *la gente bien,* the good people. Nonetheless, the revolution against General Somoza most certainly did not occur as my Leftist American friends have since carefully explained it to me: by a sudden uprising of the masses. Somoza left the people alone, if the people left him alone. Not to be openly against Somoza was to be with him.

Early opposition came only from those like my father, who fought openly with Somoza and was jailed twice, once in 1947, for four months, and once in 1954, for a year. Somoza never feared my father's generation, however, because he knew that the Nicaraguan political elite could never unite. Over the years the members of the political class had compromised themselves so egregiously and had been manipulated so often that no true organized opposition to the Somozas developed until the Sandinistas provided leadership in the mid–70s.

Of course the Sandinistas hardly spoke for the people either. The genius of the Sandinistas was that they understood that if the country's political center could be manipulated, they could attract a viable power base and the masses would follow. Sandinistas were Marxists to those who wanted Marxism; they were social democrats to those who wanted social democracy. They were deceitful in their soul.

In this spirit of cynical pragmatism, the faction led by the Ortega brothers—the *terceristas*—stopped talking about class warfare and began talking about democracy instead. Their new tactical game was to stop using Cuba as the model for the "new Nicaragua," and instead to present Costa Rica as the type of regime with which they wanted to replace

101

Somoza. Their lies were so bold and shameless that people believed them. This was the great historical achievement of the Ortega brothers. They told Nicaraguans they wanted a society based on Costa Rica's democratic model, and Nicaraguans believed them. In their hearts, of course, they continued to be Castro's children.

The Sandinistas understood something else: that for most Nicaraguans, political struggle is a personal rather than an ideological matter. Most of the participants in the Nicaraguan revolution identified with faces, not ideas. For them, the war was more of a boxing match than a political contest. Part of the Sandinistas' success came from their understanding of how to fashion heroes, as when they created Eden Pastora as a challenger to go against the champion Somoza.

I joined the Sandinistas in 1978. By then it was clear that the Sandinistas had managed to unite the political center, that the people were behind them, and that President Carter's commitment to Somoza was shaky. It was unclear to us how the Sandinistas would govern when in power, because we were all Sandinistas, and we did not know ourselves. We did not know which of us would rule, or how. At the time, the educated elite were all Marxists or technocrats. (The technocrats were the Chicago boys: they had gone to the University of Chicago and had come back imbued with monetarism). My friends and I joined the Marxist side, because I knew the country required radical economic change and I preferred Karl Marx to Milton Friedman.

Now, with nine years behind me, I also see that I became a Sandinista because I did not want to be left off the train of history. We all wanted to be present at the creation of the new Nicaragua. Creation is a terrifying act, but it would have been more terrifying to have been left out of creation altogether.

From 1979 to 1981 I was the Sandinistas' man in Washington in charge of handling Congress. It was my task to negotiate the $75 million assistance package the Carter Administration was arranging for the Sandinista regime. It provided crucial balance of payments support on very generous terms. The money came from the Special Support Funds which were reserved only for very close allies of the United States like Israel or Egypt. Not only was the U.S. Government giving us economic aid, but quality aid. And not only Special Support Funds, but also PL 480—food for peace funds—and loans for development projects from AID. The U.S. government was also supporting us in our requests to renegotiate our national debts with the private New York banks. Finally, the Carter Administration was using its good offices with the World Bank, the Inter-American Development Bank and other multinational organizations to be very generous with the revolutionary regime. With enemies like this, one doesn't need friends.

The line I took as the Sandinista representative in Washington was that if the U.S. was generous with us we would not go to the Soviets for aid. But in reality, even while the U.S. was providing us this generous financial support, we were signing every possible agreement under the table with the USSR and the other Communist governments for military support and to establish Party to Party relations. What we Sandinistas wanted was to establish a division of labor: the west would provide the money for socialist economic development, while the Communist states would provide us with the weapons and technical support in setting up the institutions of power—the army, the police, the "block committees" charged with spying on the population. So while America and the other western democracies supplied advisers to our economic ministers, the internal and external security ministers and the ministries responsible for the new ideological apparatus—communications, education—were reserved for foreign advisors from the Soviet Union, Cuba, East Germany, Bulgaria, North Vietnam and North Korea.

Gradually it dawned on me that the Sandinistas did not wish to reach an understanding with the United States, an understanding that I felt was necessary. The Sandinistas interpreted the war in Angola as a Cuban victory over South Africa. This intoxicated them; in their view, for the first time in history, a Third World power had met a First World power in combat and triumphed. Cuba's image changed from that of a glorified Soviet naval base in the Caribbean to that of a true global power. The Sandinistas decided that the United States feared Cuba too much to interfere in Nicaragua and thus there was no longer any reason for caution or subterfuge.

I was in the FSLN's Department of International Relations, but I found it difficult not to criticize the Soviet invasion of Afghanistan, which the Sandinistas resolutely refused to do. I remember once, just after the 1979 Soviet invasion, I went to a cocktail party in Washington with the first Sandinista ambassador to the United States, 27-year-old Rafael Solis. Anatoly F. Dobrynin, the Soviet ambassador to the United States, was telling our ambassador how baffled he was by the strenuous American objections to the invasion. After all, Dobrynin said, Afghanistan "is in our sphere of influence." Solis came over to me, shocked at Dobrynin's imperialistic attitude. "That's a classic example of great-power behavior," he said. He couldn't believe it. Welcome to the real world, I said to myself.

It was devastating to me to see that while my comrades were pretending to be the liberators of our country, they were actually helping to destroy it by disastrous policies and delusionary ideology. Nicaragua had undergone rapid changes under the new regime, some of which were beneficial. But certain traits of the Nicaraguan character, traits that for centuries have enriched our country, were being ravaged. The most devastating of all has been the loss of our open character. Nicaragua had always been a country of conversation, even under Somoza. As I have said, in Somoza's time, if you were not actively against him, you were with him. Today, however, if you are not with the Sandinistas, you are against them. We once lived in a society where the houses were unlocked, where people used to sit in the streets and complain about politics. Today the security and ideological apparatuses are more efficient than they ever were under the dictators of the past. Block committees have been established throughout the country. These committees have many eyes and ears. People who used to talk to their neighbors are now afraid of them. It is something worse than what we overthrew; it is *scientific Somozcismo*.

I argued that there was no reason not to remain friendly with the United States; that the factors that make the United States an inconsistent power also make it potentially a good ally. The United States can never really dominate another country because its policies are too fractured, too contradictory. Contrary to the Marxist stereotype of the imperial Uncle Sam, a country can receive millions of dollars in economic aid and arms from America and still feel free of its yoke. The United States will never command an imperial network because it does not maintain enough internal consistency to create such hegemony. The Soviets offer a much more homogeneous force. You can count on their commitments. They are a reliable ally. So much so that they can overrun a country. All of these propositions became clear to me from what was happening in the triangular relationship between Washington, Managua and Moscow.

Publicly I praised the Nicaraguan economy but privately I was discouraged. The Soviet Union was supplying us with military hardware, not economic aid. The security of a country cannot depend solely upon weapons. But my Sandinista comrades would tell me: Look at all we have done in the last two years. We have a powerful army; a political machinery; an efficient security apparatus.

The best elements of the Nicaraguan soul were withering. I didn't trust anyone. I became afraid to disagree.

My official role as a spokesman for the government forced me to take positions opposed to my personal beliefs. For instance, we were all required to condemn Poland's Solidarity movement. The junta's stance was that Solidarity was a reactionary development rather than a social movement; that Solidarity was instigated by external Western manipulation rather than by internal dissent. *Barricada,* the official FSLN government newspaper, dutifully published imaginative reports on how the Polish economy had defeated inflation and how miraculously the socialist government had served the country. But privately I supported Lech Walesa, despite the Sandinista claim that he was a CIA agent.

What we had done, while devastating the economy, was to establish dictatorial power. That was the Sandinista concept of good government: one that provided for their own power. I privately disagreed, but I wasn't allowed to disagree publicly.

My father quit the Sandinista government early in 1982. I heard that the *comandantes* were planning to use me against him. Obviously I could never let that happen. Because of family loyalty but also because of the monstrosity the revolution had become, I quit the government and left my country.

CHAPTER 3

GOOD IDEAS ARE NOT ENOUGH

Fausto Amador

To live in Nicaragua at the beginning of the '60s was to live in a political environment with three outstanding features: a personal dictatorship supported by the U.S. government, a very backward economy, and dire social poverty in the midst of the most shameless privilege.

In my own case, it was very difficult to avoid taking a stand on the plight of the nation. My family lived at the very heart of the political and social contradictions. My father, Fausto Amador Aleman, was the manager and chief administrator of Somoza's most important business enterprises, and also his personal friend. On the other hand, my brother Carlos Fonseca Amador, was the most outstanding anti-Somocista youth leader. Arrested several times and then expelled from the country, he was active in rebel movements. Strangely, those brutally incompatible ways of life never prevented a very affectionate family relationship. This was so because my father, a man of firm convictions, fully respected people whose ideas differed from his own. This was especially so with his children.

My brother Carlos was a Marxist. At his side, I began to read revolutionary texts at an age when other children were still reading fairy tales. At 12 years of age, I had conducted classes for revolutionary cadres in a shoemakers union. In those years there was founded, with the sponsorship of the Cuban ambassador in Nicaragua, Quintin Pino Machado, the so-called *Juventud Patriotica Nicaraguense* (Nicaraguan Patriotic Youth), the kernel of what would later become the *Frente Sandinista de Liberacion Nacional*. With this movement, terrorism appeared in Nicaragua. Adolescents, almost still children, were sent out to place bombs.

The basic political ideals of the radicalized Nicaraguan youth of those years were very simple: democracy, economic development, social justice

107

and national independence. It is important to ask why Marxism appeared to be the only theoretical context offering an understanding of the social problems, the only hope of a definitive solution, and the only practical organizational experience to carry out the objectives of social justice. How could we have been so naive? How could we have been so impoverished in terms of our political vocabulary?

Somoza was always able to buy off or kill his conservative opponents and those wanting liberal democracy. Those citizens who saw the need for change were gradually left with no alternative but to collaborate with the FSLN. The growing list of national and international martyrs and the ideological shift of large sectors of the Church towards Marxism, exemplified and stimulated by the death of Camilo Torres, ended in creating a political monopoly for Marxism in the mass movement for social change.

Within this general framework, there were great differences between my brother and me. I advocated developing a broad civic movement against Somoza without the necessity for guerilla warfare. I thought it necessary to give non-violent methods of struggle a chance. But there was a deeper difference. For Carlos the positive side of the social crisis was that it created the conditions for the birth of the new society. The revolutionary's task was to sharpen the existing social contradictions, never to resolve them; to use violence to midwife the arrival of the new order.

For me, then as now, the crisis in our society had flesh and bones. Those who were suffering under an unjust order had to face their problems to solve them. The future shape of Nicaraguan society was a hypothesis; their sufferings were an immediate reality. It was neither just nor humane to let the real social situation—Somoza's status quo— deteriorate further in order to realize a hypothetical one—the new Marxist order. I was showing myself to be a poor Communist.

For Carlos, this discrepancy divided the reformists from the revolutionaries. But for me, it separated the humanists from the fanatics. The difference between me and my brother became deep enough that we could no longer get along in the same organization. As a result, we followed independent political paths. Carlos's FSLN never fought a single social battle with specific concrete objectives on behalf of the poor. By 1967, however, I was one of the best-known independent leaders of a mass movement. The organization that Roberto Amaya and I had developed in the barrios had a much greater following than anything the FSLN had created.

But then came the war proclaimed by the FSLN. Despite our political differences, I continued to be emotionally close to my brother. From 1966 on, Carlos entrusted his personal security to me. In the process of passing him from one house to the next, of escorting him to and from the mountains—to protect his life—I began to use up the personal and organizational resources of groups I was trying to build. Innocent companions were captured, tortured, and murdered. I myself was eventually discovered and had to leave my home and my 6–month-old daughter and flee underground.

In an attempt to understand Carlos's point of view, and at the same time to understand the sacrifice of my brother Roberto, who had been brutally tortured and murdered by the Somoza dictatorship, I went to Cuba to receive military training.

That experience was decisive. In Cuba I saw how information was totally controlled and freedom of expression was ruthlessly suppressed even among the revolutionaries themselves. I saw the arbitrary way those in charge of every social and political association were appointed. I saw the fear of making any suggestion contrary to the whims of the *caudillo*. At that time the theme of the Castro regime was to get an enormous sugar harvest of 10 million tons, and although all the leaders of the Cuban Communist party with whom I spoke told me such a thing was impossible, no one had the courage to say so to Fidel.

The Cuban system threw away all democratic aspirations and in exchange for what? The undeniable advances in education and health care were rendered sterile by the systematic implanting of a statism in which all individual initiative, all cultural creativity and even family intimacy were lost. And none of this entailed the disappearance of social inequalities; much less did it lead to national independence or development. While in Cuba, I saw other things: the repression of the intellectuals; the absurd fear of poets; the attack on homosexuals; the support of the Soviet tanks which crushed the Prague spring; the effects of Marxist irrationality and willfulness on the Cuban economy.

The true face of socialism which I saw in Cuba left me in a state of crisis. But one thing was clear: this was not the kind of society for which idealistic youths should give their lives. Inevitably I came to think that neither by their political goals nor by their organizational methods could the FSLN represent in Nicaragua a humanist and progressive alternative to the Somoza dictatorship.

When I returned to Nicaragua all of my friends were dead or dispersed. The *barrio* organizations had been destroyed. I felt a moral obligation to make a public statement of my political conclusions. In a nationally televised press conference financed by my father, I broke publicly with the FSLN and I spoke in detail about the totalitarianism which menaced us unless we formed a new type of organization to oppose the Somoza dictatorship.

In a very few days, I became a highly controversial public figure. During that time, Carlos broke the family tradition of respect for each others' ideas and in an act of fanaticism publicly declared that I was no longer his brother, that his only brothers were his followers. We never had any personal contact again.

After a while, it became clear that if I were to continue my political fight in Nicaragua, I would have to face a violent confrontation not only with Somoza but also with the FSLN. Old and good friends in the Church, priests with whom I had studied since infancy, had undergone an important ideological shift. During 1968–69 —the period of my absence in Cuba—there was born in Nicaragua the *"Iglesia Popular"*, that eclectic absurdity wherein the Christian aspirations of fraternity and charity are sewn together with Marxism and the Communist cause.

I had no intention to enter a shooting match for influence in the popular movement. I left Nicaragua and spent several years in Europe, always involved in social movements; I finally established myself in Costa Rica.

When I was a Marxist, I did not entirely lose sight of the human being who suffers and needs solidarity and help in his fight against his miseries; likewise, my present anti-Communism does not submerge me in individualism. With much more experience now and a greater capacity to deal with social struggles, I remain actively committed to organizing the poor.

My present situation is defined by my participation in COPAN—the *Comite Patriotico Nacional,* of which I am the executive director. This is the largest social organization that has ever existed in the history of Central America. It organizes more than 30,000 people to fight for housing in the *barrios,* for health and ecological issues; it organizes youth committees, trade unions, feminist groups, intellectual associations, cultural clubs in a broad and diverse movement for social justice and reform.

From the FSLN of the '60s to the COPAN of today, a great many things have changed for me. The thing that remains is that I continue to fight for the same principles of human solidarity which took me in bygone days to a medieval convent in Assisi, and in Nicaragua to its rain-soaked mountains.

CHAPTER 4

MARXISM IS NOT PROGRESS

Xavier Arguello

The theme for this conference is reconsideration. *What made us change?* Our friends often pose this question, whose answer, needless to say, is not simple. Certain external elements can be referred to in explaining one's decision to take up the struggle against the FSLN: the inefficient, intriguing, and all-powerful bureaucracy of the State; the Cuban presence; the offensive privileges of Party members; revolutionary frivolity; militarism; the never-ending manipulation of information; the Bulgarian soap operas. But disenchantment also has something to do with a slow, personal process of maturation.

To open one's eyes takes time. It is only when one asks himself what he will do with his life that problems begin. Will I carry on forever as the cheerleader of a vain and irresponsible revolutionary leadership? Must I live forever confined in my own interior world, faking what I am told is necessary, and renouncing all personal ties for a role in shaping the collective direction of my country? Can I remain indifferent, being a witness to how the FSLN takes advantage of the ignorance of the most unwary, in order to sow indelible fanaticism? Shall I live, for the rest of my life, subject to the capriciousness of a neighborhood commissary, just to meet the basic needs of myself and my family?

One also begins to cherish those fundamental values of individual liberty and democracy which one facilely despised in the name of Marxism, and which only now, after they are irretrievably forfeited, become precious. That is why it is so important for us Nicaraguans to return to our country: to apply what we have learned about liberty during our exile.

The duty is a hard one. Can anyone learn from another's experience? I recall how we turned a deaf ear to the Cubans who denounced the tyranny of Castro. For us, that was heresy and required no examination. We made no effort to put ourselves in their place; we dehumanized Castro's victims a second time. They were retrograde and reactionary, Batistan worms. Now we play the same role they did. That is why we wonder if our preaching will convince any of those who think that spiritual and political peace are attainable under the Sandinistas.

Though it is true that now we value the element of liberty more highly, we have not stopped believing in the urgent need for social progress, in a just distribution of wealth and property, or in education and national dignity. In other words, we believe in the same objectives as we did when we supported the revolution. I must insist on that. What has changed is this: before we did not value liberty. We thought that liberty was superfluous, a bourgeois attribute, almost an enemy. And we felt that we must sink the revolutionary dagger into the heart of that decadent luxury.

Liberty cannot be achieved by decree. Liberty is a personal goal, an act of individual independence, or, if you will, of manhood. What is important is that a political system have enough flexibility so that citizens who wish to be free, different, rabidly individual, can be able to be these things without being crushed by the police.

That is why democratic societies are so much more dynamic than Marxist-Leninist ones. Their best talents find the space needed for their development and uniqueness. This is the reason behind so many defections to the West of Cuban and Soviet artists and intellectuals, and of those Nicaraguans who are creators. It is not only artists and intellectuals who desert the suffocating paralysis of Leninism. Ordinary citizens with a spark of ambition, or audacity, or energy, flee too. The humble peasant woman—for whom supposedly the revolution was fought—she flees, and now earns her living in Miami cleaning houses, and her savings go into contracting a Mexican "coyote" to help her sons cross the Rio Grande. The humble peasant man whom the Sandinista dispossessed of his little plot, obliged to turn over his crop and sell his animals, flees into the ranks of the counterrevolutionaries in Honduras and comes back across the border with a gun in his hands.

Some might argue that to speak of liberty in a country where there is no bread is a sterile exercise, even a demagogic one. The trouble is that Marxism, which pretends to speak to hunger, guarantees neither progress nor development. The problems of under-development are almost unthinkably complex, but this much is clear. It is the individual in charge of his own destiny, and not a gigantic, inefficient State bureaucracy, which can begin to solve these problems. Many liberal North Americans fall into the temptation of denying the small countries to the South their opportunity to be at once prosperous and free, condemning them, by a stroke of the pen, to medieval Cubano-Soviet totalitarianism. Not only is that position simplistic, it is cruel. Development and not repression is the surest way to solve the problems of the Third World.

The Marxist not only eliminates public liberties, but frustrates all progress. Marxist economics doles out misery, not well-being, while allowing revolutionary elites to live in the midst of abundance. To believe that condemning the countries of the Third World to regimented Marxism will mean an end to photographs of children with swollen bellies is naive. Ethiopia fills the mind with such photographs to a degree unequalled by any other contemporary state. And the Soviet-modeled Marxist-Leninist single party state of Ethiopia has already celebrated its 10th anniversary.

To believe in the traditional values of democracy necessitates, of course, a reevaluation of our attitude towards the United States. The facile irrationalism of blaming all our woes on the *Yanqui,* when in fact they are the result of our corruption and egotism, must be put behind us. The United States, too, has changed. Thirty years ago, it would already have invaded Nicaragua 30 times. Fortunately, the United States is a country capable of learning. The dynamism intrinsic to this society permits it to adapt to modern times. The international stage, too, is different. We smaller countries now have a greater say in world affairs. Economic power has been diluted in several directions, and the military and political power of the United States is no longer so overwhelming. All this has brought us closer together, Nicaraguans and Americans.

Let's be realistic. Among those who fight under the banner of democracy there is also egotism, opportunism, and spiritual poverty. That is why the solution to our problem of subdevelopment and lack of social justice must not lie in blind trust of any particular system of excessive government. The only possibility of attaining development and liberty is allowing the people to be master of its own destiny. Nobody can do the work for the humble and meek in improving themselves. The State must carry on a fiscal task, contributing to a better distribution of wealth through fair taxation policies, subject always to popular will as manifested in the electoral returns. But only the people can resolve their own problems.

But at present we have no such situation in Nicaragua. The embittered ranks of the Communist parties of Latin America, and their guerrilla armies, are not moved by compassion, nor a just wrath at the injustices which the people suffer. They are moved by rancor and the thirst for vengeance, but above all for personal power. That is why the circle in which Nicaragua lives is not only vicious, but bloody.

We have faith in the small proprietor; in the taxi-driver with his own cab; in the peasant who owns his little plot; in the entrepreneur who, without breaking the laws nor exploiting his workers, uses the honest fruit of his effort and creativity. We believe that the challenge is not to overthrow dictatorships, but to build democracy. For that, one must have faith in mankind. One must be an optimist. After seeing the true face of the revolutionary made in the image and likeness of Moscow, we have become optimists. We have understood that not only is history on our side, but so too is the inexhaustible hunger for liberty which characterizes human nature.

CHAPTER 5

SECOND THOUGHTS AND THIRD THOUGHTS

Bruce Cameron

My journey to the left, as for so many of my generation, began during the Vietnam War. But until 1973, I was always on the periphery. The turning point for me was September 11, 1973. That day, President Salvador Allende was overthrown in a bloody coup. I believed instantly at the time and believe today that the coup would not have taken place without U.S. involvement.

I was angry and felt an overpowering need to act. I had been living in Ann Arbor, Michigan and had just started a job as a research social scientist at Bendix Aerospace, where my work was in the field of work safety. In October 1973, I took leave to go hear Tom Hayden, who with his wife Jane Fonda and others, had started the Indochina Peace Campaign. I saw the war in Vietnam as the war of the people against a foreign aggressor. My stock line was that the government of South Vietnam was a U.S. creation, held together by a vast network of corruption and held in power by terror. Much of that was true, though it was more complicated; but I could not even hear the nuances that were put forward by our leader, Tom Hayden.

After joining the Ann Arbor chapter of the Indochina Peace Campaign, I looked around the world to see who the United States supported: the Park dictatorship in South Korea, the Marcos dictatorship in the Philippines, the Suharto government in Indonesia that had massacred thousands of leftists and Chinese, the Shah's Iran, fascist South Africa, fascist Rhodesia, Mobutu's Zaire, Pinochet's Chile, the military dictatorship in Brazil which we helped install, and the military dictatorship in Uruguay.

From South Vietnam and Indonesia, through Tehran to South Africa and on to Chile and Uruguay (Argentina would soon fall), there was a gulag of Leftists and many democrats whose only crime was to have been a member or supporter of a previous government or to oppose a bloody dictatorship.

The only position that made sense at the time was to support revolution. So much did I recoil from U.S. imperialism that for a brief period of six weeks in the spring of 1975, I adopted the Weather Underground position of believing that the U.S. should be turned into a holding company for the distribution of its assets and goods to the Third World.

Over time, many things caused me to question the American Left fundamentally, but it was a slow process.

The Ann Arbor Indochina Peace Campaign was the last anti-war group created. It was founded in 1972 when other Leftists had already dropped out or moved on to other issues. Our chapter, which became the largest in the country, had two foci: (1) educating the University of Michigan community about the "truth" of the Vietnamese revolution and the horror of U.S. intervention; and (2) attempting to mobilize pressure on the four swing votes in Michigan and persuade liberal members of Congress to initiate legislation to limit U.S. involvement in Indochina.

The political culture of the Ann Arbor Indochina Peace Campaign was unusual to say the least. There were three power centers. I was one. I had contacts in the Democratic party all over the state and had aggressively sought out contacts in the churches and church-based peace groups. Off the campus of Ann Arbor, I was the Ann Arbor Indochina Peace Campaign, including the city of Ann Arbor. The second power center was a Maoist media collective led by a very intense and charismatic former member of the Communist party. He and his people were capable of working 70 to 80 hours a week. The third group was the remaining 10 to 15 independent activists.

For a year, the Maoist media collective supported my leadership. I had the contacts in the state, in Congressional offices, in the churches, and even our office derived benefits from my personal relationship with a professor on the campus. And in that year more legislation challenging U.S. policy in Indochina came from Michigan Congressmen than all the other states combined.

Then I was challenged by one of the independents as being unresponsive to the organization, of being sexist by virtue of my relying on four male independents as my advisors and assistants, and being elitist. The Maoist media collective supported the challenge.

In retrospect, though I did not appreciate it at the time, their goal was clear. They were isolated even on campus. Their hard-core political beliefs and intense work style put them at odds even with most of the other political groups. Their agenda was sectarian. While it was interesting and useful in terms of the struggle against U.S. imperialism to be part of an effort working with the U.S. Congress to end U.S. involvement in Indochina, their priority lay in expanding their organization on their terms even at the expense of the goal of moving Congress.

They skillfully exploited the charges of elitism and sexism on my part in a step-by-step take over of the organization. When I would resist their efforts, they would direct their attacks at my allies. After three months of "struggle," I capitulated and let them take over. Then they began the purge of their allies. And I participated in every purge. Fortunately, the war ended before I and every other potentially sane independent became a total zombie. Afterwards, all of us, one by one, drifted off and the organization that had once been the strongest IPC chapter in the country disappeared.

The end of the war showed me something else. It was sad and disorienting, because what were we going to do now? How could we recreate that excitement? But also that month Josef Smrkovsky died. Smrkovsky had been the leader of the Chamber of Deputies during Prague Spring in Czechoslovakia in 1968. He was the most charismatic of the Communist leaders who had changed their mind about Communism and who had wanted to build "Communism with a human face." He almost single-handedly kept the Czech people from engaging in a hopeless attack on the Soviet invaders. He was dead. I thought a dream was dead. And no one, especially in the Maoist collective, thought it was significant at all.

Both of these events should have sent up giant alarm bells. But one becomes accustomed to a line of thought and a way of acting and it is hard to give them up. And at that point I could not. I could see that once the independents came under the power of the collective, they lost their ability to speak to the people of Michigan. They had the fervor, the commitment, but not the voice. And I still had hopes for the revolutions in Vietnam and even Cambodia. I was to be proven desperately wrong in both cases.

When I arrived in Washington in January of 1976 to begin work as the foreign policy lobbyist of Americans for Democratic Action, I still had the same mindset and became a part of another collective, a group of IPC leftovers guided by a Vietnamese inspired anti-American anti-imperialism. One of our leaders used to talk confidently of an American revolution (we called it the "Big R") within 25 years. My first break with the Left came that same year.

The Democratic Congress had forced on the Ford Administration legislation that required concern for human rights in the conduct of diplomacy with governments which received military assistance. One part of that amendment allowed the Congress to require of the Administration special reports on the human rights practices of governments which received U.S. military assistance.

I thought we should test that law. I also thought we should add to our list of Chile, Argentina, South Korea, and Indonesia Leftist governments which received U.S. aid. I was not concerned about human rights in the two countries I chose at this time, but I thought we should give the Congressman assisting us in this effort political cover. I chose Peru, which was ruled by a vaguely Leftist military junta, and Ethiopia, which was ruled by a military junta that would soon embrace Marxism-Leninism.

I was greeted with a torrent of criticism by the leaders of the human rights community in Washington. To them the issue was simple. "You never attack the Left, ever." With Congress, my position prevailed, but the Human Rights Working Group of the Coalition for a new Foreign and Military Policy would not endorse the effort.

The whole episode made me ask myself what was going on with these people. A person put to death for a non-violent political crime is still dead whether killed by a Rightist or a Leftist government. But my colleagues made the crime of the Left an excusable crime.

In 1977, I began to work with Raul Manglapus of the Philippines, who was a former foreign minister (and coincidently was reappointed a week ago). His commitment to human rights was absolute. In the years I worked with him, he did human rights investigations all over the world. And yet, Leftists, principally Filipino, but some Americans, opposed his association and work with our community consistently. The pettiness of his opponents seemed ridiculous. I had arranged for him to be interviewed by the *Christian Science Monitor* after Congress and adopted legislation holding back a paltry $3 million in military aid to the Marcos dictatorship. A delegation of Filipino Communists living in the United States came to my office to register their complaints.

What was his crime? He was a democrat and a human rights advocate concerned about the people's rights in all countries in the world. He represented an obstacle to the forward progress of world revolution because he also opposed Communism. It did not matter that he was more effective than his enemies in dealing with Congress. Their agenda was larger than human rights.

By the end of 1978, I had ceased to believe in any concept of revolution led by Marxist-Leninists as being the true vehicle for national liberation. But I retained a fundamental anti-Americanism. I continued to believe and to preach that the Third World was best off without U.S. intervention, which I broadly defined to include all forms of U.S. aid and assistance.

My first work on Nicaragua began in June 1977 when I supported then Representative (now Mayor) Ed Koch (D-N.Y.) in his effort to prohibit military aid to the government of Antonio Somoza Debaye. This began 10 years of activism on the affairs of this little country.

In 1979 for the first time, I visited Central America, specifically Nicaragua, El Salvador, and Guatemala. U.S. policy toward these three countries was at best non-existent and at worst, inconsistent. Non-existent or inconsistent were vintage Carter. People were dying in serious numbers and we had no policy. In Guatemala, which we visited for only a day, I was always terrified. You could even see terror on the faces of our guides from the American Embassy.

Since 1978 I already had contacts with business opposition to Somoza (all are now Contra officials.) I began to look, with their guidance and conviction, to the Sandinistas as a possible third way, neither a puppet government within the American orbit nor a Marxist-Leninist one-party state.

On July 19, 1979, the revolution was victorious. The next day, the Sandinista leadership, side by side with their colleagues from the business opposition, triumphantly entered Nicaragua. These were heady times. Children with sticks and home-made Molotov cocktails had overthrown a bloody dictatorship. A whole people and a whole world had put aside their other divisions to see this day. Nicaragua could be an example to other Latin American countries of a gentle revolution which sought social justice and economic progress, not just power. In Washington, many of us believed, like the Sandinistas, that El Salvador or Guatemala would soon follow.

Three or four months after the Sandinista triumph, President Carter proposed a $75 million aid package to help Nicaragua rebuild itself. The war had destroyed many of the factories and an even greater percentage of their inventories. I lobbied very vigorously for this bill. Unlike my colleagues on the Left, I did not sing the praises of the Sandinistas, but rather I based my arguments on the statements of three Nicaraguan leaders who had been part of the business opposition: Adolfo Calero, Alfonso Robelo, and Arturo Cruz. They continued to support the aid package even when Robelo resigned and Cruz took his place in the Government of National Reconstruction.

We were successful. We won. But I became tagged as a "Robelista," someone not marching in step with the others who favored only the Sandinistas. In 1980 following the passage of the aid, I attended a party for a former Washington Office on Latin American (WOLA) staffer who had left for Nicaragua after the Sandinista takeover. She asked me what I would do "when we go after the bourgeoisie." I was dumbfounded. The Contras were not a serious force in 1980. Very few top businessmen not connected with Somoza, had left Nicaragua, and Calero, Cruz, and Robelo all still had hopes that a workable arrangement could be made with the Sandinistas. Only late last year, did I finally learn that for much of the time she had worked at WOLA, she had also been a secret member of a Sandinista cell here in the United States. And at the time I did not take her seriously. I still believed in the promise of a third way.

In 1976, I was a co-founder of the Human Rights Working Group which eventually merged and became part of the Coalition for a New Foreign and Military Policy. Unity within that group was at times strained as I indicated above, but was basically solid as long as we focused on the dictatorships of Latin America, South Korea, the Philippines, Indonesia, Zaire, and South Africa.

That unity began to fracture in 1980. The human rights community was almost universally fulsome in its praise of the revolution in Nicaragua and condemnatory of the government in El Salvador.

In 1981, the Deputy Director of Land Reform in El Salvador, Leonel Gomez, after evading assassination by the Salvadoran army, fled to the United States and lived in my home for three and one-half years. Instead of embracing him, the majority of the human rights community scorned him as they did Calero, Cruz, and Robelo. One WOLA staffer spent a year trying to discredit Leonel Gomez. The reason was simple. While Leonel Gomez spoke out very forcefully about human rights violations and corruption by the Salvadoran army, he also made it very clear that the intention of the guerrillas was to impose a Communist government in El Salvador.

In April 1982, Alfonso Robelo left Nicaragua for the last time. Before he left, as president of the Democratic *Coordinator,* a coalition of four political parties, two union confederations and the major business groups, he called for negotiations leading toward national reconciliation in Nicaragua and in El Salvador and Guatemala as well. He was embracing the liberals' and the Left's call for dialogue in El Salvador, but also saying if dialogue was appropriate there, it was urgent in Nicaragua. He also—for me—called into question for the first time the legitimacy of the Sandinista government. Because of their massive human rights violations, that was easy in the case of Guatemala and El Salvador, but to think that way about Nicaragua was revolutionary.

The government of Nicaragua was not in 1982 engaging in massive human rights violations. People had been killed by security forces for their non-violent political opposition. Testimony by one defector in 1985 put the number of special executions at 2,000 by the end of 1984. But that number is unproven and seems high.

The Sandinistas' major sins were two. They were preventing the rise of opposition political forces by limited censorship, mob violence, and a program of indoctrination through the educational system. And they were building a party and party-led mass organizations whose purpose was to permeate all aspects of civil society and thereby control it. They were not building a third way, they were laying the foundations of a new dictatorship and political nightmare.

From that time on, I came to believe that for there to be peace in Central America, there had to be an agreement that put equal demands on the Nicaraguan government and the Salvadoran government for national reconciliation. At that time, I thought in terms of power-sharing for both countries. At this point I basically stopped working with the American Left at all on any issue.

In 1984, Arturo Cruz, who had resigned from the Sandinista government in 1981, made an aborted run for the Presidency of Nicaragua. There are many unanswered questions about U.S. government actions at that time to stop his participation, but one thing is clear. Twice, the Cruz coalition offered directly or through mediators a set of conditions under which he would run and twice the Sandinistas indicated acceptance and twice sharply withdrew from negotiations.

Still, he and even some in the Contra leadership believed that there would be an opening in Nicaragua following the election of President Daniel Ortega and the termination of aid to the Contras by Congress. Instead, there was an immediate reimposition of censorship and harassment of opposition leaders.

Also in 1983 and 1984, I saw that a relatively unified Reagan Administration could demand reforms from the Salvadoran army and achieve some of them. More importantly, elements of the Salvadoran army began to take certain American liberals at their word about not wanting a Communist victory, but a reform of the military, and they began a set of discussions with retiring Sen. Paul Tsongas (D-Mass.) which led to other reforms. And Napoleon Duarte was elected President in May of 1984 and in October began a dialogue with the Salvadoran guerrillas.

In the first six months of 1985, the Reagan Administration supported the inclusion of moderates Cruz and Robelo in the umbrella leadership of the Contras with Adolfo Calero to take charge. To me Cruz and Robelo represented two things: first, they were small "d" democrats who could be the catalysts for building a more effective military and political force; and second, they were Latin Americans of international stature who supported a political, not a military solution to the conflicts—that is, a negotiated settlement that would leave the Sandinistas in power if they would agree to true political pluralism.

Over 10 years, I had come to understand that the true goal of Third World revolutionaries inspired by Marxism-Leninism was absolute power and nothing less. They and their American allies would use the rhetoric of human rights and democracy, but their use was tactical. Their goal was always the same.

Following U.S. withdrawal in Indochina, I had watched from afar what can happen when Marxist-Leninists who have achieved total power are able to put in practice their ideas. I watched the unfolding mass murder in Cambodia and the hundreds of thousands of Vietnamese who fled in boats across the South China Sea and the hundreds of thousands more who remained and were put into prisons or forceably relocated to desolate areas.

I now looked in retrospect at the rise of Soviet imperialism as a global phenomenon after America's defeat in Vietnam in 1975. In that year, the Soviet Union with its new sea- and air-lift capabilities was transporting Cuban troops to Angola, and later, Ethiopia. In 1979, the Soviets themselves invaded Afghanistan.

I had come to the realization that the greatest threat to human rights and democracy was Marxism-Leninism in its Soviet variant and that Cuba and Nicaragua had both put themselves in the service of a world revolution led by the Soviet Union. It was also beyond doubt that revolutionaries from all of Nicaragua's Central American neighbors were being trained and supplied by the Sandinistas.

In 1985 I had come to also believe that while the Reagan Administration had made many mistakes, many of its leaders had learned from them and wanted now to make a real partnership with democrats in promoting democracy and human rights. As a result I supported the restoration of so-called "humanitarian aid" in 1985 to the Contras and worked diligently to achieve a similar bipartisan aid package in 1986 which would include military aid.

For my change of mind, I was asked to resign from ADA on June 14, 1985, and did so five days later.

I now believe that I was fundamentally in error in 1985 and 1986 in my assessment of the Contras, the Reagan Administration, liberals, and the Soviet Union. I have not changed my mind that Marxism-Leninism is not a doctrine of national liberation or that the Soviet Union remains a threat to human freedom. But in particular, I have come to reject the Contra policy as a response to the Sandinista challenge and, in general, I have serious doubts about the effectiveness of the so-called Reagan doctrine as a response to these challenges.

I believe that many of us, certainly the whole conservative movement, have engaged in what the Marxist-Leninists call the error of volunteerism, that is the belief that by sheer force of political will, one can surpass and overcome stubborn and recalcitrant social realities. Despite all efforts to change it, the Contra army remains basically what it was in 1982 at its creation: a peasant army, a collection of men and women who have their individual grievances against the Sandinistas, an army without a vision of the future society it would create, and an army without a network of civilian supporters except in the remotest areas. By reciting the sins of the Sandinistas, which are legion, and by evoking the suffering of the Nicaraguan people including those who have joined the Contras, one nonetheless cannot change the stubborn reality that the Contras cannot win in the foreseeable future.

It is perhaps the case that the whole notion of a democratic vanguard leading an insurgency is an impossible one. It may be that democracy by its very nature, with its emphasis on process rather than goals, does not lend itself to providing the emotional fodder absolutely necessary for a guerrilla army. The history and social realities of different countries also may make a democratic vanguard impossible. And finally, we do not know how to build a genuine democratic counter-revolution. We do not have the skills, certainly not in the CIA, to nurture a democratic political culture in a resistance movement that will animate guerrilla soldiers.

In 1985, I came to believe that the Reagan Administration genuinely believed that it had to pursue a two-track approach of military pressure and negotiations. That clearly was not and is not the case. The Guatemala City Accords, when coupled with direct negotiations with Sandinistas on our legitimate security concerns, could produce a settlement that is good for our security concerns and will produce a political opening in Nicaragua. Nonetheless, the Administration stubbornly refuses to embrace the peace process preferring to have another round of debate on Contra aid so that it can pursue its true objective: Total military victory over the Sandinistas.

In 1986, I wrote that there was a wing of the Democratic party that was "soft on Communism." That there are activists in the party and a few members of Congress who fit this description is true. But there is no wing of the party that is "soft on Communism." What there is are very committed small "d" democrats who have an appreciation of the limits of U.S. power and a concern for the unintended consequences of its use that bring about greater involvement that is undersirable, or unintended consequences no one would want, e.g., the rise of the Khmer Rouge after the U.S. invasion and massive bombing of Cambodia.

I also engaged in another error I fear is all too common, confusing the anti-democratic and anti-American elements of the Left with liberals. They are not the same. Liberals, with few exceptions, are anti-Communist and pro-American. And liberals, unlike too many conservatives, tend to be consistent in their condemnation of tyranny by both the Right and the Left.

I think my assessment of the projection of Soviet power in the 1970s was in error. It is true that a number of small and vulnerable governments slipped into the Soviet orbit in that time. The larger story, however, was the loss of China—the real loss of China—and the loss of Egypt.

It is also not clear that all those countries that embraced Marxism-Leninism in the 1970s and an alliance with the Soviet bloc are frozen in history. Mozambique, a Marxist-Leninist government, now has as its principal supporters, Margaret Thatcher, the Italian government, as well as a large U.S. aid program (for over $80 million). How it will move ideologically is not clear, but the question is open.

Over my 17 years of activism, I have gone through many turns of mind, from embracing the Left, to moving away from it while maintaining an anti-American isolationism, to becoming a cautious liberal willing to countenance certain types of U.S. intervention, then passing on to become a strong interventionist including support of anti-Communist insurgents, and finally after a year of working with the Contras and the Reagan Administration returning to a moderate liberalism. Although while on the Left I embraced a notion of participatory democracy in the framework of Marxist centralism and while leaning Right too often settled for too little democracy, I have always been—and still am—guided by the desire to be faithful to the principles of human rights and political freedom.

CHAPTER 6

TRUTH AND CONSEQUENCES

Robert S. Leiken

Many of you may know me from a critical report on the Sandinistas I wrote in 1984 entitled "Nicaragua's Untold Stories." Through the promotional flair of *The New Republic* it became better known as "Sins of the Sandinistas." David Horowitz and Peter Collier asked me to recount some of that article's post-publication career. How could I turn down the opportunity I'd been awaiting to hatch the title "Son of Sins of the Sandinistas?" Yet, in light of my ensuing excommunication from the Left, perhaps, this talk should be called "Sin of Sons of the Sandinistas."

It was not a pro-Contra piece. I wrote that "there is a general impression among those in the United States properly aghast at the C.I.A. mining of ports and U.S. support for the professional torturers among the Contras that the Sandinistas are the victims not the victimizers. Inside Nicaragua, however, the image is reversed." And, though the article was prompted by indignation at Sandinista hypocrisy and by compassion for their victims, it was not a diatribe. Today, it would hardly seem controversial, so much has the radiance fallen from the Sandinista regime.

The article stated that Nicaraguans' standard of living had deteriorated well before the Contras turned to economic sabotage in the spring of 1983 with real wages falling sharply in the first 2½ years of "workers' government;" shortages had dramatically driven up prices mainly because peasants were forced to sell their goods to the state and private investment frightened off by arbitrary expropriations and revolutionary rhetoric; rationing cards were employed as political coercion; the shortage of basic necessities had bred pervasive corruption; profiting from this corruption, the Sandinista leadership was living the same swinging lifestyle they denounced in bourgeois countries; former *Somozistas* had

125

gained prominence in local and even national government; popular support had declined drastically and the government was resented by most of the population. The final part of the article focused on the upcoming elections and particularly a political rally in Chinandega which demonstrated the popular support for the opposition and the Sandinista government's intention to stifle it.

It became clear to me, and to my brother who accompanied me part of the way on that visit to Nicaragua, that many of the vaunted achievements of the revolution, such as a literacy campaign, had not borne fruit. Most of the graduates of the literacy program we encountered couldn't read their diplomas.

Nicaraguans often used the word *"engano"*—hoax, fraud—to describe their experience with the Sandinistas. I wrote: "The Sandinistas' *engano* has been most successful among the resident foreign press. Journalists familiar with the atrocities of the Right wing tyrannies of Central America, wish to believe quite understandably that the Sandinistas present an alternative. In today's Nicaragua, it is easy to confuse desire with reality. The resident press also frequently merges with a larger population of *internationalistas,* a term which embraces all those foreigners expressing solidarity with the Sandinistas from Bulgarian and Cuban apparatchiks to idealistic North Americans and West Europeans. It is a general feeling among Nicaraguans that the foreign press in Managua strongly sympathizes with the government."

When I returned I was asked by the press and by others, "Why have you been able to discover things which the press hasn't written about?" Ironically my "breakthrough" owed something to the Left. For most of the previous decade, as a revolutionary in Mexico, I had lived and worked among workers, peasants and intellectuals, taught in labor union schools, in Marxist study circles and in revolutionary cadre schools.

Those experiences provided good footing for revolutionary Nicaragua: among other things, familiarity and ease with Latins, particularly peasants and workers. In the summer of 1984 you could still rent a car in Managua. I would drive to the bus stop and pick up hitchhikers who were waiting for the inevitably late and overcrowded buses. In the privacy of a trip from Managua to Matagalpa conversations could develop at a leisurely human pace, often followed by an invitation to eat or spend the night.

The world of the Nicaraguan people was utterly different from that of the revolutionary tourists and journalists who resided at Managua's Intercontinental Hotel travelling only in government arranged tours, on solidarity tasks or for specific assignments. Revolutionary tourists, whose mental backpacks contained voluminous literature about "the psychology of the oppressed," seemed to assume that their contact with Nicaraguan workers and peasants was unmediated by class, state, or imperialism; as if in two days or two weeks or two months, with or without Spanish, they could apprehend directly, people whose history, culture and living conditions, by the Left's own account, were so different. Yet when one considers the enormous gulf between Western revolutionaries and their own "masses," it is not so shocking that these political pilgrims could speak so confidently and ignorantly of the Nicaraguan people. The same arrogance, class prejudice and incomprehension that I had seen among revolutionary students in the '60s and vanguard revolutionaries in the '70s, reappeared when revolutionary tourists recounted their experiences of Sandinista Nicaragua.

I suppose it was natural to expect that such people and their colleagues would take umbrage at my *New Republic* article. But after its publication my career took an interesting turn. I became the object of anonymous letters to my employers, rumors, and blackballing. I also became a household oath in those homes which subscribed to publications like *The Nation, In These Times, The Village Voice* and *The Guardian* or who tuned into Pacifica radio. I was guilty of "lies and slanders," I was "a propagandist for the Reagan administration," the entire piece was nothing but "calumny and falsehoods which formed an adroit piece of anti-Sandinista propaganda." The former Central American correspondent for *The New York Times* Ray Bonner returned from a two-day visit to Managua to spread the word that I had obtained all my information from the U.S. Embassy, had refused to meet with any Sandinistas, etc., etc.

Representative George Miller of California, in a letter penned by his Leftist aide who was also working part-time at the Institute for Policy Studies, accused me of employing "innuendo" instead of "the more time consuming effort of research and analysis." Witness for Peace said that my article was a bunch of "rumors, smears and cheap shots" and Noam Chomsky compared me unfavorably to Abu Nidal.

But later my critics got harsh. The editor of *The New Left Review* said that I was "a familiar haunting the underworld of Contra intrigue and central intelligence consultation," and Tony Jenkins of *The Nation* called me a "nitwit." An article in *In These Times* reported that "informed sources in Managua" had disclosed that I was part of a "secret Reagan administration operation" preparing the invasion of Nicaragua. Later the pro-Sandinista editorialist of *The Boston Globe* was to echo the view that

I "was methodically engineering a major U.S. intervention in Nicaragua."

During this educational process I learned that I had been "a supporter of Pol Pot," "a press agent for Eden Pastora," and inevitably "a CIA agent." Needless to say, it was impossible to begin to answer all these charges. This difficulty was compounded by the fact that I worked at a research institute anxious to preserve a reputation of un-controversial, mainstream policy analysis. Moreover, though I would have enjoyed a debate on the Left over Nicaragua, I did not relish replying to personal attacks. Alexander Cockburn of *The Nation,* my dearest foe, met my responses in *The New York Review* to his attacks with more slander, but he studiously ignored my refutations. Curiously, publications like *The Nation* and authors like Bonner previously had praised me lavishly for articles and testimony which used similar methods of research to criticize the Reagan administration policy in El Salvador and for a study which the media considered the Democratic alternative to the Kissinger Commission Report. These were the experiences which led me to tell an interviewer that I had realized to my chagrin that I'd been "keeping bad company all these years."

Doubtless part of the success of the article and the reason for its harsh reception on the Left was precisely because it was written by a former sympathizer and a former Leftist. Part of the reason for this response was their perception of the article's influence. President Reagan cited it in speeches; it was reprinted in *The Reader's Digest* and elsewhere; and it was quoted often in editorials. Liberal and Conservative Senators placed it in the Congressional Record and it was employed so frequently in Congressional debates that editorialists referred to the "Leikenization" of the Congress. The article helped to bring about an interesting transition in which Congressional opposition to Reagan's Central American policy shifted from support for the Sandinistas to opposition to the Contras.

"Sins of the Sandinistas" received a very different reception from Nicaraguans from that of their American "friends." *La Prensa* had put out a clandestine edition of the article, after a regular edition was censored. A small opposition party paper published it as did *La Nacion* in neighboring Costa Rica. The clandestine diffusion of the piece made me a kind of local hero, and I began to use reprints as calling cards. I learned I could overcome Nicaraguans' distrust of foreign journalists by letting it precede me.

Even at the Socialist Party, the former Moscow-backed Communist Party of Nicaragua, I was received with great eagerness. The Party's vice-presidential candidate told me it was the best piece he'd seen on his country.

The Sandinistas felt otherwise. I was informed that I would be granted no further interviews because of a decision taken at the "supreme national level."

To prepare for today's talk I reviewed some of my critics' notices. Sometimes their innocence was stunning. One wrote that "Robert Leiken charged that high level officials enjoyed all sorts of privileges, including dining at special restricted restaurants and shopping at hard currency stores. When I asked Tomas Borge about the special privileges of the high party officials he laughed and said that a French journalist who had just interviewed him would not believe that his home was his because it was so modest." I don't know how this California-based "Central America expert" felt if and when she read Merle Linda Wolin's remarkable set of interviews with Sandinista officials published in *The Los Angeles Herald-Examiner* in May 1985. Her portrait of Borge pointed out that in fact Borge's demonstration home was not the home in which the *comandante* resided but the one he used for receiving journalists and Leftists. Wolin, a veteran New Leftist herself, noted that Borge also employs an alternate office decorated with crucifixes for receiving religious and human rights delegations.

The American Left has been of enormous importance to the Sandinistas' effort to consolidate and preserve their domination over the Nicaraguan people and undermine their resistance, but the Sandinistas have been just as important to the American Left. They have revived the notion of American imperialism on which the Left nourished itself, and provided new heroes now that Fidel and Mao have lost their luster; they have renewed the faith.

For these reasons above all others, it is important to blacken the reputation of those who reveal even a part of the truth about the Sandinistas, especially if they come from the Left. I speak of myself, but I'm just one of many. Everyone on this panel, and many of you out in the audience have had similar experiences. That we came from the Left makes our criticisms more disturbing, more threatening, more dangerous and more effective. In my case *The Nation* and other Leftist magazines strove to persuade their readers that I was not in fact truly a Leftist (something they may have convinced me of) but only a "Maoist," and therefore an oddity.

Steeling the ranks also has to do with preserving what the Reverend Neuhaus referred to this morning as "the hermetically sealed" character of the Left, preserving it as a cult, as a sect, as a social and cultural calling.

Also, among my critics is another and related strain, the true believers, people who need to believe in socialism, because they need to believe that there is some alternative to capitalism. People who rightly criticize capitalist societies want to believe an alternative exists and particularly want to believe that a non-totalitarian alternative exists.

This is all fueled by the tendency that David Hawk mentioned this morning of conferring virtue on the victims of U.S. foreign policy and looking the other way when those victims become oppressors. Underlying this tendency, often, is the Left's own Vietnam syndrome, the desire to relive those great days, in which of course anti-Americanism was a principal theme.

Many of the letter writers and critics felt that the United States was responsible for Somoza and responsible for the war, and felt a great deal of guilt about it and experienced an inability to imagine anything more evil than Ronald Reagan. Indeed, for many, there was simply the hatred of Reagan. One of the accusations made over and over again was "all this may be true but don't you see that the effect is to help Reagan." This was particularly strong among liberals. Most liberals, I found, did not mind my criticizing the Sandinistas. But they did mind when my position evolved to one of support for the Contras. The liberals worried about domestic politics; they saw Contra support assisting Reagan just where he was weakest. Among Leftists and liberals solidarity with the oppressed tended to weaken dramatically when the oppressed were allies of the American Right wing.

I noticed that in many news stories and in the media (especially in outlets like National Public Radio) I suffered a change in status once I began to support conditional aid for the Contras. Before I was presented as an "analyst" (i.e. when I opposed aid to the Contras); afterwards I was presented as a partisan.

Let me just conclude with a few reflections, however partial and incomplete. One is that McCarthyism reigns on the Left—a Left which flees discussion and debate preferring character assassination, guilt by association and even red-baiting. In my case, the attack was orchestrated from Managua.

Truth hurts the Left, and the Left makes sure, therefore, that it hurts those who tell it. There are penalties for opposing the Left. Attack capitalism and businessmen will invite you to lunch and offer you a consultantship. But, if you offend the Left, watch your reputation and even your job (especially if you work in the university system). The Left does have influence—in the media, the academy, and within the Democratic Party, though it is still a limited influence which though growing should not be exaggerated. It is an influence which depends on its capacity to influence and manipulate liberals, who as a group are more numerous and significant.

It is worth mentioning that the Right has been a very difficult ally in this political and ideological battle. The Right lagged far behind the efforts of democratic Nicaraguans to reform and modernize the Nicaraguan resistance movement. The Administration withdrew its unconditional support for the authoritarians at the behest of moderate Democrats. Contra aid was passed last year because of the efforts of moderate Democrats, primarily, sometimes over and against the efforts of some people in the Administration. With the complicity of the Right and the Left, the rescue of Nicaragua from imperialism and totalitarianism became an ideological project of the Right not a strategic policy of the nation.

At bottom the Republicans have not cared much about Nicaragua. Much more important in this town has been lowering the tax rates and funding SDI. But I don't want to end without acknowledging that the Right has been basically correct all along about Nicaragua: right about the Communist nature of the Sandinistas; right about their relations with the Soviet Union and Cuba; and right about the danger this alliance signifies for the long-term security of our country.

CHAPTER 7

CUBA THEN, NICARAGUA NOW

Ronald Radosh

Twenty-five years ago the New Left saw in the Cuban revolution a beacon of the socialist future, a revolution that was neither Communist nor capitalist, but politically democratic and socially just. A revolution made without the witches of the old Cuban Communist Party. It was a revolution that gave us hope, that we quickly identified with, defended, and held up as an example for the oppressed of Latin America. A revolution that provided the very qualities missing in imperialist America.

The United States was so evil, we thought, that the other side had to be forgiven for its own crimes, if indeed we ever admitted or recognized that such crimes had taken place. When we were confronted with Fidelista repression we ignored it since the truth was viewed as a potential weapon in the hands of the imperialists. We went to Cuba and became "revolutionary tourists" *par excellence*—ever eager to bring home an enthusiastic report despite the reality that we saw. The trips we took bring to mind Hans Ensenberger's classic observations:

> In Havana in the 1960s I kept meeting communists in the hotels for foreigners who had no idea that the energy and water supply in the areas of the working class had broken down; that bread was rationed; and that the population had to stand two hours in line for a slice of pizza. Meanwhile, the tourists in their hotel rooms were arguing about Lukacs.

In 1968, when a Cuban confidant of Todd Gitlin hinted in a letter the awful truth of what was really taking place in Cuba, Gitlin went so far as to express some personal doubts privately to his friends on the Left. The result was that he was deemed too unreliable to be included among the cadre then forming the first *Venceremos* Brigade.

133

And so the pattern is repeated, this time in revolutionary Nicaragua. It is most noticeable in two recent books by Salman Rushdie and Peter Davis, both of whom see the revolution through the eyes of its sponsors and offer their political support to the *comandantes,* who are described by Mr. Rushdie as "definitely not dictators in the making." Peter Davis concurs: "Their suppression of political liberty is understandable, if regrettable. After all, the freedom Americans prize never had a place in Nicaraguan life anyway." The same argument would have applied to Somoza.

It is repeated by Staughton Lynd who wrote two weeks ago in *In These Times* that "the Sandinista trade unions have been the first to build workers control, and a genuine free trade union movement." Lynd toured Nicaragua as the Sandinistas' guest and failed to interview any leaders of the independent trade unions or to observe any of the state sponsored brutality against their union members. Thus Lynd—a man who has publicly admitted that he was snookered by the North Vietnamese in the 1960s—is now snookered anew by the Sandinistas.

Even when New Leftists acknowledged negative developments in revolutionary states like Cuba, these developments were always explained as the fault of the United States. The fountainhead of these "explanations" is yet another myth: that U.S. hostility to these revolutions pushed them away from their original commitment to freedom and into the hands of the Soviet Union and the old line Communists.

This position was first propagated by my mentor, William Appleman Williams in his much quoted 1962 book *The United States, Cuba, and Castro.* His argument was simple: Castro, a radical nationalist, had to break the old binding ties with the American Empire in order to honor the promises of the 1952 Cuban constitution. Castro came to the United States to seek an economic loan in April 1959. That loan request was turned down. Meanwhile, Castro's agrarian reforms were opposed by the United States and in the face of this opposition, the revolutionary coalition in Cuba split. As Williams put it:

> By giving up on Castro and becoming increasingly negative and antagonistic, the United States closed off the one main chance Castro had to make his revolution without turning to the Communists in Cuba and the Soviet Union.

To Williams and the Left, the responsibility for the direction of the Cuban Revolution lay with the United States. First, because the U.S. refused to help Castro except on its own terms, and then because it planned unilaterally to destroy the Cuban revolution. It was a cliche of the New Left, given currency in other books like David Horowitz's *Free World Colossus*. The Left likes to downplay its influence and evade its responsibilities, but the record shows that these ideas had consequences: Carter liberals like Anthony Lake and Robert Pastor, head of Carter's National Security Council staff for Latin America, for example, refused to act to push Somoza out of power at a time when a moderate democratic coalition could have taken over instead of the Marxist-Leninist Sandinistas; to do so would be "interventionism;" what influenced this crucial decision not to exert pressure in behalf of the democratic forces in Nicaragua? Robert Pastor told one interviewer the reason: "Horowitz's *Free World Colossus* had a dramatic impact on me and taught me the truth of the radical critique of the cold war mentality." David is apologizing for that right now at this conference.

What do we know about all this in the 1980s? The answer is best provided by an important (and neglected) book by Richard E. Welch, *Response and Revolution: The U.S. and the Cuban Revolution 1959–1961*. A careful and balanced academic study, Welch's book reveals that the version of events propagated by Williams and others is a politically inspired myth. The reality was quite different. The first U.S. Ambassador to post-revolutionary Cuba, Phillip Bonsal, was a man of good will who hoped to help Cuba recognize that the United States truly offered friendship and desired to provide solid guidance to the new regime. Bonsal, we might add, was to the Cuban revolution what Carter's Larry Pezzullo was to the 1979 Nicaraguan revolution. Even the Eisenhower Administration, Welch shows, sought to discuss economic aid to Castro but Castro rejected such discussions, because he believed that a request for a loan might endanger the momentum of his revolution. Castro decided against making a request for U.S. aid—capital and technical aid—*before* he came to Washington.

Moreover, Phil Bonsal and the United States gave full support to Castro's agrarian reform law, contrary to the version of events propagated by the Left. It was *Havana,* not Washington, that shaped the U.S.-Cuban relationship at a time when the United States was ambivalent and not hostile, or aggressively mobilized against the revolution. What do we know about Castro's intentions? The cat, of course is now, out of the bag. Tad Szulc's recent biography, based on interviews with Castro and other leaders of the revolution, reveals that from the day he seized power Castro had set up a secret shadow government, knowledge of which was kept from his own July 26 Movement *cadre* to plan how and when to turn power over to the old line Communists and Marxist-Leninists of Cuba.

This reality is now acknowledged by Castro groupie Saul Landau, who in 1960 told us in no uncertain terms how Fidel had made a revolution *against* the Communists and had developed a true third way to humane socialism. Writing in a recent issue of *Monthly Review* twenty-five years later when Cuba has become a Soviet satellite, Landau claims that of course everyone on the inside *knew* then that Fidel was a Marxist-Leninist and had forced Communists on a reluctant 26th of July Movement and moved them into strategic places in the revolutionary government. That only proves, Landau writes, that there can be no genuine revolutionary thought in Third World countries that is not Marxist-Leninist. Indeed, says Landau, Fidel personally told him that he had been a Leninist since his imprisonment by Batista in 1954.

Now it is 1987 and we hear the same arguments concerning Nicaragua. If only we give the revolution some breathing space its true moderate nature will be revealed. This argument was brilliantly refuted by Larry Harrison, the Carter Administration's Director of the aid program to Nicaragua from 1979–1981. In an important article appearing in the *Wall Street Journal* and reprinted in the very first uncensored edition of *La Prensa* two weeks ago, Harrison explained what happened in that time period. Moderates in the Nicaraguan junta had resigned in April 1980 when they learned that key portfolios were taken over by the *comandantes,* whose actions showed that real power had not resided in the *junta,* but in the leaders of the FSLN who held the guns. To insure receipt of $75 million in U.S. aid that had been voted by the U.S. Congress, the Sandinistas held a meeting with their opponents, agreed to hold local elections, and to allow opposition parties complete freedom to organize and to have access to the media; in addition they promised the establishment of a system of due process to prevent illegal confiscation of property. Arturo Cruz then joined the junta and it seemed, as Harrison writes, that the Sandinistas were demonstrating that they were not doctrinaire ideologues, that their commitment to pluralism was genuine, and that they were sincerely concerned about good relations with the U.S.

But four months later, after the appropriation of the $75 million, the Sandinistas turned their backs on the agreements they had negotiated with the opposition. Humberto Ortega announced that when the Sandinistas held elections, they would not be like the corrupt ones held in the United States. Instead of conciliation, they continued to march toward totalitarianism and towards confrontation with the United States. A turning point was reached—the end of the honeymoon, as Tomas Borge refers to it in the current edition of *New Left Review*—when the Sandinistas killed the anti-Somoza labor organizer Jorge Salazar. "When they made the right noises about democratization," as Harrison puts it, "they were pursuing the Leninist strategy of two steps forward, one step back." As *comandante* Borge says, "There was this honeymoon period, when the bourgeoisie and even *La Prensa,* and all the pretty girls, thought they were Sandinista. Why?" he asks. "They thought we were going to just establish a democracy."

Despite all of this evidence the support of the Sandinistas in the United States continues to increase. New Left thinking confined to the political fringes in the 1960s has spread to the political mainstream. Jesse Jackson, a strong Democratic party Presidential candidate, sees no reason why the Sandinistas should trust Ronald Reagan, but plenty of reasons why the United States should trust Daniel Ortega. And a new film, which opened in Washington last night—*Fire on the Mountain*—presents a picture of the Sandinistas as a humane force and a hope for liberation in the entire hemisphere. The film's North American creator edits out any shots of *"Comandante Zero,"* Eden Pastora in the scenes of the 1979 Sandinista triumph. Shades of Joseph Stalin.

Twenty years ago such naivete may have been understandable (even if the duplicity was not); today, in 1987 it is inexcusable, even criminal.

PART IV

SECOND THOUGHTS ON A POLITICAL CULTURE

Glenn Loury
Carol Ianonne
Michael Medved
Joshua Muravchik

CHAPTER 1

BLACK POLITICAL CULTURE AFTER THE SIXTIES

Glenn Loury

Some time during the 1960s we Americans began to fall prey to various conspiracies of silence about the black condition. This was especially so among black intellectuals and politicians.

Those of us who, with trepidation, return to the places where we were raised, now communities unlike any we had known, who look despairingly at the tenements which once housed poor families in dignity but no longer do, and who, having found a long though unsatisfying list of whites to blame for this state of affairs are still bewildered at the profound changes that have occurred in less than a generation. We remain unwilling to express that bewilderment, or to ask today's residents: *"How can you live like this?"* We are a part of this conspiracy.

We have tolerated incompetence in the social and political institutions serving this population, because its source has been black. We have made excuses for and sometimes even glorified the supposedly rebellious actions of thugs, though those thugs have made poor black people their victims. We have strained our imaginations, and our fellow citizens' credulity, to find apologies for the able-bodied, healthy, and intelligent young men who father children and then walk away from the responsibility to support them. We have listened in silence, or sometimes with enthusiastic encouragement, to middle-class young black men and women at the best colleges and universities who explain their failure to make full use of the opportunities presented to them in the terms of an ideology of racist exploitation that was not even valid in the 1960s, and is much less so today. In the name of racial loyalty, and in an effort to keep alive the sense of oppression which fueled the revolts of our youth, we have engaged in an almost criminal abdication of responsibility.

Moreover, we have encouraged and enforced the exclusion from good standing in our ranks of those few (called "bourgeois elitists" on many campuses today, though usually their origins are anything but "bourgeois") who have had the insight and courage to object to this transparently inadequate series of rationalizations. And the poor have paid the price for this folly.

We have adhered to a false, enervating conception of racial loyalty, one which, while avoiding "giving aid and comfort to the enemy"—that is, to the "white man"—requires abandoning the dictates of our parents' traditions and most deeply held values. In the wake of the moral relativism introduced in the '60s, we blacks now in the best position to do so, have shown ourselves to be without the will and self-confidence to provide leadership and set standards for our people. We have lapsed into the position of assuming that true commitment to the cause of black people requires that we be uncritical of the deeds of blacks and silent about the implications of our own accomplishments. We act as though the historical fact of slavery and the associated culpability of America have endowed us with a fully paid insurance policy excusing whatever behavior now ensues: Every personal failing of blacks (even the illegal behavior of corrupt politicians) becomes evidence of the discrimination of whites, every individual success is taken to be an exceptional event. And in this we have been encouraged by the Left.

Remarkably, we think that the mere announcement of the small number of blacks who attain a certain achievement constitutes an indictment of society, and not of us. Thinking thus, we engage in an *exhibitionism of non-achievement*, hurrying to advertise our every lack of success. It never occurs to us, in doing so, that we are advertising failure, for the first axiom of the credo of loyalty is that when blacks do not succeed it is whites who have failed. We display the false security of those who, having been violated historically, somehow think they can do no wrong—that "right" must inexorably be on their side. Demagogues can run among us spewing hatred and venom, and we express the barest annoyance, reasoning that these haters are but the natural result of that ever-present, ultimately cleansing, oh so convenient hate we call white racism.

ILLUSTRATING THE EXTENT OF THE PROBLEM

Lest you think the foregoing too extreme, consider some of the enormities which have driven me to these conclusions. In Atlanta several years ago there erupted a series of child killings which gripped the community in fear. All of the victims of these crimes were black. The black mayor, black police chief, and substantially black police force threw themselves into the hunt for the killer. They called on the FBI for assistance. A man was found, tried before a black judge for two of the murders (though evidence implicated him in others) and convicted of the crimes. That man was black, and this was a great disappointment for many blacks across the country. Some insisted that the Ku Klux Klan was behind the child disappearances; others agreed with popular black activist Dick Gregory that the Centers for Disease Control in Atlanta were kidnapping and murdering young black boys for an exotic cancer-fighting drug to be found in the tips of their sex organs. The (largely black) jury's verdict, to this day, is rejected by blacks throughout the land.

It could hardly be otherwise, given the extent to which prominent blacks had used the killings to exemplify the fact that blacks continue to suffer the ravages of racism. Indeed, in 1981, before the trial of the accused Wayne Williams, Jesse Jackson had said of the killings: "It is open season on black people. . . . These murders can only be understood in the context of affirmative action and Ronald Reagan's conservative politics."

One victim's mother, derisively referring to the mayor as "the fat boy," led a campaign against the middle-class black Atlanta establishment, accusing it, in collaboration with the white "powers that be," to have found in the accused a convenient scapegoat. Rather than celebrate the cessation of a murder spree, the victims of which were black children, many chose instead to absolve the apparent perpetrator and use the case as a platform for expressing their discontent with American society. Evidently, no act of a black man, however willful and depraved, is unfit for exploitation in this manner. For the "sophisticated" observer, one seeing "beneath the surface" to the "true" nature of racial oppression, the formula injustice (a black man on trial for murder in white America is by definition a victim) proved more politically salient than the reality of mass killing being finally brought to a halt. This is a kind of collective madness whose roots can be traced, I believe, to the excesses of the 1960s. We learned too well during the upheavals of that decade how to be America's pre-eminent victims.

Consider, for a graphic example, the response of black Congressman Charles Rangel (D-N.Y.) to the efforts of prominent New Yorkers to get him to issue a condemnatory statement before Minister Louis Farrakhan's Madison Square Garden speech of October 7, 1985. The Muslim

Minister's speech on that occasion, greeted by wild cheers, was described in one eyewitness account as follows:

> "The scriptures charge your people [the Jews] with killing the prophets of God." Farrakhan contended that God had not made the Jewish people pay for such deeds. However, if something happens to him, then God will make the Jews pay for all the prophets killed from biblical times to the present. "You cannot say 'never again' to God because when God puts you in the oven, 'never again' don't mean a thing. If you fool with me, you court death itself. I will not run from you; I will run to you!" Farrakhan reserved a little of his hatred for black political leaders, telling the audience that "when a leader sells out the people, he should pay a price for that. Should a leader sell out the people and live?"

Not only did Representative Rangel refuse to issue a statement condemning this event in response to the entreaties of his fellow New Yorkers, he went so far as to suggest that the pressure for him to do so constituted yet another example of white racism. Writing five days later in the *Washington Post,* Rangel declared "most objectionable [the] assumption that I and other elected leaders who happen to be black have a special obligation to issue denunciations of Farrakhan on demand." He likened efforts to get him to make a statement to the requirement that he carry a "South African-like passbook stamped with issued denunciations" of the Muslim leader.

Rangel further suggested that "to [have] renounce[d] Farrakhan prior to his scheduled appearance at Madison Square Garden" would somehow have interfered with his Constitutional rights. He urged that we "differentiate between . . . the anti-semitic garbage and the advocacy of discipline, self-help and black pride" in Farrakhan's message, explaining that the real problem here is "the despair in the black community, the frustration and rage over America's failure to come to terms with its racism."

It is a measure of the great pressure which this member of the U.S. House of Representatives was under that he would resort to such a transparently faulty attempt to evade his responsibilities as the principal national political spokesman for the blacks of Harlem. How would the public expression of his opinion regarding Farrakhan have limited the latter's right to speak? Why should it matter that "black pride" is also touted by one who preaches that no "leader [should] sell out the people and live?" While there were many thousands of his constituents in that auditorium cheering on Mr. Farrakhan, many thousands more reject his hate-filled message. To whom else ought concerned observers have gone to ascertain whether the sentiments as were expressed there represented the views of the majority of black New Yorkers? Were Rangel the black representative of a farm district in Iowa one might take more seriously his cry of "South Africa-like" racism at being asked to respond. As it was, his talk of politicians who just "happen to be black" seemed, at best, disingenuous. He would, after all, be among the first to insist that blackness is a primary qualification for one who would occupy the seat once held by Adam Clayton Powell.

There is a stunning *moral insensitivity* here, born of being too long in the habitual status of victim. For Rangel ends up absolving Farrakhan's supporters of their anti-semitic bigotry with his reference to "America's failure;" yet no white politician could similarly dismiss the expression of anti-black sentiments among his constituents, however impoverished.

In December of 1984 the so-called "subway vigilante" Bernhard Goetz shot four black youths who, he claimed, were about to accost him on a New York subway. He instantly became a folk hero among many urban dwellers, black and white, living in fear of victimization. In the ensuing public discussion of the problem of urban crime one of the most eminent living black social scientists, Kenneth Clark, offered the theory that in today's big cities it is not poor young men, but instead "society", that is the "real mugger." Writing in the *New York Times,* Clark condemned the unseemly vigilante sentiments evoked by the Goetz case, and ascribed to "society" responsibility for the criminal acts of urban muggers. Those committing most street crimes, he asserted, have been "mugged" themselves. They are the victims of "pervasive community, economic, and educational muggings" perpetrated by a "hypocritical society," at the hands of which "their humanity is being systematically destroyed." The theft and violence which many city-dwellers fear are, for Clark, but "the inevitable criminality that comes out of the degradation of human beings."

This is a remarkable argument, not only for its questionable sociology—some impoverished urban minority populations have very low crime rates—but more significantly for what it reveals about Dr. Clark's view of the values and capacities of the inner-city poor. Quite simply, he is willing to avoid judgments about the behavioral differences among blacks in the interest of portraying the problems of the community as due to racism. Yet it is factually inaccurate and morally disturbing to say of poor black persons generally that their economic deprivation has destroyed their humanity. Even in the harshest slums the vast majority of residents do not brutalize their neighbors; they can hardly be taken as aberrant exceptions to some sociological law requiring the unemployed to become "mindlessly anti-social" (Clark's usage).

Moreover, even the black poor who are violent must be held responsible for their conduct. Are they not made poorer still when they are not accorded the respect inherent in the equal application of the obligations and expectations of citizenship? What is most dangerous about the "social muggings" analogy is that it invites society, blacks and whites, to see the black poor as morally different, socially distorted human beings. What such a construction (which is but a restatement of the old "blaming the victim" argument) may "achieve" by way of fostering guilt and pity among the population at large would seem to be more than offset by the extent to which it directly undermines the dignity of these persons.

LEADERSHIP AND THE DICTATES OF RACIAL "LOYALTY"

These examples serve to illustrate the contemporary crisis in black political leadership. To call for "law and order" in the nation's ghettos, or to openly criticize politicians who fail to do so, is to invite (as I have now done) attack by advocates of blacks' interests, attacks which I believe are at base motivated by a sense of betrayal: such problems of the group are not to be discussed in public, at least not while whites can hear. One should put the best face on things.

Yet given the extent of the problems which plague black society, especially the poorest of blacks, it is obviously necessary for writers, artists, intellectuals, political leaders, and ordinary folk openly to examine what is happening so as to formulate effective responses. This kind of dialogue disappeared from black intellectual life during the "black power" years, as demands for solidarity took precedence over the dictates of reason. For black Americans, in light of the objective failure of the conceptions and approaches ritualistically endorsed by the Left to improve matters, it is vital that there occur a critical discourse regarding what went wrong and what might yet work. We blacks must try to recreate an environment where such critical intellectual exchange can occur without it undermining the basis for our cooperative association. The natural distrust of those espousing what some may regard as heretical thoughts must somehow be suspended at least long enough for there to occur a serious reflection on whether the received verities continue to serve the group's best interest.

How is this to be done? A necessary first step is to understand the nature and extent of the problem, and carefully to examine its root causes and its enormous consequences. This has been my purpose in my work on racial politics in recent years. The difficulties about which I am concerned are cultural, as well as political. They run very deep, and will not be reversed overnight. Yet they must be confronted, and should be understood, I think, as a detrimental legacy of that infamous decade.

PLAYING THE "VICTIM"—A COSTLY ROLE

The signs of intellectual exhaustion, and of the increasing political isolation of the current black leadership class are evident. This isolation is exacerbated by its reliance on a basically adversarial approach in dealing with the rest of the polity, an approach toward which our leaders gravitate because of the way in which the claims of blacks are most successfully pressed. These claims are based, above all, on the status of blacks as America's historical victims. Maintenance of this status requires constant emphasis on the wrongs of the past and exaggeration of present tribulations. He who leads a group of historical victims, as victims, must never let "them" forget what "they" have done; he must renew the indictment and keep alive the moral asymmetry implicit in the respective positions of victim and victimizer. He is the preeminent architect of what British philosopher G.K. Minogue has called "suffering situations." The circumstance of his group as "underdog" becomes his most valuable political (and cultural) asset. Deployment of this "asset" was elevated to an art form by black activists in the '60s. Yet, this posture, especially in the political realm, militates against an emphasis on personal responsibility within the group, and induces those who have been successful to attribute their accomplishments to fortuitous circumstance, and not to their own abilities and character.

It is difficult to overemphasize the self-defeating dynamic at work here. The dictates of political advocacy by America's victims require that personal inadequacies among blacks be attributed to "the system," and that emphasis by black leaders on self-improvement be denounced as irrelevant, self-serving, dishonest. Individual black men and women simply cannot fail on their own; they must be seen as never having had a chance. But where failure at the personal level is impossible, there can also be no personal success. For a black to embrace the Horatio Alger myth, to assert as a guide to *personal* action that "there is opportunity in America," becomes a *politically* repugnant act. For each would-be black Horatio Alger indicts as inadequate or incomplete, the deeply entrenched (and quite useful) notion, born during the "revolts" of the '60s, that individual effort can never overcome the "inheritance of race." Yet where there can be no black Horatio Algers to celebrate, sustaining an ethos of responsibility which might serve to extract maximal effort from the individual in the face of hardship becomes impossible as well.

In short, the nihilism and moral relativism of '60s counter-cultural thinking, together with the New Left's adoption of blacks as the system's leading victims, have had a devastating impact on the most vulnerable of Americans.

CHAPTER 2

THE FEMINIST CONFUSION

Carol Iannone

It's pretty embarrassing to have to admit now that I was first seriously drawn to feminism by its messianic dimension. I was never a hands-on, political, activist feminist and I've never owned a pair of red stockings. But I was first introduced to feminism in graduate school in the mid-Seventies as it was making its long march through the institutions. Soon I was teaching it in the context of women in literature classes and shaping my intellectual life by its tenets. I enjoyed, reveled in the utterly systematic property feminism takes on when used as a tool of analysis, especially when to the exclusion of all others. Like Marxism, feminism can explain everything from advertising to religion by following its single thread, the oppression of women. How comprehensible everything became! All injustice and evil were caused by patriarchy; dismantle patriarchy and we would have the brave new world of feminism: humane, generous, peaceful, good. Women had been defined by men; let women define themselves and then we'll change the world.

When I defected from the feminist philosophy some years later, it was largely out of simple, gut-level, personal disillusionment. As time went by, however, I began to see more clearly the extent of the damage feminism has done to women and to our cultural life. I would like to focus on the damage feminism as a way of thought has done to women, although some of the cultural issues will be discussed by implication.

First of all, feminism is a series of self-indulgent contradictions and anyone following it for a while is going to find her thought coarsened. Women are the same as men, women are different from men, according to the ideological need. Women are strong and capable. And yet have been the slaves and victims of men throughout history. Women are angry, rebellious, even murderous in patriarchy, but also superior to

149

men because loving and tender. Women are the humane and nurturing sex, but can put their children in child care centers for ten hours a day. Feminism sponsors choices for women, unless the choice is the domestic role. Feminism is for the social good, even though it openly advocates dismantling the entire social order. Feminism is a legitimate academic and intellectual approach, but it cannot be judged by ordinary academic and intellectual standards. Women writers have been wrongfully excluded from the mainstream tradition, but they have also been wrongfully seen outside their separate "female tradition."

Second, feminism encourages women to look at their experience only within narrow feminist terms. Consciousness raising inflames the discontent that is bound to be in every woman's life and then in the ensuing disarray invites her to see it as the oppression of being seen as a sex object, or whatever, and to look to alleviate it in political terms. To the extent that the personal becomes political, the woman loses contact with herself. She is constrained from seeing how many "feminine" problems are more moral and characterological than social or political, and that regardless of origin, can only be overcome by the individual—vanity, self-centeredness, the tendency to want to idealize men, even the tendency to surrender to emotional weakness.

Then there is the hidden destructiveness and the various female poses and postures of helplessness and dependency which women have always been loath to acknowledge, and which feminism has helped them avoid acknowledging too. When Susan Brownmiller argues that "while the extremes of masculinity can harm others (rape, wife-beating, street-crime, warfare . . .) the extremes of femininity are harmful only to women themselves in the form of self-imposed masochism," she is revealing a terrible ignorance about the ways of human nature. How apt seems the Saturday Night Live parody of the Phil Donahue Show in which a woman sociologist comes on to discuss her new book entitled *Women: Good; Men: Bad.*

The preliminary result of the politicization of the internal life may seem liberating but the end result is enslavement, since it diminishes the individual's sense of control over her own destiny and weakens her self-discipline by encouraging her to blame others. Much New Left thought began with the demand for greater individual freedom, but the subsequent fear of the real demands of freedom lead to a rush into collective, pre-fabricated identities, with feelings, thoughts, and ideas dictated by ideology. Thus feminism has enabled women to behave childishly, demanding equality and independence, but also preferential treatment and special protection as a group.

Third, feminism has made many things worse by preventing women from seeing their experience clearly, as in the unspeakably dishonest comparison of women with blacks, or in the pretense that female biological needs are the result of male indoctrination. Feminism refuses to see how much of a hand women have had in creating the despised system, and how much it has served not only men's but women's needs as well. Feminism also joins the rest of the New Left in disdain for the Western tradition for its purported oppression of women, although it is only on the basis of this tradition that a campaign for greater freedom for women could ever have been mounted. With all its faulty but rigidly held convictions about certain matters, however, feminism is utterly and foolishly amoral about a whole host of issues, unable, for example, to decide if prostitution is exploitation of women, or a praiseworthy example of women controlling their own sexuality in patriarchy. Similar debates go on over pornography, surrogate motherhood, etc.

After its original insistence that women are the same as men, much feminist thought now derives from differences. In literature, for example, feminists have managed to make headway by insisting that the canon of great works was founded by white males and that therefore they can discard the standards upon which this canon is based and single out works for study based on female standards which thus far have eluded clear articulation. Academic feminism is even able to influence some of the work being produced by women writers today and it is not uncommon for a poet or a novelist to appear at conferences and on panels, reading some creative adaptation of the feminist vision. For example, I recently heard a poem extolling the decision of Lot's wife to disobey God's directives and to turn and look at the city of Sodom while it was being destroyed because as a woman, she felt the pull of communal identity. Recently, too, I heard a prominent feminist scholar denounce Eudora Welty's memoir, *One Writer's Beginnings,* for presenting too sunny a version of its author's life. Welty does a disservice to women, the feminist critic insisted, by hiding her anger at patriarchy. Again, I can't resist pointing out the contradiction between the two versions of women's experiences— they have special, loving, communal female values, they are full of anger and patriarchy. If one argues that patriarchy creates their anger might it also not be argued that patriarchy also creates their nurturing and communal female values?

A recent study by feminist psychologist Carol Gilligan of Harvard which posits separate male and female moral sensibilities has aroused a lot of positive commentary, some even from conservative critics, who are happy to see differences asserted. Gilligan argues that women tend to see moral choices more in terms of responsibilities and men more in terms of rights: women tend to be concerned with who else will be affected by their choices, not only with the absolute rights and wrongs of the case. Gilligan does argue for an eventual integration of both types of morality, but, as more than one commentator has noted, the emphasis in her works falls on difference and she implicitly glorifies the more relational, caring, selfless qualities of the female over what comes to look like the emotional deficiencies of the male.

Such thinking when codified into an intellectual approach, can serve to encourage self-flattery and self-righteousness among women, in the retrograde manner of a 19th century American female sentimental writer documented by Ann Douglas in *The Feminization of American Culture*. These writers created and peddled a false, fulsome, meretricious view of redemptive womanhood that was a caricature and that cheapened the terms of cultural life. To the extent to which such formulations have been adopted by feminism in our time—and it is to a considerable extent—intellectual life has suffered, with reality split into artificial dichotomies.

Recently, I sat in on a Columbia graduate fellowship seminar and heard a young woman state that women's poetry must be taught to off-set the "male values" advanced in poetry by men. Homer, for example, sponsors martial values which must be balanced by the more nurturing values of female writers. This dichotomization leads to a terrible flattening on both sides, but one in which female writers especially are seen to be mainly talking from, and about, the gender or gender-related experiences which supposedly give rise to their female experiences such as menstruation, child-bearing, sex, motherhood, courtship, etc.

All of this emphasis on spurious differences—so there is a denial of genuine difference and an elevation of spurious difference— brings me to my last point, which is how feminism has hurt women: it has denied to them any possibility of transcendence or universality. The modern thinking female lives and moves and breathes in a world more gender inflected, to use the current jargon, than that of the most benighted and reactionary Fifties housewife. Academic feminism has created separate disciplines through women's studies—we have women's language, literature, forms, traditions, history, philosophy, theology, science, morality and art. The only activity that miraculously is allowed to be neuter is child-rearing.

In popular culture too, in movies, television shows, magazines, fiction, it seems that if a woman is asked to take any view at all on the meaning of her existence, it is on the basis of her problematic position as a female in patriarchal culture. One almost begins to feel that the reason some women are trying desperately to get into men's clubs is to have a respite from the womanized world feminists have created. A generation of women has sacrificed real intellectual growth to this parochialism, until it is actually incapable, it seems, of understanding that ancient Greek philosophy, for example, is not a white male view of the world.

The extent of the feminist depredation on the intellectual life of women was graphically illuminated for me some time ago when I heard Allan Bloom participate in a panel discussion. In the general course of an attack on Bloom, a woman professor defended the relativism of the universities, insisting that different modes of thought had a right to be heard, since there are no absolutes. Later in her remarks, she said she hoped her own students would come to renounce racism and sexism in their own lives. Professor Bloom set aside a lot of other questions she had posed and probed this weak spot. "Do you consider sexism an evil," he asked. She said she did. "Then," he said, "you cannot be a relativist, since you believe that there is something which is absolutely evil. Unless, of course, you consider sexism being evil only your opinion, and consider another view—that sexism is not evil—just as good an opinion. You see, you can't have it both ways." The woman professor was completely at a loss. Having shot this arrow, Bloom went in for the kill: "When you have spoken in contradictions like that you have said *nothing*," he declared. At that moment, a distinctly uneasy panel moderator stopped Bloom by insisting that it was time to move on to the next speaker. Later the room was filled with bristling women denouncing Bloom for his sexist treatment of the woman professor. And, it seems, there were a number of men who agreed with them.

Feminism rode into our cultural life on the coattails of the New Left but by now it certainly deserves its own place in the halls of intellectual barbarisms. In a way it is too bad that the inevitable advance of women into a greater role in public life had to be accompanied by feminism, but in a way also it is good. As women are forced step by step to overcome the falsities of feminism, they will be working their way to true intellectual and emotional freedom.

CHAPTER 3

A GATHERING OF IDEALISTS

Michael Medved

Let me begin by recalling some of the long ago days when I was working for the Vietnam Moratorium as one of the organizers who went out into the high-schools to recruit students. In those days I learned a very interesting rhetorical trick. I would begin my pitch in assemblies (we had tremendous cooperation from the high school administrations), by saying this: "What I'm going to speak to you about today has nothing at all to do with politics. I know that you're soured on politics, you're not interested in Young Republicans, you're not interested in Young Democrats. But we're not talking about politics. We're talking about human decency. We're talking about whether you care enough to reach out and try to help human beings who are suffering and are in pain." That was the basic pitch. What's interesting about it is that over the last twenty years, though my own personal political perspectives have changed decisively, the Left, in all of its organized manifestations, and particularly its cultural manifestations, is still striking precisely that same rhetorical pose and is still pressing precisely that advantage.

There is a notion abroad in the land—and it's extraordinarily common and very widely accepted—that somehow Left-wing political activism is non-partisan, is non-political, is humanitarian, is simply a matter of peace and social justice. Let me share with you a few examples that I've experienced from one of the worlds in which I function which is the world of television and motion pictures.

Recently I had the opportunity to observe that high level forum of political thinking "The David Letterman Show." I was in a hotel room and it was late at night— that's really my excuse—in any event, I turned it on and there was an actress named Annie Potts on the show, talking to David Letterman. She was talking about the fact that her own show had recently been cancelled but there had been a letter writing campaign, with thousands of people urging the station to put her show back on the air. All of a sudden, while she was speaking, her eyes sort of glistened and you could see that they were filmy and wet and she was deeply moved. She said, "You know, it makes me think. What if all those thousands of people instead of writing about a little T.V. show had written in about the anti-nuclear thing. Wouldn't that be great?" The entire audience applauded wildly. Now I have no idea what she meant by "the anti-nuclear thing." Was she against nuclear power plants? Against nuclear weapons? Nuclear families? Or all of the above? I don't know. The audience loved it. Can you imagine if some actress had been on there and said "Wouldn't it be great if everybody wrote in to support the Democratic Resistance in Nicaragua?" Do you think for a moment the audience would have applauded? David Letterman would have fallen out of his chair. The screen probably would have gone black. But "the anti-nuclear thing"—that's fine.

Another high level exchange of political information that I happened to witness took place about six months ago involving two of our leading thinkers on defense issues, Jane Alexander and Mariette Hartley. Mariette Hartley was interviewing Jane Alexander on the "CBS Morning Program" and Jane was telling her how she was taking six months off her career to work with the Soviet Peace Committee and with Helen Caldicott in an effort to try to decrease the nuclear arsenal of the United States which is menacing peace throughout the world. And what was astonishing was not that Jane Alexander used this forum to push her political ideas—after all, she was the guest—but that the host of the show, Mariette Hartley, said, "You know Jane, you're such a wonderful example to people; what is it that we can do to get other people to follow your example so they too will care more about issues of war and peace?" It was a breath-taking moment. She was talking about a campaign for unilateral nuclear disarmament as if it were a campaign for muscular dystrophy. How can we get other people involved? It's just a simple humanitarian matter. That seems to be the idea that is accepted in the general culture, particularly in the television culture.

You can see it also very strikingly in the public reception given to various film and television programs. For instance, I'm sure you all remember the tremendous public service that was performed by the American Broadcasting Corporation, ABC, when they ran "The Morning After," a show about the disasters of nuclear war that everybody heralded as a great contribution to America's consciousness. Two years later, however, when the same network ran "Amerika" which purported not to show the nuclear devastation wrought by the joint imperialisms of Russia and America, but to show what America might be like after a Soviet victory, it was condemned before it even aired. It was savaged by critics because it was "political," which it was. But the same critics had praised "The Morning After," as though it was non-political, which it was not. Now I'm not going to make a brief for "Amerika", I didn't watch it, or "The Morning After" which I didn't watch either. But the fact is that the response to those two different shows evidently went far beyond the quality of either of them, and had to do with one being perceived as a public service program, and the other as a Right-wing and red-bashing vehicle.

One sees the same response to the various Vietnam movies. There have been very few pieces published that even begin to suggest that there might be a political agenda behind Oliver Stone's "Platoon", let alone Stanley Kubrick's "Full Metal Jacket". These are non-political movies; they show us the truth about Vietnam. But then a movie is released like "The Hanoi Hilton" and it is absolutely creamed by mainstream American film critics. It was an astonishing spectacle. Stanley Kauffman began his review in *The New Republic* with the sentence: "The Hanoi Hilton is filth." And why? Because it portrayed the suffering of American POW's in Hanoi during the war and because there was a three minute segment showing a character who looked and sounded very much like Jane Fonda, doing very similar things to what Jane Fonda actually did when she visited Hanoi during the war, except the film softened the reality.

I had a personal experience with this phenomenon when I was reviewing Oliver Stone's film "Salvador" on my TV show. You can say what you will about the movie, but it's a very slick piece of propaganda. Whenever the government troops of El Salvador appear there are ominous chords that sound like the background music to 1950s monster movies, while whenever the guerrillas are on screen there are little strumming guitars and a hopeful boys' chorus singing inspirational peasant songs. It seemed to me that one could say that such a film has a certain political ax to grind. I dared say that on PBS. And the response was astonishing. I've reviewed now hundreds and hundreds of movies on the air and I've never had a response comparable to my review of "Salvador". People wrote in saying you are allowing your politics to get in the way of your appreciation of this wonderful film, and how can you review it from a political perspective? My position was that when a film was so profoundly political as "Salvador", how could you not introduce politics into the equation, at least to some degree? You must. But the fact is that for most people the film was non-political because it represented that point of view of humanitarian concern, of a quest for social justice, of good people. Therefore, by definition, it was non-political.

So what do we do about all of this? And what does it all mean? I think one of the things that you have to take into account is that this double standard matters. It matters for several reasons. First of all, Americans instinctively are so distrustful of politics in any form, that anytime you have a debate where one side is overtly political and the other side can claim to be non-political, a lot of public sympathy is naturally going to go to the non-political side. And second, it matters because it so clearly encourages Left-wing activists whether they happen to be movie stars, or writers, or producers, or journalists of any stripe, or sports figures, or you name it, to step forward proudly with their commitments and their associations.

In fact, there is a group of young actors and actresses right now in Moscow making a film in cooperation with the Soviet Peace Committee and SANE and a lot of the publicity concerning those people features the fact that this group of people—Mary Stuart Masterson, Daphne Zuniga—have a great depth that we hadn't perceived before. Being political on the Left actually helps one's public image whereas on the other side it has a chilling effect. Except for a few singular exceptions such as Mr. Eastwood, I think that you will find that in the Hollywood community, in the motion picture and television community, there is genuine political fear—particularly on the part of screenwriters and directors, and technical people—who have political opinions that don't mesh with the standard Norman Lear "People for the American Way" perspective. People with those opinions will largely keep them to themselves, because to speak out could hurt their careers. What is happening currently in Hollywood is a sort of McCarthyism in reverse. For people who do not share the prevailing point of view a chilling effect is induced by this double standard.

Finally, permitting this double standard to flourish creates a situation in which all Left-Right questions can be stated very simply. You've all heard it a thousand times: it's not a question of Left or Right, it's a question of passion versus passivity; of commitment versus complacency; of idealism versus selfishness. As long as we accept those kinds of formulations of reducing complex issues to issues of selfishness versus idealism, we lose. This formulation is a disaster for those who are defending the cause of America.

To be sure, it is a disaster that is to a certain extent imposed on us by circumstances. I believe that those critiques are correct that point to a certain bias in the media, in the way things are reported, and the way things are framed. And beyond that there is something in the Left–Right dichotomy itself. Those on the Left generally claim to be building a new world, a utopia, a brighter tomorrow. Such a claim, however fanciful, is obviously more easily associated with idealism in people's minds than the skeptical realism of the classic conservative point of view, a view more concerned either with incremental change or simply preventing the world from being more loused up than it already is. The classical conservative position doesn't inspire the same idealistic sentiment that is available to the Left. But Ronald Reagan's success would seem to indicate that it is at least possible, under certain circumstances, to associate the cause of the Right with idealism, with selflessness, with noble goals. It is extraordinarily important that we do just that.

Obviously we need to do more than simply rehash Ronald Reagan's rhetoric of optimism. The time for that is probably over. We have to insist on different terms in the way that we portray ourselves, and the way we portray our own commitments. It's critically important that when we enter any public forum we insist that what we are doing is every bit as noble, and selfless, and humanitarian, and as yes non–political as any of those Hollywood airheads on all of their smug pilgrimages to Managua and Moscow.

When people asked what I would be doing in Washington I told them that I would be attending a gathering of dreamers, crusaders, and idealists, who have committed themselves to the anti–totalitarian struggle and to opposing oppression in Eastern Europe, in Afghanistan, and Nicaragua, and all other places in the world. We have to insist on those kinds of terms in describing our own activities and commitments. Most of all, we have to insist on the proper terms in describing our own political journeys. One of the things that infuriates me most is the notion that somehow my own progress represents some kind of fall from grace; that in moving from the vaguely focused instinctual anti–Americanism which characterized my years in college and law school to my current opposition to totalitarianism, that I have sacrificed my idealism. I refuse to accept for one moment that I am any less idealistic today than I was in the 1960s; that what we are engaged in is in any way inherently less humanitarian, less concerned with social justice, less concerned with peace, than what we were involved in back in the 1960s. The anti–totalitarian struggle in which we are engaged is every bit as brave and challenging and compassionate as some of those vague and unfocused instinctual feelings that many of us had years ago.

I can think of no better way to conclude than to paraphrase John Kennedy and say: Let the word go forth from this conference that the idealism of the 1960s generation is still alive, but this time its hopes are focused on something more definite, and tangible than a vague entity like the Woodstock Nation, or on failed, evil utopias like Cuba, Vietnam, or even Algeria. Instead, we now make clear our commitment to the cause of America, which is still the most dazzling and persuasive focus of all mankind's idealism and much more than ever before, man's last, best hope on earth.

CHAPTER 4

A CURE WORSE THAN THE DISEASE

Joshua Muravchik

From 1968 until 1973, I was the National Chairman of the Young People's Socialist League (YPSL), the youth section of the Socialist Party of Norman Thomas and Eugene V. Debs. Its creed was democratic socialism.

The YPSL's reaction to the New Left was ambivalent. Culturally we were a part of it. We were radicals; we even thought of ourselves as revolutionaries. Not that we proposed to overthrow the government, but we sought a "revolutionary" transformation of society from capitalism to socialism. Still we were largely at odds with the New Left.

While the New Left ranged from pro-Communist to anti-anti-Communist, we were adamantly anti-Communist, regarding Communism as the great betrayal of the socialist ideal. While the New Left preached "participatory democracy," we were skeptical, wondering if their real aim wasn't to vitiate representative democracy.

On these issues we stood to the right of the New Left, but in at least one respect we saw ourselves as standing to its left. The New Left (at least in the early years) eschewed formal ideology in favor of a vague sense of political direction or, more likely, a mere posture. To us this smacked of reformism. We believed in socialism, and we saw the struggle to replace capitalism (and Communism) with socialism as the single overriding political question—the key to man's destiny, the framework in which all other political issues had to be viewed. We were Marxists. Not Leninists, but Marxists. We believed in the economic interpretation of history, in particular that history was shaped by the struggle of classes and that political systems were best understood in terms of the classes whose rule they respectively expressed. Socialism would express the triumph of the industrial working class which was therefore the chief

161

progressive force, the repository of our hopes, and of mankind's. We scorned the New Left's view that students or blacks or any other group could substitute for the workers as the main agency of progress.

Looking back, there is much in this record that gives cause for pride and for reaffirmation rather than regret. But there is ample room for second thoughts, as well. The second thoughts concern socialism, and especially Marxism, and the erroneous evaluation of the American experience that made socialism seem necessary to us.

The motivation for socialism arises from the yearning for justice. If all men are made in the image of God, if each alike possesses an immortal soul, then how can it be right for some to enjoy a share of the earth's bounty many, many times greater than others? How can it be right for some to enjoy opulence far beyond what they can dispose of while others haven't enough to eat? Granted, talents and accomplishments may vary, but the vast discrepancies in individual wealth under capitalism—where some people have a thousand or a million times more money than others—seem way out of proportion to the degree of variation in individual talents. And would anyone argue that all variations of reward under capitalism arise from variations in talent or accomplishment? Although America's founding fathers were not socialists, if one believes as they did that "all men are created equal," then it is hard to accept the vast and sometimes illogical inequalities that arise under capitalism.

Socialism presents itself as the remedy to this injustice, but at best it does not work. More often, it provides a cure worse than the disease. It has failed miserably in its totalitarian versions (Communism) and its authoritarian ones (in the Third World). In its democratic variants it has been successful, but only by abandoning its main goal. That is, the socialist parties of Europe and Israel have contributed much to the success and development of their societies, but they have backed away from the essential socialist vision of a fundamentally different type of economy. All have come to recognize severe limits on the degree to which the economy should be owned, administered or planned by government. They have opted instead for an economy that is largely privately owned and governed by markets, but in which inequalities of wealth are cushioned by taxation and social security—in short, the welfare state.

Socialism's failings are not merely pragmatic; they are spiritual as well. Although socialism is motivated by humanitarian sentiment, it rests ironically on an image of man that is wooden, that robs him of much of his individuality and creativity. The idea that an economy consists of static elements that can be centrally administered or "planned" leaves little room for inventiveness and ingenuity, for individual drive and ambition, or for changes in consumers' tastes and desires.

But the defects of socialism are only a small part of those of Marxism. In the YPSL we believed in Marxism in its most humane and democratic interpretation. We abhorred Leninism as a betrayal of Marxism because it substituted the revolutionary vanguard for the proletariat itself. The beauty of Marxism was that by assigning the task of liberation to the majority (the proletariat), it assured a democratic outcome. And though we were right in saying that Lenin had betrayed the democratic content of Marxism, it seems to me now that Lenin may have been more faithful than we were to other essential components of Marxism that render its democratic content meaningless.

In Marx's conception, man is a quintessentially economic animal whose "consciousness" is a mere by-product of his occupational category. His public acts are of no consequence except insofar as they express the role of the class to which he belongs, and his inner life is at best meaningless, and more likely contemptible. Ideas and feelings, esthetic sense and religious convictions are all but an insubstantial excrescence of material life. It may not be true that Marx led inevitably to Stalin, but by denying the worth of so much of what makes man human, Marx surely paved the way to Stalin's gulag.

Marx's historicism, moreover, is a kind of religious belief devoid of the ethical content and love that graces most other religions. Marxian historicism treats History itself as possessing a will, thus attributing to this divine abstraction exactly the quality it denies to man. And History has a place it wants to go, an ultimate endpoint called the classless society or socialism. That indeed is the value of socialism. "Communism is the riddle of history solved," said Marx. If history has a goal, if Communism or socialism is the riddle solved, then the only possible standard for judging men's acts is the degree to which they further the design of destiny. As Trotsky put it: "Only that which prepares the complete and final overthrow of imperialist bestiality is moral, and nothing else. The welfare of the revolution—that is the supreme law!" In this framework, liquidating ten or twenty million "kulaks" (or implanting an ax in Trotsky's skull) can be condemned only if it does not in fact contribute to the advance of socialism; it cannot be judged intrinsically wrong.

Moreover, if one observes, as Lenin in fact did, that without the Party the proletariat will fail to fulfill its appointed mission, then is History's goal to be abandoned? Who can blame Lenin for charging into the breach and taking on his own shoulders the responsibility for completing the divine plan by creating a vanguard party to fill the vacuum left by the recalcitrant *proles?*

The democratic Marxist will protest, of course. He will say that substituting a vanguard party for the proletariat defeats the whole purpose of the plan which is to empower a ruling class that for once comprises a majority. If the proletariat has not embraced socialism, we must be patient and we must redouble our efforts to imbue it with socialist consciousness, he says. (I said it myself, God knows how many times). But the counsel of patience grows tattered now 140 years after the publication of the *Communist Manifesto*. And why should we have to imbue the proletariat with the consciousness that ought to grow organically out of its class conditions? Above all, the argument rests on the premise that the proletariat constitutes a majority. Democratic Marxists contemporary with Lenin pointed out that in developing countries (such as Russia in 1917), the proletariat was not yet large enough to constitute a majority. But since then we have seen that highly developed countries quickly progress to the stage of "post-industrialism" in which the size of the proletariat shrinks. Thus if the proletariat ever constitutes a majority, it is only for a brief moment in a nation's development, and in none of the countries that have passed through that stage has the proletariat seized the occasion to usher in socialism. In short, majoritarian Marxism is a chimera.

My final "second thought" concerns the evaluation of the American experience. In early adolescence, the first news stories that I read, the first news broadcasts that I watched on TV, depicted the electrifying struggle by American blacks (and their supporters) for civil rights. Snarling police dogs attacking prayerful marchers. Redneck thugs knocking peaceful black students off lunch counter stools. Pipe-wielding mobs setting on freedom riders fleeing burning buses. Bombs in churches blowing little girls in their Sunday best to bits. These were the images that gripped me and many of my generation. They reflected a struggle of elegant simplicity between good and evil. Racial discrimination was an unalloyed evil, for which no rational defense could be offered. On the other hand, the civil rights movement was exemplary in its methods and its goals.

I did not realize then how anomalous this issue was. I did not know how rare the issue is, especially in domestic politics, in which the moral lines are so clearly drawn. I did not know that most political issues involve choices between competing goals each of which contains at least some merit, and equally difficult choices between alternative means of achieving agreed upon goals. The impulse to radicalism thrives on the illusion that ·political conflicts can generally be reduced to easy moral choices.

The civil rights issue was anomalous in still another way that misled me and others of my generation. It made it easy for us to believe ill about America. Having seen how our country could so badly mistreat its black minority, we could readily believe indictments charging it with mistreating innumerable other groups both at home and abroad. Our embrace of socialism flowed from the axiom that America needed to be fundamentally overhauled.

Racial discrimination was indeed a monstrous evil, but it seems clear to me now that far from typifying the American experience, it was the single greatest anomaly: the meanest blemish on a polity which is otherwise probably the most humane, most praiseworthy that man has ever created. Indeed, America's capacity for moral responsiveness and constructive change was demonstrated dramatically in the triumph of the civil rights movement. We are well on the way to being a multi-racial society of genuine civic equality. How many of those has history known? The major form of legally sanctioned racial discrimination that still flourishes is called "affirmative action." It prescribes preferential treatment for members of oppressed minority groups to compensate for past discrimination. To appreciate how remarkable this is, try to imagine analogous compensatory policies between, say, Romans and Jews, Turks and Armenians, Frenchmen and Algerians, Englishmen and Irishmen, Ugandans and Indians, Russians and Tatars, Arabs and infidels. Need I continue?

America is arguably the freest country on earth, the most socially egalitarian, and the most generous and peaceful great power in history. (If you think you can name another country that is in some respects more free or egalitarian or generous, you will necessarily be naming a country inspired to some large degree by the American model and relying on America as its protector). Whatever reforms America may need today—and its success is the product of constant experiment and change—the highest imperative is not the radical transformation of America but the preservation and perfection of its values and the extension of its liberating model to as much of the rest of the world as possible. This is the most important second thought of all.

PART V

SECOND THOUGHTS: A GENERATIONAL PERSPECTIVE

Martin Peretz
Hilton Kramer
William Phillips
Irving Kristol
Norman Podhoretz
Nathan Glazer

CHAPTER 1

MARTIN PERETZ

I want to thank Peter and David for asking me to be chairman of this panel and for giving me license to make certain remarks without the compulsion of being a panelist, that is, without the compulsion of ordering my remarks into coherence or even making my ends meet. Which is what I suspect some of you have thought I have not been doing in any case for a great many years.

I'm grateful to be here because at least today's sessions were a remarkable event. And if we gauge by the applause earlier from some quarters of this audience, the American Right, or at least a large part of the American Right, has today acceded to several revolutionary propositions. For example, there was applause when one of the Nicaraguans mentioned the desirability of the eight-hour workday. [Laughter] There was applause when some speaker spoke about free trade unions. There was applause when there was the implication that perhaps the security provisions of the McCarran-Walter Immigration Act might be rescinded. And there was applause again from large sections, or important sections of the American Right when one of the speakers suggested that socialists might be appropriate allies of the United States.

So it's not only we ex-Leftists who are having second thoughts but also some Rightists, and for that we are always grateful.

It is a vocational hazard of editors to get abusive mail. Is that not right, Norman? Bill? [Laughter] And I myself have gotten a decent amount of abusive mail about this very event even before it happened. How dare you, was the drift of these letters, appear in such homogeneous and such homogeneously retrograde company? Most of the mail came from people, those at least whom I knew, who had never had a second thought in their entire life. [Laughter] Which is really like not thinking at all.

So I want to remark a little bit on the intellectual and spiritual diversity, at least as seen earlier today, of the assembled free spirits. It was a reflection at least of a part of the contentious parliament of

169

American life. Up here on the platform we have five men. Four of them ostensibly founders of the intellectual movement called Neo-Conservatism. They're all lumped together, but in fact they are each of them very, very different. One, I at least think, is perilously close to being an isolationist; another my colleague with whom I'm teaching a course at Harvard in the spring, Nat Glazer, in my view has an insufficient appreciation of the desirability and morality of deterrence and in any case, and perhaps more important, is much too dovish on Israel. And one of the gentlemen on this platform isn't a neo-con at all. Guess who? [Laughter]

Lest the few representatives of the media who thought this might be an important or interesting enough event to cover get it wrong—as if one can actually preempt deliberate error by stating the facts in advance [laughter]—it's important to point out that not only was there amazing diversity earlier in the day (and I suspect there will be diversity on this platform this evening), but that in general this is not a gathering only of people on the Right. For example, myself. I find it hard to vote Republican. The Psalmist says, "if I pull the Republican lever, let my right hand wither." [Laughter] And worse, "let my tongue cleave to the roof of my mouth." [Laughter]

Some of us—and I don't mean this at all haughtily— some of us separate ourselves from some of you because we dissent seriously from what we see as two at least of the mainstreams of contemporary Conservatism: (1) the Libertarian stream, with, in my view, its implicit enthronement of greed, and (2) the Moral Authoritarian stream, looking somewhat more shabby in recent months but still present with its implicit suggestions of coercion. So I believe that some of us are here despite our disagreements and particularly our fundamental disagreements on the role of the state in social affairs. We are here because we disagree with the mainstream of the active Liberal Left, of which we were a part and which we helped form, which either has an awful foreign policy or no foreign policy at all. The Liberal Left, by the way, only has the barest inklings of a domestic policy also. And that is why it has foreign policy obsessions to fill the void.

John Kenneth Galbraith once self-mockingly—when Ken is self-mocking he's actually being arrogant [Laughter]—said that the Democratic foreign and defense policy means the defense of Israel. And of course these days we can't even be sure of that. But I do have a formulation for it. It means the eagerness of Democrats to provide weapons to Israel which these Democrats don't think the United States should build at all.

The real difference then between those of us who are here and those who are not is our appreciation of the phenomenon of totalitarianism. I reread with my class this week Hannah Arendt's *Origins of Totalitarianism*, and there is a passage in which she talks about the fascination of the mob and the fascination of intellectuals with coercion and cruelty, which I think is still appropriate today. In any case, totalitarianism is a phenomenon which we take seriously. We even believe in the difference between totalitarianism and authoritarianism, an issue which Norman Podhoretz' magazine has illumined and has illumined relentlessly with some stubbornness and also I might say with some bravery. But it also takes a little bit of bravery for me to say something nice about Norman Podhoretz in public. [Laughter] And since we take the phenomenon of totalitarianism seriously, we are appalled by the cynicism of this present administration over Tibet and China. I notice, however, the enthusiasm in this Congress for Tibet, and of course that's because the Congress is not being asked to do anything. In fact the only form of new aid the Democrats seem enthusiastic about, or at least the only form of new aid that some important Democrats seem enthusiastic about is aid to Vietnam, perhaps in a package with withdrawal from Korea.

I used to count myself on the extreme right of the Left. One of my children, not appreciating the new subtlety of my position, suggested to me that now I'm on the extreme left of the Right. I don't know. I try from time to time to place myself in the present and even portentously situate myself in history. Which brings to mind a story. I once had lunch with that extraordinary man, genius, rogue, patriot, God knows what else, poet, raiser of orchids, James Jesus Angleton, and he told me about the Soviet mole who was on my staff [Laughter], and my curiosity got the best of me and I said, "you know, when you were running that illegal CIA surveillance operation of the Peace Movement, did you know about me?" And it felt like a very long time elapsed before he answered and he said, "Yes," and I breathed a sigh of relief. But then very quickly and deflatingly he said, "But you know, we never worried about you." [Laughter] Downcast, crestfallen, literally crushed, even though I'd converted already, I said: "Why?" He said, "Oh, we were always sure that your Zionism would save you from the Russians." [Laughter]

Once wringing my hands at Hazen's Cafeteria in Cambridge over some particularly egregious act by the local chapter of SDS, wringing my hands and complaining to my companion and thesis supervisor, "ah, why did they do something so silly," he said: "I have as much sympathy for you as did Czarist guards for the Mensheviks they met in Bolshevik prisons." [Laughter]

Still the making of distinctions, even fine distinctions, is a right of all men and women, and an obligation of intellectuals. "We are condemned to err," writes Octavio Paz. "We wished to be brothers to the victims and we found ourselves accomplices of their executioners." On this score, with reference to Vietnam, which was not Paz' frame of reference, fine distinctions don't help us. So at least it's correct to admit that even if there was not then available or discernible an acceptable alternative over Vietnam, our way failed; our way was being an accomplice to executioners. While some of us rather finickly were saying that a defeat in Vietnam would be containable, it would cause no ripples, the cadres were saying—to prepare for the future, I believe—"One, two, three many Vietnams." And I think I know why some of them were saying it. I was glad to see Todd Gitlin here, a very honest man and certainly among the most honest in the Left, and when he asked someone in the panel earlier today about their assessments of the motives of some people in the anti-war movement, I thought all of the answers were plausible but I have an answer which I want to put on the record.

Some things are true, even if Joe McCarthy believed them. There were Communists, disciplined, driven, dedicated, in those movements whose filial devotion was to foreign powers. Their filial devotion even extended to what Norman Mailer once called subpoena envy. [Laughter] Hoping for persecution. I can't tell you how many times during those days I would get a phone call in the middle of the night about someone's phone being tapped or someone's taxes being scrutinized. Professor Robert Lifton thought that all of us were being watched day and night. It was a hope for a sign that we were really important, that we were the determinate negation—as Herbert Marcuse portentously would call it. Just thinking about Herbert Marcuse—he was a teacher of mine—reminds me that you can lose your second thoughts. You have to repeat to yourself why you have them. I have no excuse for the '60s, for my role in the '60s, because I was at Brandeis in the '50s and the '60s happened at Brandeis in the '50s. I, for example, heard Herbert Marcuse defend the Soviet suppression of Hungary; and need I have heard anything else to know? And the truth is that it did not help.

And speaking about these dedicated, disciplined, driven Communists, I might risk saying that I do not think that even the present movements or even some of the present campaigns, are entirely without their influence.

Having said something about influence, let me say just one thing more and I'm almost done. My colleague Michael Kinsley, has a concept that he calls "upward failure." You screw up and you're promoted. And that happens in our intellectual and political life also. You make a cataclysmic misjudgment and you lead people behind it and your error is visible and palpable to some, but it somehow does not hurt you. You go on to give advice on the next crisis. And I ask myself—and this is a rhetorical question and it addresses a disease of our culture—why should anybody believe a journalist who wrote in the *New York Times* about Castro having a Montesquieuian view of law and authority. Why should one believe a journalist like that about anything? But some people, having been wrong about Cuba and wrong about Vietnam and having been wrong about detente and wrong even about the desirability and the circumstances of the revolution against the Shah—how do we not simply laugh them out of court?

And so what is our moral authority or intellectual authority? It is in fact the moral and intellectual authority of having second thoughts. Of admitting error. Not as Koestler's Rubashov did as a faithful act of dogma, but as a reflection of our honest and painful and contentious and disagreeing-with-one-another explorations in search of the truth. Which is why we are unashamed to celebrate—with all its faults and warts—America. Which is not—as Dr. Neuhaus counselled Dr. King—"the greatest purveyor of violence in the world," but is the only hope for freedom and economic development in the world. So we are not ashamed to celebrate America. And after all, what else do those loathsome English journalists who so loathe America exhibit, but their contempt for America, by choosing not to cover and abuse this country on foreign assignment, but to come and live in our midsts?

One other matter. I had never met Fausto Amador and Fanor Avendano until today. In fact I didn't really properly meet them, but I heard them. But I've known Xavier Arquello and I know Arturito Cruz pretty well. I have not encountered in my life individuals more worthy of calling the old-fashioned word, comrade. I wish we were worthy of you.

CHAPTER 2

HILTON KRAMER

When I said to Marty Peretz earlier today in a rash moment that I felt I was the only person at this conference who had nothing to confess, of course I was only talking about the war in Vietnam and some of the other things that were on the agenda today. Except for once having agreed to write a book review for *Dissent* magazine, I don't think I could really ever have been considered a sort of *bona fide* member of the Left. So in that sense I really don't have much to confess or anything to confess today.

And, by the way, just to sort of fill in the picture of the period that everybody's repenting here today [Laughter], when I wrote that book review it was a long time before Irving Howe got around to publishing it. And even for a quarterly I thought it was really a remarkably long time. But in about nine or ten months I discovered why when I picked up an issue of *Commentary* and found that the book that I had written a review of for Irving, which was Richard Chase's *The Democratic Vista,* was reviewed in *Commentary* by Irving, and that his review not only contradicted my review but actually attacked my review in *Dissent* before it had been published. [Laughter]

Yes it was a very amusing time, the 1960s, even for those who were not in the Movement. [Laughter] However, to turn to more serious matters than Irving Howe [Laughter, applause], I have to say that this morning's session was deeply dismaying even to someone like myself who expects very little of the survivors of the '60s. First thoughts, second thoughts, fourth thoughts.

There's something about the '60s that got into the personality, that got into the brain cells, got into the psychology, that is inexpungible. And it seemed to me we saw it on full parade in this morning's session. In a conference devoted to second thoughts about the '60s, I heard an incredible amount of praise for the Movement. I even heard one ex-'60s activist say—and how vividly it evoked that spiritual vanity of the '60s—

I heard one ex-'60s activist say that he was not ashamed of a single thing that he did in the '60s. Now is there any adult morally conscious person who can say that about any decade of his life? But this was a concept that the '60s introduced into American life. The concept of not being ashamed of even the worst things.

But even more interesting and illuminating and to me morally catastrophic to the tone of this conference, there was not in this entire day a single mention of the counterculture. Now I know that's probably going to be on the agenda tomorrow and there'll be all sorts of *mea culpas*, but still, is it really possible to separate the politics of the Movement from the counterculture? Was it possible to do it then? Did anybody in the Movement believe that it could be done or should be done? The Movement, if I may use a term that's come to be associated with the religious fundamentalists and the Reagan administration, the Movement had what we now call a social agenda. It was the drug culture, the rock culture, the sexual revolution, the assault on the family and the middle class, the assault on high culture and the aggrandizement of popular culture, the devastation of the universities as the centers of cultural and intellectual life. That was part of the Movement, too, and I didn't hear anybody mention it this morning.

Much as I admired certain things that were said in the discussion this morning, there was also that incredible smugness and vanity which was so suffocating to many of us in the '60s, all on parade again. Despite the born-again appreciation of democracy, there was the same old moral smugness, and what I kept thinking of was something that was written some years ago by a figure that I'm not a great admirer of but who had his one moment of illumination, namely John Maynard Keynes, who when he came to write his memoir of his friends in the Bloomsbury group, looked back and said to them and to the world: we were all immoralists. I didn't hear anybody say that this morning.

We were all immoralists, Keynes said. And he went on to say, we didn't understand, we didn't appreciate what a fragile thing our civilization and its standards of respectability really are. Didn't anybody who had been in the Movement of the '60s who is here today have any second thoughts about that? Didn't anybody have any understanding of the wreckage that was left in the wake? The wreckage in family life and sexual life and academic life and intellectual life, in the whole structure of Western Culture? Well, you were all immoralists and we are now all paying the price for the social agenda that your immoralism let loose.

There was another speaker this morning who said, well, Watergate was not a product of the New Left—totally forgetting that it was the

New Left in 1968 that gave us the Nixon presidency. Now whether one liked the Nixon presidency or didn't like it, it was the New Left in 1968 that guaranteed it. And it's really something not to be forgotten.

What I miss in this whole discussion is some really morally vivid sense of the relation in which the '80s stand to the '60s. The only trace of it was in establishing—and there we are in debt to our friends from Nicaragua—the relation of the struggle in Nicaragua today to the war in Vietnam in the '60s. That was the only reference to the real relation in which the 80s stand to the 60s. Otherwise, what we heard was what I hope my Catholic friends will forgive me for describing as the rosary of virtue. Everyone stood up to say, well, they might have been wrong about the Viet Cong, but they nevertheless still believe in civil rights and the rights of women. Like nobody else does! But what nobody really thought to talk about in regard to the relation that obtains between the '80s and the '60s, is that things are worse now than they were in the '60s when you were all having such a wonderful time, being young and stupid.

The difference between the '60s and the '80s is that the radicals in the '60s were on the outside beating on the doors, demonstrating, trying to get in. In the '80s they're on the inside running the institutions and that is a catastrophic difference.

One of the things that I wrote some years ago about this whole subject—the year was 1976 to be exact—in the *New York Times*, was a piece called "The Black List and the Cold War." It's a piece I'm very proud to have written but I have to confess that it really wasn't my idea. Amazingly enough it was the idea of one of my editors at the *New York Times* who had been to see a screening of the movie called "The Front" in which Woody Allen plays the lead. And he said, "I want you to go see this movie and write something around it." And in those days art critics weren't taken very seriously at the *New York Times,* or indeed anywhere else, and they were always trying to persuade me to do something more serious, like writing about movies [Laughter]. It was what my wife called, "What do you want to be when you grow out?" And I said, "I don't want to review movies." They said, "No, no, you don't have to review it, but go to see it and when you see the movie I think you'll have some idea about what you should write about or what you might want to write about." So I went to a screening of "The Front." It was the moment that *Scoundrel Time* was in the ascendant and there was another documentary movie at that time about the Hollywood Ten. So I wrote a piece that was on the front page of the Art Section of the *New York Times*. When I showed it to my wife before I turned it in she said to me, "Well, it's wonderful but don't you think we should leave town for a few weeks?" [Laughter]

But an amazing thing happened. The letters began pouring in—and this is what I mean about these being really worse times—the letters began pouring in, talking about first thoughts, second thoughts, other thoughts. The two strongest letters in support of my article, which were subsequently published in the *Times*, were written by Alfred Kazin and Arthur Schlesinger, Jr. Arthur Schlesinger, Jr wrote that in his opinion everyone born since 1940 should be compelled to read this article. The principal letter written attacking my piece was written by Ronald Radosh. [Laughter] So, life has changed.

There are two things I will say about that article. One is that it was my introduction to the keen appreciation that newspaper people have about First Amendment rights. Upon the publication of this article my then-colleague on the *New York Times*, Seymour Hersh, went to the editors of the *Times*, little knowing that they had initiated the article, and demanded that I be fired. Big First Amendment buff. [Laughter]

And the other thing which I'll say, which is not amusing, is that today that article could not be published in the *New York Times*. And those are not second thoughts.

CHAPTER 3

WILLIAM PHILLIPS

I go back further in my political history, I would guess, than most people here, maybe all people here. That of course has given me the opportunity to make more mistakes. I, too, have a kind of *deja vu* feeling when I hear the talk about second thoughts. Obviously I was one of a number of people who had second thoughts in the 1930s. But it was so long ago that I've almost forgotten what my second thoughts were. [Laughter]

I don't have to have any second thoughts about the 1960s because I was not young enough then to be part of the New Left or the counter-culture. The only possible criticism that could be made of me for any association with the counterculture—well, perhaps not the only one, I'll mention another one in a minute—was that a member of the New Left at that time said I was the only person over 30 whom she trusted.

The other mistake we made in the '60s which could be associated with the counterculture was that we printed a few pieces that failed to distinguish between popular and more serious culture. In particular, we printed one famous article praising the Beatles and claiming that they were as important as T.S. Eliot. The article went on to assert that the Beatles should be approached with the same kind of sophisticated literary methodology that is used to approach the work of T.S. Eliot. That was a big mistake. [Laughter] But there were extenuating circumstances. As I've been hearing all day, there are always extenuating circumstances for mistakes.

What I really want to talk about in the few minutes that have been assigned to me, is a question that was raised by several speakers: What is there, what magic is there, what historical formula is there, what historical explanation is there, for the periodic recrudescence of the foolish and inauthentic Left, especially in this country but also in Western Europe? I assume that 20 years from now there will be another meeting—second thoughts, third thoughts, fourth thoughts—of people who had

179

occupied some new inauthentic left positions on some new issues, some new Vietnam, some new Nicaragua.

I want to address the question, 'What is the magic attraction of the fashionable Left?' But I want to introduce that by first speaking of the differences between the Left in the '30s and the Left today, and the difference between the Liberals in the '30s and the Liberals today. Some people have said that the terms Left and Liberal don't have any meaning anymore. I don't agree with that. I think they do have a meaning but they have a different meaning, and certainly different meanings to different people. When we at *Partisan Review* first came out as an independent journal critical of the Communists—Stalinists as they were mostly called then—it was easier to be anti-Stalinist or anti-Communist, because everybody knew what Communism was; everybody knew who the Communists were, even though some of them kept denying they were Communists, and everybody knew who the fellow travelers were. The main issue was that they were supporting Russia. Today I think that's changed almost completely, although obviously there are some continuities—for example, in the editorial policies of *The Nation*.

I've had a long time to think about this question. I may be wrong in some matters. You may disagree with me in others. But it seems to me that this is one of the most important political questions before us in the present period. The Left today, in my view, is no longer revolutionary. It really doesn't intend to make revolutions, especially in this country. Moreover, Marxism is very much attenuated, watered down, distorted among Leftists nowadays. Many members of the New Left don't even think of themselves as Marxists, although some do. What we call the Left is today composed of a kind of addiction to a number of causes. And I can enumerate all these causes. In fact, when you speak of somebody being on the Left today, I can tell you for example, what they're going to think about various questions. I'm an expert on this by now because I've been spending my summers at Cape Cod [Laughter] which is a Liberal Left summer retreat, and I know exactly how these people think. I also am a member of a university—a professor in partial good standing at Boston University—and I'm surrounded by people who don't call themselves Leftists but whose opinions are on something called the Left. One professor there was talking to me one day about something on the phone, and he said to me: "What am I talking to you for? You're for Star Wars, you're for the Strategic Defense Initiative." In other words, that was a signal for him—the fact that I was for Star Wars—to stop talking to me. I can also tell you what he thought on all other questions, about the Contras, Poland, Israel, the Third World, the Black esthetic; I could go on and on and on.

Liberals today are also not what Liberals used to be, in this country at least. Generally speaking, we've always thought of Liberalism as a kind of centrist position between the Right and the Left, a position that maintained certain independent attitudes, approaches, values and so on. If this position hasn't already disappeared, it's fast disappearing because Liberalism has been infected by what I have tried to describe as the attitudinizing Left in this country. I wonder whether anyone has noticed this, but the Left doesn't attack Liberals today. In the '30s, Liberalism was attacked by the Left every day. There was a standard Communist joke about Liberals: during an elevator strike, they ride up and walk down. [Laughter]

Now I want to carry this a little further by suggesting that we have here more than a political phenomenon. We have a cultural phenomenon. I think that Hilton is right when he talks about the connection of the counterculture to the political culture, to the political stance of the New Left in the '60s. But I want to expand that concept even further. I think we are talking about a culture in an anthropological sense. It's almost like a different country. For example, you expect a Frenchman to have certain attitudes and values, regardless of whether he's right, left or center, certain ideas about his country, certain feelings about Germany, about history, about the French Revolution. When you visit France you expect certain responses to certain questions, even by people who think differently. The same is true, culturally speaking, of most of the Left.

To put it another way, it's futile to try to argue with attitudes that are culturally ingrained rather than rationally arrived at. My friend and colleague Edith Kurzweil keeps telling me that I shouldn't write people off, particularly on vacations. You have to talk to them, she says, to argue with them, to present your point of view. The net result is that I was told this summer, that I have a morbid fear of Russia. [Laughter] That was the result of a two-hour argument. [Laughter]

What I'm trying to suggest is that you can't win the argument on any one issue because no given issue is decisive. It was Vietnam yesterday, it is Nicaragua today, it'll be something else tomorrow. It's literary theory, it's to some slight extent deconstruction, although there is some flexibility on deconstruction, mostly because it is not understood. [Laughter]

Now having said this, I must say that I don't know the answer. How do you combat a culture? I studied philosophy at City College under the great logician Morris Raphael Cohen and learned how to argue, even how to win an argument. But I never learned how you win over a culture, how you change a culture. Even if you win any one point there's always a retreat to 15 other points. There are always fall-back positions. There are always explanations, justifications.

Before going on, let me remind you that in the '30s I, and Phillip Rahv, and a few others like us, were fellow travelers. I was never a Communist Party member but I was close to the Party and knew a lot about the Party and how it worked. It was a valuable experience because many people who didn't have that kind of experience don't realize how canny the Communists are, how shrewd, how devious and ruthless in pursuing their ends, in organizing opinion, in concealing their program, in winning over converts, in infiltrating organizations. The Communists could put 3 people in an organization of 400 and capture the organization. That's something I learned then and I don't know how else I could have learned it. You don't really learn it by reading about it.

When several of us broke with the Communists, we were called "agents of imperialism," "reactionaries"—which is worse than being called a conservative. We were called literary snakes. And we were called Trotskyites. Now a Trotskyite, for the Communists, was somebody who was opposed to totalitarianism and critical of the Soviet Union—but from the Left. So we were Trotskyites for years. That predated the kind of attacks that some of you have encountered when you left the Left. But there's a continuity and a similarity.

Let me go on and say certain other things that characterize the so-called magic of the Left, regardless of its specific beliefs. It is thought in the West—and this perhaps is a heritage almost of the French Revolution—that to be on the Left is itself sufficient. It doesn't matter what given problem is being faced or what given position is taken at any given time. The fact is that you're on the Left, which is superior to being on the Right, to being a conservative or of course a reactionary. It is automatically better, regardless of the position on the issues. And I don't know how you combat that kind of attitude, frankly. You can stand on your head, trying to prove that you're interested in the welfare of people, that you're not against rights for women, you're not against rights for children, you're not against rights for animals, you're not against any kind of rights. It doesn't do you any good. Because you're not on the Left.

As I have said, I don't know the answer. What I do know is that you have to be critical of the Left by approaching it as a culture, as a set of beliefs, attitudes, assumptions, as unified as those of a country, or a religion. How you do that, maybe some of my fellow panelists will tell you.

CHAPTER 4

IRVING KRISTOL

I confess that when I got this invitation to a conference on second thoughts, my heart sank and in the immortal words of Yogi Berra I thought *"deja vu,* once again." [Laughter]I have been editing magazines now for just about 40 years and I suppose in that period of time I have rejected at least 50 articles of second thoughts—that is, of people who have broken with the left, usually with the Communist Party, who are convinced they have a story to tell, and insist that you tell it, or at least permit them to tell it. In a way, it's like everyone who has had an unhappy love affair and is convinced there is a novel about it to be written and published. But I have strict editorial standards, and in fact we published very few of those articles. Nathan Glazer, who was with me at *Commentary* back in the late 1940s has reminded me of the people who came trooping up, a former editor of the *Daily Worker,* a former editor of the *New Masses,* people who had "important" jobs and whose experience, they were absolutely confident, really told you something new about what had happened. It turned out what had happened to them is what had happened to everyone else. Nothing new, nothing interesting. Such political disillusionment is an old, old story.

Nevertheless I decided to come here because I felt this was my last chance to get in touch with the generation of the '60s, with whom I've had very little contact, and Lord knows the way they're going they'll soon be eligible for Medicare, so I thought I'd better see them while they last. Twenty years from now they'll be up here explaining to another generation having second thoughts why it is all such a familiar theme. Also, I must tell you that my experience with second thoughts was rather different from some of those here tonight, and different from all those people whose articles I rejected.

I was a young Trotskyist for 18 months or so, a fellow traveler for perhaps a year before that. I have no regrets whatsoever about that experience. I had my radical days; I enjoyed them enormously. They were very fruitful—I met my wife then; I made lifelong friends then; I got a good education then, reading a lot of books—not necessarily the books that were prescribed for me by my political associates. I did read *Partisan Review* regularly and broke my teeth trying to understand those articles. It was good intellectual discipline.

By the time I left the radical movement, I really felt fine. I felt I had been through a special kind of college and had come out with something to show for it. In a way, for me, it is not a case of a God that failed. First of all, it wasn't a God; it was just a radical movement. I suppose in a way I was untypical; I was always rather snotty about radical movements, including my own. I don't know why, but even when I was in it, I couldn't take it quite seriously.

My de-radicalization proceeded very quickly. I got into the army with a Midwest regiment. It turned out that most of the guys there came from a town called Cicero, a town I had never heard of. I said to myself, I can't build socialism with these people. They'll probably take it over and make a racket out of it. [Laughter]

That was a decisive experience. I was caught between the hierarchical authoritarianism of the army and my fellow soldiers from Cicero, Illinois. I quickly decided I was on the side of the army. I appreciated military discipline. Someone had to stop those young thugs from shooting me, which they might have done if I irritated them a little bit.

So I had my second thoughts really even while I was in the Trotskyist movement; my third and fourth thoughts happened within a short period thereafter, and then came the period of fifth thoughts. Neo-conservatism I guess is my sixth thought stage.

I think it's very important to have more than two stages of thoughts. That really is a serious point. Two thoughts get you nowhere. You start out as a Communist; your second thought is you are an anti-Communist. That's not necessarily progress. You have to go beyond that; you have to understand something about Communism. You have to understand, above all, why Communism appealed to you, why it still appeals to people, why the Left is the Left, why the culture is on the left.

These matters require a kind of intellectual work that simply rejecting one's radicalism doesn't solve. I am particularly interested, I must say, in the radicalism of the 1960s which was so very, very different from the radicalism I knew in the 1930s and early 1940s. Ours was a political radicalism. Entirely political. It had no teachings about sex—the issue of homosexuality never arose, though I think we rather disapproved of it. There were some debates, I remember, on free love in the Trotskyist movement, but the Marxists didn't know what to do about free love. Of course, there were a couple of essays by classical Marxist thinkers that seemed to suggest it was a good idea, but on the other hand the 1930s' radicals didn't really like it. Basically, Communists and Trotskyists were all prudes. They couldn't reject free love, so they just didn't practice it much. Not enough to suit me anyhow.

The radicalism of the 1930s was entirely a political movement in the sense that it was young people echoing their elders and following in the path of their elders. It had almost no non-political dimension: sex didn't play a role; drugs didn't play a role; nothing played a role except politics and, to some degree I guess, economics.

What interests me about the 1960s, and what I find so absolutely fascinating, is the counterculture. This was a different kind of radicalism from the radicalism I knew. It was—to use a terrible word—an existential radicalism, rather than merely a political radicalism. Most of us, when we were radicals, had radical ideas in our heads and nothing else changed. We went on living the same lives, doing the same things. We were anti-bourgeois in theory, but on the whole quite bourgeois in fact, except for the painters in Greenwich Village; even the writers in Greenwich Village on the whole were quite bourgeois.

It interests me that this radicalism went so deep into people's personal lives. It seems to have been a conflation of bohemianism, Marxism, existentialism, nihilism, and a distorted religious impulse. I take that as a significant fact about the radicalism of the 1960s and while I think P.J. O'Rourke gave us a wonderful picture of it* I want to know why it happened. I need to know why it happened because the basic fact about second thoughts is that we have been hearing them now for 200 years. Ever since the French Revolution which imported utopianism into our political discourse, there have been second thoughts. Very few of them are memorable. Who had second thoughts about the French Revolution? Well, we know Wordsworth did and he wrote some nice poems out of his disillusionment, but they were apolitical; he did not have *political* second thoughts about the French Revolution. Name me a major book of second thoughts about the Russian Revolution by one of the participants. The books that were written were all very boring, as a matter of fact. Are there any interesting ones? I can't think of any.

There have actually been two pretty good books of second thoughts in 200 years, one coming out of the revolution of 1905 in Russia (I can't remember the Russian name of it), that's now available in English. It's a collection of essays by people of considerable distinction—Berdyaev,

---

*See below, P.J. O'Rourke, "The Awful Power of Make-Believe."

Shestov, Bogdanov—who were deradicalized by the failure of the 1905 revolution and moved toward religion. That was a book that one can go back to and read with some interest.

Then there is Arthur Koestler's *Darkness at Noon,* which is still a book one can go back and read with some interest, too. But two books in 200 years is not all that many and I must say they don't stand up really that well, as Norman Podhoretz pointed out writing about *The God That Failed.* You read it again today and it isn't as good as you thought it was when you read it the first time. It turns out to be rather shallow.

This seems to be part of the process of political disillusionment, which is why, of course, we are all doomed to have second thoughts. Every generation seems to go through this bloody ritual again and again, and if not every generation, then every other generation—of demanding of the world more than it can give, finding the world as it is not just unsatisfying but intolerable in some basic respect, and reacting.

This is the problem we have now, not with politics but with the culture, and—William Phillips is exactly right—this is the problem. We non-radicals can win elections, we keep winning elections. What good does it do us? A little bit of good, no doubt, but in the end the basic temper and mood expressed by those who have not had second thoughts is what dominates the novels, the poetry, the painting, the movies, all the things that affect our cultural life and all of the things that eventually shape our educational system and shape the minds and souls of our children.

Every society is faced with a barbarian threat, since children are being born every minute. They have to be reared and given character and given definition as persons. To do this against the weight of a culture is enormously difficult, as many of you here, I'm sure, have experienced. It's really a one-on-one job, the saving of souls from the culture. Until we can somehow figure out why it is that we have to keep having second thoughts about something we have had second thoughts about now for two centuries—namely that these gods have failed, that these revolutions get betrayed, that the world is such, human nature is such, reality is such, that these kinds of messianic enthusiasms that find expression in political movements always are doomed and are always reborn.

So, I must tell you, I'm rather serious when I say it's important to get on to third, fourth, and fifth thoughts. Because what's the point of saying no more than I used to be a Marxist, I used to be on the left, now I believe in democracy and capitalism? That's good—but, on the other hand, what is the 20th Century except a series of rebellions against democracy, liberalism and capitalism. Whether on the left or on the right—nazism, fascism, communism, socialism, of one kind or another. That is the history of our century. Those are the movements that have vitality and the question is: Why? What is missing? What—to quote a wonderful phrase of Matthew Arnold—are the elements that are wanting in our own civilization that give rise again and again to these first thoughts that always lead to disillusionment?

So, I am very glad to have been here to share my thoughts with you. I hope they don't depress you too much. Most of you are young enough so that you can look forward to having third and fourth thoughts—and not only that, you can publish them. And not only that, you can make a career out of them. Some of us here have almost done that. And that is the way it should be in this best of all possible worlds.

CHAPTER 5

NORMAN PODHORETZ

Irving Kristol, in his inimitable style, said to me earlier, I see that we're on the geriatric panel. [Laughter] When David Horowitz asked me to participate in what he, in his inimitable style, called a panel of elders [Laughter], I tried to tell him and I've been trying in vain to tell him for months now, that I am scarcely three or four years older than he is. But the penalty for having been around for so long and looking the way I do is to get promoted prematurely to the ranks of the aged and elderly. People often confuse me, as Irving Kristol knows, with him. He and I are frequently sent letters addressed to the other. I have received—or Irving has received—fan mail on my books. I never get any fan mail on my books. And so on every occasion on which Irving and I share a platform I always make a point of saying that we are not, as you can plainly see, the same person. And what is more, Irving is 10 years older than I am. But I'm catching up.

I always was a very dutiful student and my assignment was to give a generational perspective. But before I get into that, I thought I might help to throw some light on the question of definitions. We heard a very good definition this morning of a conservative. Someone said a conservative is a Liberal with a 13–year-old daughter. I had that experience myself three times and I can attest to its accuracy. In a new novel by Tom Wolfe, an advance copy of which I have just read, he defines a liberal as a conservative who has been arrested. [Laughter] Think about it for a bit. Irving Kristol is the author, of course, of the most famous definition of neoconservative. He said a neoconservative is a liberal who has been mugged by reality. My son, John Podhoretz, has defined a neoliberal as a liberal who has been mugged by a neoconservative. [Laughter] So I think that ought to help a bit in our thinking on these matters.

Like Hilton Kramer I, too, was dismayed by some of the proceedings this morning, though for slightly different reasons. Because indeed it was *deja vu* all over again. I really am too young to have experienced the process of deradicalization in the 1930s since I was only 10 years old by the end of the decade. On the other hand, I did join a front group, American Youth for Democracy (AYD) in 1943, when I was 13 and I suppose that gives me some claim on a generational link. I have also spent a good deal of time reading and thinking about the 1930s. And I've done some writing about it, most recently in an essay to which reference has been made, a long essay on *The God That Failed,* a book which I reread after approximately 30 years for the purpose of writing an introduction to a new edition. And when I reread the book I was amazed at how different it was from my memory of it. I won't go into the details of that difference except to say that in general I remembered this book— and it did indeed have such a reputation—as a hard-line anti-Communist testament. And what struck me most when I reread it was how little it corresponded to the impression it has left in the world.

Certainly it was an anti-Communist document. There were six testaments of prominent intellectuals, literary people who had been Communists and had broken with the Communist Party and who certainly were now anti-Communist. But it was not by present standards or even by the standards of that period, as I look back on it, a hard-line anti-Communist document. I have written down a couple of quotations from Arthur Koestler and others that give some notion of the character of the anti-Communism of that book.

As the author of *Darkness at Noon,* Koestler was regarded as what I suppose in today's parlance would be the number one Cold War intellectual in the world. And yet what he said in describing what was only just beginning to be called the Cold War was that it presented us with a choice between a gray twilight and total darkness. In other words, the Soviet Union and Communism were total darkness, he had no question about that. But the best he could say about the alternative represented by the West, and particularly by the United States, was that it was a gray twilight.

Stephen Spender, who had been one of the young Oxford Communist poets of the '30s—not a very distinguished poet but there in the pantheon along with Auden and MacNiece and Day Lewis—said in the course of his essay explaining why he had broken with the Communists, "America, the greatest capitalist country, seems to offer no alternative to war, exploitation and destruction of the world's resources."

This was written in 1949–50 when America, capitalist America, was in the process of offering democracy to formerly fascist countries which it had just defeated in the war—Germany, Japan, and Italy—and was offering prosperity to its allies in Western Europe. It was offering defense against the new totalitarian threat from the left, having just shed blood and spent enormous amounts of treasure to defeat the totalitarian threat from the right—this America seemed to Spender to offer no alternative to war, exploitation and destruction of the world's resources.

Now when I first read *The God That Failed* as a senior in college that sentence just passed me by. I didn't notice it. I probably just assumed that it was correct. I grew up in a metier and a milieu that were ready to believe that kind of charge against America. And so I was not only surprised and shocked but appalled, morally and intellectually appalled, to come upon that sentiment in my rereading of *The God That Failed* thirty years later.

It suddenly struck me that here we had the source of a lot of the troubles that were to develop later, particularly in Europe. Not a single one of the contributors to *The God That Failed* had virtually a kind word to say about the major alternative to the system they had just rejected and were, by the way, very fearful of—these were people who were afraid of the Soviet Union, afraid of Communism. That was the whole point of writing this book. Richard Crossman, who was the editor, had persuaded Koestler and the others to write these pieces on the ground that only someone who had, as Crossman said, lived with the devil and grappled with him, could really convey the urgency of the threat emanating from that quarter. The devil—that was how Richard Crossman (who had been a Communist himself) referred to Soviet Communism. It wasn't Whittaker Chambers and it wasn't Joe McCarthy, it was Richard Crossman, prominent member of the British Labor Party, prominent socialist intellectual, who was identifying the Soviet Union and Communism with the devil. You could hardly find a more dramatic measure of how things have changed.

Yet, these people, who thought of the Soviet Union as the devil and were not afraid to say so, could see nothing more than gray twilight, almost equally vicious institutions and habits, when they looked at the living embodiment of the alternative, the United States of America. What this meant simply is that having rejected the Soviet Union or Communism, these people were still caught up in the utopian greed that we've heard talk of here.* There was still a refusal to make choices among real available alternatives.

And what grew out of this attitude, this refusal to give up the utopian dream, this spiritual greed, this clinging to utopian fantasies, was the refusal to make a serious political commitment to the other side of the

---

*See P.J. O'Rourke "The Awful Power of Make-Believe below."

political struggle, the side that would protect them and would defend the values they cherished. Why? Everybody keeps asking why? What is it that causes people to maintain such perverse attitudes? One answer, which has been given several times here but I think is worth repeating— particularly in this context when we think about the second thoughts of the generation of the '30s in its struggle with Communism—is that the ruling passion of all those people was to hold on to an idea of themselves as men of the Left. They would do virtually anything in order to maintain that identity. It was all right to give up on the Soviet Union, it was all right to give up on Communism in the Soviet Union and on a Communist Party subservient to the Soviet Union; that didn't mean you had to give up on Marxism; or it didn't mean that you had to give up on Socialism; or it didn't mean that you had to give up on Trotskyism. There was some refuge you could find somewhere that would maintain your integrity and would keep you within the true church of the Left.

This attitude has, I think, been responsible for the exfoliation of the neutralism that was almost explicit in *The God That Failed* and particularly in Spender's essay. Orwell had something to say about it in those days. He ridiculed the neutralist intellectuals, the anti-American intellectuals who were shielding themselves behind the guns of American power. The whole framework of moral equivalence, as it is now called, the refusal to make a distinction between the United States and the Soviet Union, or between the West and the East, has its roots in a refusal to make a choice between the available alternatives, a refusal that was so vivid in *The God That Failed* and for which I think we are paying a heavy political price.

I might just say, parenthetically, with no real organic connection to the point I just made, that I can't remember a time when there has been so much uncritical Soviet-loving as there is today. I mean, when I was a kid, in World War II, we had an atmosphere something like it, but I would never have believed that the kind of favorable press that the Soviet Union is getting today could ever come back again to haunt us. But it has.

In *The God That Failed*, Louis Fischer, the forgotten contributor, introduced a highly valuable concept, what he called the "Kronstadt"— the experience that was decisive in leading to a break with the Communist Party, and named after the sailors strike in Kronstadt in 1921 that was suppressed brutally by Trotsky and the Red Army. Some broke with the Communist Party then; Kronstadt was their Kronstadt. For others it was the Moscow trials. For others it was the Nazi-Soviet Pact.

For still others it was Khrushchev's de-Stalinization speech or the Hungarian Revolution.

As I sat here this morning listening to some of the talks, I was struck by the relevance of the Kronstadt image. I realized the difference between me and most of the people up there, many of whom are, as I say, not that much younger than I am, is that their Kronstadt came a little later than mine, and over slightly different issues.

My own Kronstadt was—that is, my own break with the Movement, with the Left, with the radicalism of the '60s—was not associated with any single episode, except that I remember a dinner (of course it being the '60s this was at an extremely expensive restaurant, the Palm in New York), where I first heard from a friend of mine the comparison between the United States and Nazi Germany. This was a very new idea at that point. It was early on. And I found myself appalled beyond anything I might have imagined, even though I myself had been saying nasty things about this country. The comparison with Nazi Germany just seemed to me unbelievable, incredible, and we had a screaming fight. And that was the opening phase in my own Kronstadt because what finally alienated me from the radical movement of the '60s was its hatred of America. David Horowitz is absolutely right when he talks about the "hate America" Left. I totally disagree with whoever it was who said from the audience this morning that the New Left was neutralist. The New Left was not neutralist; the New Left was anti-American. And its major passion was hatred of this country. It differed from the old Left in that it defined itself by what it was against, namely America and everything it stood for. Whereas the Old Left in the '30s had defined itself by what it was for, namely the Soviet Union and Communism.

Well, I guess that most people here who have had second thoughts probably found their Kronstadt in the aftermath of the Vietnam war, and to some extent Nicaragua under the Sandinistas. But since there was no way of breaking with the New Left without in some sense changing one's mind about America, the kind of neutralist refuge that was offered to Spender and some of the others in *The God That Failed* was not available to this generation. You couldn't break with an anti-American movement without at least becoming anti-anti-American and perhaps even pro-American. And I think to a certain extent that is what happened with a lot of people here. And yet what gave me the Yogi Berra sensation, the *deja vu* all over again, this morning, was the feeling I had of a desperate effort on the part of some of the speakers once again to cling to their idea of themselves as men of the Left in some sense, social democrats or liberals. And some people here congratulated themselves on their virtue and courage in maintaining their commitment to what they take to be the values of these lesser Left positions, these refuges from the Movement.

Let me suggest that these refuges are themselves a utopian delusion in disguise. Let me suggest to you that the available alternatives remain what they were in 1950. There is still no viable third force that is neither this nor that but something combining the virtues and eliminating the vices of both possibilities. This is a utopian delusion no less than the God that failed. Let me suggest that the abstract commendations of capitalism, as Irving Kristol says, are not enough. There is also the very serious question that has been raised by some critics in recent years about state control over the economy as an issue not only of efficiency or economic freedom alone, but of freedom in general: the question of whether indeed it is possible for a high degree of state control of any economy to co-exist with personal freedom. I think the answer is no, and I think it is a delusion to go on dreaming of some magical formula that will unite the two possibilities.

What about being a Liberal? Harmless enough. [Laughter] There was a time when I regarded that as a highly honorific epithet, liberal. Some of us spent many hours, many sterile and fruitless hours, contesting for possession of that label. For years I got angry with people who called me a neoconservative. I was not a neoconservative, I said; I was a liberal. A certain kind of liberal: a real liberal, a genuine liberal, a 1950s liberal, or whatever. But to no avail. I finally surrendered and I am perfectly happy to be called a neoconservative these days, thereby following Irving Kristol's lead in this as in so many other things.

But forget for a minute about the intellectual or philosophical pedigree of liberalism, and ask yourself what *is* the community of people today known almost universally as liberals? What does this community represent? What does it stand for? I'm now talking about foreign policy, since we don't have time for the other issues. What do the liberals, the people who are called liberals, (even though some of us don't think they deserve to be called liberals, that they've stolen the title)—what do these people known as liberals think about the Soviet Union, or the Soviet threat, about American power, about the Soviet-American conflict, about Nicaragua, about the whole issue of the struggle between totalitarianism and democracy in our time? The liberal community generally thinks that the kind of view I hold, that I think most of us in this room hold, is a paranoid delusion at best, and at worst a wicked incitement and provocation that will lead to war. The liberal community of today does not take these threats seriously. I once was told by a rather famous liberal when I was one of the early members of the Committee on the Present Danger that "The Committee on the Present Danger is a greater danger to this country than the Soviet Union." In short, I don't think there is a refuge in liberalism, as presently constituted, for people who have had serious second thoughts about totalitarianism in our time and about the anti-Americanism that is so essential a component in the progress of the totalitarian mentality and the political triumphs of totalitarian power.

I don't know what to do about "the culture," William, Irving. I don't think any of us quite knows what to do. We have our own notions of how to go about it from day to day, conducting the argument, trying to persuade. But I would appeal at least to *this* segment of the culture, to continue with your second thoughts, not to rest content with these illusory refuges which will in the end prove politically sterile and even damaging. I would appeal to those who have started on this journey not to stop happily at some midpoint but to continue on to where the logic of the experience and the logic of the idea lead. I won't give a name to where those logics lead. I don't much care by what name you call it, but an essential component of it is a serious commitment to the institutions of this country, a serious assessment of the threats to those institutions, both from within and from without—and when I speak of the threats from within I'm not merely talking about subversion or moles, I'm talking about certain cultural tendencies, ideas, attitudes, many of them indeed flowing from the counterculture which was absent, as Hilton has noted, from the discussions this morning. Anyone who has seriously thought about those dangers and who has seriously assessed the dangers from without, will find himself driven, as many of us have been driven, into surprising new third and fourth and fifth thoughts, into revelations, some of which are shocking when they first enter one's mind, but I think are essential if we are ever to do anything about the corrupted and poisoned culture which in this country is our major problem.

CHAPTER 6

NATHAN GLAZER

Reading some of the material Peter Collier and David Horowitz sent me, material which may have been distributed to you, and which assisted me in thinking about the issue of a generational perspective as they put in it, I was taken by one element in their discussion of the '60s. That is their discussion of the "hatred of America" theme, which came up in Norman Podhoretz' comments and to some extent in others'. And I realized that was one difference between that generation and mine; and a substantial difference. We didn't hate America.

But I'm also not so sure just how important that "hatred of America" issue was. I think in Berkeley in '64 that was not an issue. I think maybe by '68 or '69 it was. There was then a kind of irrational and mad aspect to it—America spelled with a "k" and so on. But it didn't begin that way.

Thinking of my generation, however, perhaps I am here under slightly false pretenses, because I did not have a chance to have second thoughts. Some of us grew up in families where the question of Communism and Soviet Russia was already settled, so why would we have need for second thoughts? The only problem was to get *other* people to have second thoughts. I understood the issues, I argued with Communists in high school and college and so on.

But in my generation, some of whom were socialists, as I was, some of whom had come out of Trotskyism, and some out of Communism, I don't recall any hatred of America. Rather, we had a Europhilia, whether it was a Marxist Europhilia, or a Modernist Europhilia, or both. We didn't read American books, only European: Marx, of course, or Bukharin on dialectical materialism, or Erich Fromm on *Escape From Freedom.* Only the Europeans had something to say. Marty Lipset would grab me now and then and say, "A wonderful new European has just arrived," Lew Coser perhaps, he had a new study group, and he had the truth.

197

And at that time the truth was not Russia, we all knew about that. It was not the United States. It was variants of European radicalism.

When our "second thoughts" did emerge, the Europhilia was broken in the early '50s and that was an interesting phenomenon. It didn't have the same power as breaking with a hatred of America, which made it easier to develop in counter-response an excessive and undiscriminating love of America. Our situation was rather that we saw Europe didn't help us. All those clever European Marxists and those wonderful Modernists, some of whom were reactionary, they didn't help make a better country. *Partisan Review* ran its important symposium, "Our Country and Our Culture" in 1952 or thereabouts. We ran a piece in *Commentary*, I don't know if it has been reprinted, titled "America the Beautiful: the Philosopher in the Bathtub," by Mary McCarthy. She lives in Paris, but then she wrote, "What's all this about Europe? America has a lot to offer." And so it was a milder turn to America and a milder and less excessive love, and appreciation, of elements of the American culture. The pluralism, the diversity, the pragmatism, the fact that the cultural elite was not taken so seriously, those were all good things. We didn't have cultural emperors like Sartre. So, at least for one generation—I think there are at least three generations represented here, or four—there was neither an initial hatred for America nor a later immoderate love. Rather, we just didn't know much about America; our experience of it was limited.

So there was first a great appreciation of Europe, and then a developing appreciation of America for all sorts of reasons. Now, nevertheless I will make a claim to "second thoughts" even if I didn't have them in connection with Communism. My second thoughts were on other issues and I don't think they played a role in this conference, looking at the agenda and the speeches. If you recall, the term "neoconservatism was first launched by Michael Harrington, or Irving Howe, or whoever it was, not so much to criticize us on grounds of our foreign policy stands. Harrington and Howe have no illusions about the Soviet Union; that was not the problem. The attack on neoconservatism was sparked by domestic issues. Our leftist critics were concerned that we were not maintaining the tradition of liberal social reform, that we were losing faith. And after all, *The Public Interest*, which was regularly coupled with *Commentary* as the source of neoconservatism, does not deal with foreign policy at all.

Yet the discussion here has been entirely on foreign policy. But there was another group of issues and it was around those that I had that "second thoughts" experience. There was no great revelation, but a lot of things one was enthusiastic about or at least willing to think positively about in '63 or '64 did not look as good in '67, '68, and by '71 one was getting other thoughts. Things weren't working out. Social problems were more intractable than we thought; we weren't very good social engineers; no one was very good at dealing with social problems. And if you are a socialist, that is a disappointment.

One of the things that has not been mentioned here is the notion of, shall I say, orderly social reform. I remember the days when I was a socialist, we would always think of redrawing the boundaries of the United States, I mean internally—the State lines were irrational. I think we once ran a piece by Dan Bell in which he suggested just this, among other things of course, in *The Public Interest*. This socialist impulse to rational order is an important motivation in socialism, in communism.

So why should Wyoming be a perfect square, when you can run the boundary down the Rocky Mountains? The eastern part of Wyoming should be part of one State, the Western another, that's how the rivers run and so on. That's a very small example. But then we began to doubt, and we weren't so convinced that we could do it better, or that there was any reason to change an arrangement that had lasted a hundred years.

I have been thinking about whether there is any connection between these two kinds of second thoughts or these two branches of policy that initially formed the neoconservative outlook. I haven't gone through all of the domestic issues—affirmative action and others—but basically our view of how one can manage society and make it better changed; and that really didn't have much to do with the international conflict with Soviet Russia and Communism.

In fact, there is a very peculiar set of non-connections between the two which intrigues me. I remember Norman Podhoretz until quite late was willing to call himself a social democrat, while still holding the same views he has today about foreign policy. This is not a criticism, but an observation. There are still many social democrats, even socialists, who think just as the organizers of this conference do about Communism. Sidney Hook, for example. There are certainly no doubts about his views of totalitarianism but he still calls himself a social democrat.

I see thus two realms of policy-making which have developed fairly independently, the foreign and the domestic. One of the reasons I emphasize this is because I do not feel the passion I used to feel about Communism. You should have seen the editorial I wrote when Alter and Erlich were shot by the Russians during World War II. Perhaps I'm getting older or life is different or Russia is different. I do think Russia is different. And other things have happened to change our views on Communism.

I have lived to see the Yugoslavian break with Russia and the Chinese. The development in Nicaragua does not make it exactly like Cuba. Every Communist country is getting to be a little different from every other Communist country. We all have our preferences—we would all prefer Hungary to Romania for example. Hungarians do and so do the Romanians. Clearly when these differences develop our views on the monolithic and unchangeable character of Communism must change.

I believe the point of view that claims a monolithic and unchanging Communism is a permanent and overwhelming danger is somewhat overstated.

I perked up when Irving Kristol said second thoughts are not enough, that just to be an anti-communist is not enough. I don't think I mean what he meant, but I would say we should reconsider our fierce views on the international conflict. When George Schultz, Caspar Weinberger and even Ronald Reagan don't agree with us, we have to face up to realities, the kind of reality which tells us that the policies we desire will simply not go down with the American people. There's been a lot of talk here about Vietnam, but whatever caused our defeat there, we should remember the American people thought 500,000 troops in Vietnam was enough. When we couldn't win with those forces they said let's get out. 50,000 dead is enough, and the fact is they won't even risk that much in Nicaragua, which is much closer to home. They may know something we don't know, or they are just responding humanly. I think these human responses have to be taken into account and I think it's fortunate that the totalitarian Russia we face today, in view of the cautious mood of the American people, is rather different from the totalitarian Russia that existed under Stalin. I won't go through the differences but I believe they exist and are important.

I didn't have to have second thoughts about Soviet Russia. I was raised in a "second thoughts" family; no benefit to me, that's just the way it was. I have, however, had second thoughts about other things, and as others have said that is certainly not enough. You have to move on to third and fourth thoughts too.

PART VI

SECOND THOUGHTS ON A POLITICAL AGENDA

P.J. O'Rourke
Julius Lester
Joshua Muravchik
Michael Novak

CHAPTER 1

THE AWFUL POWER OF MAKE BELIEVE

P.J. O'Rourke

WHAT I BELIEVED IN THE 60s

Everything. You name it and I believed it. I believed love was all you need. I believed you should be here now. I believed drugs could make you a better person. I believed I could hitch-hike to California with 35 cents and people would be glad to feed me. I believed Mao was cute. I believed private property was wrong. I believed my girl friend was a witch. I believed my parents were Nazi space monsters. I believed the university was putting saltpeter in the cafeteria food. I believed stones had souls. I believed the NLF were the good guys in Vietnam. I believed Lyndon Johnson was plotting to murder all Negroes. I believed Yoko Ono was an artist. I believed Bob Dylan was a musician. I believed I would live forever or until 21, whichever came first. I believed the world was about to end. I believed the Age of Aquarius was about to happen. I believed the I Ching said to cut classes and take over the Dean's office. I believed wearing my hair long would end poverty and injustice. I believed there was a great throbbing web of psychic mucus and we were all part of it. I managed to believe Ghandi and H. Rap Brown at the same time. With the exception of anything my parents said, I believed everything.

WHAT CAUSED ME TO HAVE SECOND THOUGHTS

One distinct incident sent me scuttling back to Brooks Brothers. From 1969 to 1971 I was a member of a "collective" running an "underground" newspaper in Baltimore. The newspaper was called, of all

203

things, *Harry*. When *Harry* was founded, nobody could think what to name the thing so we asked some girl's two-year-old son. His grandfather was named Harry and he was calling everything Harry just then so he said, "Harry," and *Harry* was what the paper was called. It was the spirit of the age.

Harry was filled with the usual hippie blather, yea drugs and revolution, boo war and corporate profits. But it was an easygoing publication and not without a sense of humor. The Want Ad section was headlined "Free Harry Classified Help Hep Cats and Kittens Fight Dippy Capitalists Exploitation." And once when the office was raided by the cops (they were looking for marijuana, I might add, not sedition), *Harry* published a page one photo of the mess left by the police search. The caption read, "Harry Office After Bust By Pigs." Next to it was an identical photo captioned "Harry Office Before Bust By Pigs."

Our "collective" was more interested in listening to Captain Beefheart records and testing that new invention, the waterbed, than in overthrowing the state. And some of the more radical types in Baltimore regarded us as lightweights or worse. Thus, one night in the summer of 1970, the *Harry* collective was invaded by some twenty-five blithering Maoists armed with large sticks. They called themselves, and I'm not making this up, the "Balto Cong." They claimed they were liberating the paper in the name of "the people." In vain we tried to tell them that the only thing the people were going to get by taking over *Harry* was $10,000 in debts and a mouse-infested row house with over-due rent.

There were about eight *Harry* staffers in the office that evening. The Balto Cong held us prisoner all night and subjected each of us to individual "consciousness-raising" sessions. You'd be hauled off to another room where ten or a dozen of these nutcakes would sit in a circle and scream that you were a revisionist running dog imperialist paper tiger whatchama-thing. I don't know about the rest of the staff but I conceded as quick as I could to every word they said.

Finally, about six a.m., we mollified the Balto Cong by agreeing to set up a "People's Committee" to run the paper. It would be made up of their group and our staff. We would all meet that night on neutral turf at the Free Clinic. The Balto Cong left in triumph. I breathed a sigh of relief. My air-head girlfriend, however, had been actually converted to Maoism during her consciousness-raising session. And she left with them.

While the Balto Cong went home to take throat pastilles and make new sticks or whatever, we rolled into action. There were, in those days, about a hundred burned out "street people" who depended on peddling

Harry for their livelihood. We rallied all of these, including several members of a friendly motorcycle gang, and explained to them how little sales appeal *Harry* would have if it were filled with quotations From Ho Chi Minh instead of free-love personals. They saw our point. Then we phoned the Balto Cong crash pad and told them we were ready for the meeting. However we asked if their Free Clinic was large enough to hold us all. "What do you mean?" they said. "Well," we said, "we're bringing about a hundred of our staff members and there's, what, twenty-five of you, so. . . ." They said, uh, they'd get back to us.

We were by no means sure the Balto Cong threat had abated. Therefore the staff photographer, whom I'll call Bob, and I were set to guard the *Harry* household. Bob and I were the only two people on the staff who owned guns. Bob was an ex-Marine and something of a flop as a hippie. He could never get the hair and the clothes right and preferred beer to pot. But he was very enthusiastic about hippie girls. Bob still had his service automatic. I had a little .22 pistol that I'd bought in a fit of wild self-dramatization during the '68 riots. "You never know when the heavy shit is going to come down," I had been fond of saying, although I'd pictured it "coming down" more from the Richard Nixon than the Balto Cong direction. Anyway, Bob and I stood guard.

We stood anxious guard every night for two weeks, which seemed an immense length of time back in the 1970s. Of course we began to get slack, not to say stoned, and forgot things like locking the front door. And through that front door, at the end of two weeks, came a half dozen hulking Balto Cong. Bob and I were at the back of the office. Bob had his pistol in the waistband of his ill-fitting bell-bottoms. He went to fast draw and, instead, knocked the thing down in the front of his pants. My pistol was in the top drawer of his desk. I reached in and grabbed it, but I was so nervous that I got my thigh in front of the desk drawer and couldn't get my hand with the pistol in it out. I yanked like mad but I was stuck. I was faced with a terrible dilemma. I could either let go of the pistol and pull my hand out of the drawer or I could keep hold of the pistol and leave my hand stuck in there. It never occurred to me to move my leg.

The invading Balto Cong were faced with one man fishing wildly in his crotch and another whose hand was apparently being eaten by a desk. It stopped them cold. As they stood perplexed I was struck by an inspiration. It was a wooden desk. I would simply fire through it. I flipped the safety off the .22, pointed the barrel at the Balto Cong and was just curling my finger around the trigger when the Maoists parted and there, in the line of fire, stood my air-head ex-girlfriend. "I've come to get my ironing board and my Herman Hesse novels," she said, and led her companions upstairs to our former bedroom.

"It's a trap!" said Bob, extracting his gun from the bottom of a pant leg. When the Balto Cong and the ex-girlfriend came back downstairs they faced two exceedingly wide-eyed guys crouching like leopards behind an impromptu barricade of over-turned book cases. They sped for the exit.

It turned out later that Bob was an undercover cop. He'd infiltrated the *Harry* collective shortly after the first issue. All his photos had to be developed at the police laboratory. We'd wonder why, every time we got busted for marijuana, the case was dropped. Bob would always go to the District Attorney's office and convince them a trial would "blow his cover." It was important for him to remain undetected so he could keep his eye on . . . well, on a lot of hippie girls. Bob was in no rush to get back to the Grand Theft Auto detail. I eventually read some of the reports Bob filed with the police department. They were made up of "_____ is involved in the *Harry* 'scene' primarily as a means of upsetting his parents who are socially prominent," and other such. Bob is now an insurance investigator in Baltimore. He's still friends with the old *Harry* staff. And of the whole bunch of us I believe there's only one who's far enough to the left nowadays to even be called a Democrat.

WHAT I BELIEVE NOW

Nothing. Well, nothing much. I mean, I believe things that can be proven by reason and by experiment, and believe you me, I want to see the logic and the lab equipment. I believe that western civilization, after some disgusting glitches, has become almost civilized. I believe it is our first duty to protect that civilization. I believe it is our second duty to improve it. I believe it is our third duty to extend it if we can. But let's be careful about the last point. Not everybody is ready to be civilized. I wasn't in 1969.

IS THERE ANYTHING TO BE GAINED BY EXAMINING ALL THIS NONSENSE?

I like to think of my behavior in the '60s as a "learning experience." Then again, I like to think of anything stupid I've done as a "learning experience." It makes me feel less stupid. However I actually did learn one thing in the 1960s (besides how to make a hash pipe out of an empty toilet paper roll and some aluminum foil). I learned the awful power of make-believe.

There is a deep-seated and frighteningly strong human need to make believe things are different than they are—that salamanders live forever, we all secretly have three legs and there's an enormous conspiracy somewhere which controls our every thought and deed, etc. And it's not just ignorant heathen, trying to brighten their squalid days, who think such things up. Figments of the imagination can be equally persuasive right here in clean, reasonable, education-choked middle America. People are greedy. Life is never so full it shouldn't be fuller. What more can Shirley MacLaine, for instance, want from existence? She's already been rewarded far beyond her abilities or worth. But nothing will do until she's also been King Tut and Marie of Romania. It was this kind of hoggish appetite for epistemological romance that sent my spoiled and petulant generation on a journey to Oz, a journey from which some of us are only now straggling back, in intellectual tatters.

Many people think fantastic ideas are limited to the likes of Harmonic Convergences, quartz crystals that ward off cancer or, at worst, hare-brained theories about who killed JFK. Unfortunately this is not the case, especially not in this century. Two of the most fecund areas for cheap fiction are politics and economics. Which brings me to Marxism.

Marxism is a perfect example of the chimeras that fueled the '60s. And it was probably the most potent one. Albeit, much of this Marxism would have been unrecognizable to Marx. It was Marxism watered down, Marxism spiked with LSD and Marxism adulterated with mystical food coloring. But it was Marxism nonetheless because the wildest hippie and the sternest member of the Politburo shared the same day-dream, the day-dream that underlies all Marxism: that a thing might somehow be worth other than what people will give for it. This just is not true. And any system that bases itself on such a will-o-the-wisp is bound to fail. Communes don't work. Poland doesn't either.

Now this might not seem like much to have learned. You may think I could have gleaned more from a half dozen years spent ruining chromosomes, morals and any chance of ever getting elected to political office. After all, the hippies are gone and—if *glasnost* is any indication—the Communists are going. But there is a part of the world where politico-economic fish stories are still greeted with gape-jawed credulity. It's a part of the world that pretty much includes everybody except us, the Japanese, some Europeans and a few of the most cynical Russians. You can call it the Third World, the Underdeveloped World or just The Part of the World That's Completely Screwed.

Over the past four years, working as a foreign correspondent, I've spent a lot of time in the part of the world that's completely screwed. It's always seemed a comfortable and familiar-feeling place to me. The reason is, Third World countries are undergoing national adolescences very similar to the personal adolescence I underwent in the '60s. Woodstock Nation isn't dead; it's just become short, brown, distant and filled with chaos and starvation.

Marxism has tremendous appeal in the Third World for exactly the same reason it had tremendous appeal to me in college. It gives you something to believe in when what surrounds you seems unbelievable. It gives you someone to blame besides yourself. It's theoretically tidy. And, best of all, it's fully imaginary so it can never be disproved.

The Third World attitude towards the United States is also easy to understand if you think of it in terms of adolescence. The citizens of the Third World are in a teenage muddle about us—full of envy, imitation, anger and blind puppy love. I have been held at gun-point by a Shi'ite youth in West Beirut who told me in one breath that America was "pig Satan devil" and that he planned to go to dental school in Dearborn as soon as he got his green card. In Ulundi, in Zululand, I talked to a young man who, as usual, blamed apartheid on the United States. However, he had just visited the U.S. with a church group and also told me, "Everything is so wonderful there. The race relations are so good. And everybody is rich." Where had he gone, I asked. "The south side of Chicago."

We are a beautiful twenty-year-old woman and they are a wildly infatuated thirteen-year-old boy. They think of us every moment of the day and we take no notice of them whatsoever. If they can't have a chance to love us, a chance to pester us will do—by joining the Soviet Bloc, for example. Anything for attention.

Isn't this very like the relationship we "drop-outs" of the '60s had to the "straight" society of our parents? Weren't we citizens of our own Underdeveloped World, the world of American teenage pop culture?

So what are we supposed to do about all this? How do we keep the disaffected youth of the West out of mental Disney World? How do we keep the poor denizens of Africa, Asia and Latin America from embracing a myth that will make their lives even worse than they are already? How do we keep everyone from falling under the spell of some even more vile and barbaric phantom such as religious fundamentalism? We have to offer an alternative to nonsense, an alternative that is just as engaging but actually means something.

Maybe we should start by remembering that we already live in a highly idealistic, totally revolutionary society. And that our revolution is based on reality, not bullshit. Furthermore it works. Look around us. It works like a son of a bitch. We have to remember it was this revolution, not the Bolsheviks', that set the world on fire. Maybe we should start acting like we believe in it again. That means turning our face against not only the Qadhafis, Khomeinis, and Gorbachevs, but also against the Dengs, Pinochets, and Bothas.

The President and his advisors will not have to sit up late working on a speech to explain this policy shift. There's a perfectly suitable text already in print:

> We hold these truths to be self-evident, that all men are created equal, that they are endowed by their Creator with certain unalienable Rights, that among these are Life, Liberty and the pursuit of Happiness. That to secure these rights, Governments are instituted among Men, deriving their just powers from the consent of the governed.

And that is a much spacier idea than anything which occurred to me during the 1960s.

CHAPTER 2

BEYOND IDEOLOGY

Julius Lester

The Movement. It was a special time, a time when idealism was as palpable and delicious as a gentle rain, a time when freedom and love and justice seemed as immediate and seemed as ripe as oranges shining seductively from a tree in one's backyard. It was a time when we believed that the ideals of democracy would, at long last, gleam like endless amber waving fields of grain from the hearts and souls of every American. It was a time when we believed that love was too wonderful and too important to be confined to our small circles of family and friends because love was a mighty stream that could purify the soul of the nation, and once purified, the nation would study war no more, and everyone would sing "no more auction block" because we all were slaves of one kind or another. We had a vision of a new world about to be born and that vision burned us with a burning heat.

In its beginnings, in the latter half of the '50s, The Movement challenged us to sing the Lord's song in a strange land, a land in which we all sat by the rivers of Babylon and wept, though only a few of us knew we were weeping. In Montgomery, Alabama, Martin Luther King, Jr. was saying that yes, segregation was wrong, but that one was not justified in destroying it by any means necessary. "All life is interrelated," he said. "All humanity is involved in a single process, and to the degree that I harm my brother, to that extent I am harming myself." We must be careful, he admonished, not to do those things that will "intensify the existence of evil in the universe."

From a monastery in Kentucky, a monk named Thomas Merton was writing essays and books imbued with a clarity and authenticity unlike anything many of us had ever read:

> . . . our job is to love others without stopping to inquire whether or not they are worthy. That is not our business and, in fact, it is nobody's

211

business. What we are asked to do is to love; and this love itself will render both ourselves and our neighbors worthy if anything can.

And on the West Coast, in a place with the romantic name of North Beach, there came the voices of Allen Ginsberg, Jack Kerouac, Alan Watts, and Gary Snyder stripping the Eisenhower and McCarthy years of their gray-flannelled fear, and through their words we were invited to live life in all its fullness and blinding complexity. Henry Miller, the elder statesman of the Beat Generation, put it this way:

> I am not interested in the potential man. I an interested in what a man actualizes—or realizes—of his potential being. And what is the potential man, after all? Is he not the sum of all that is human? Divine, in other words? You think I am searching for God. I am not. God is. The world is. Man is. We are. The full reality, that's God—and man, and the world, and all that is, including the unnameable.

The Movement was not born from the desire to change the system. We wanted to move far beyond systems; we wanted to create community, and in the words of one of the earliest white members of the Student Nonviolent Coordinating Committee (SNCC), Jane Stembridge, that community was to be "the beloved community."

What made The Movement such a compelling force in its early years was that political action was merely the vehicle for spiritual expression. The values by which we lived were what really mattered—the quality of who we were and the subsequent quality of our relationships. Ending segregation was not sufficient as a goal. (Anybody who really thinks that the aim of the early Civil Rights Movement was to sit down at a lunch counter next to a white person and eat a hamburger and drink a cup of coffee insults not only the intelligence of black people but also our tastebuds. We had always known that the food was better on our side of the tracks). We wanted to create a new society based on feelings of community, and to do that, The Movement itself had to be the paradigm of that New Community.

Spring, 1960. I stood in the Student Union Building at Fisk University in Nashville, Tennessee, staring at the bulletin board. The sit-in movement had begun in February of that year in Greensboro, North Carolina, and it had spread quickly to Nashville and other cities in the South and become national news. That spring afternoon of my senior year, I stared at the bulletin board reading the telegrams tacked upon it. They were telegrams from schools all over the country expressing support for the sit-in movement: Harvard, Yale, Stanford, the University of Chicago, Oberlin, and on and on and on.

I was bewildered. I didn't understand their what or their why. I had lived my then twenty-one years shuddering within the lingering shadow of slavery—segregation. I had learned to walk great distances rather than sit in the back of segregated buses, to control my bodily functions so that I would not have to use segregated bathrooms, to go for many hours without water in the southern heat rather than drink from the Colored Fountains, and to choose hunger rather than buy food from a segregated eating place. I was fourteen before I ever spoke to a white person. Although I had encountered whites during a semester at San Diego State College the previous year, and although there were white instructors and a few white students at Fisk, white people had no reality as persons. They were an implacable force as massive and undifferentiated as an iceberg, and somehow I would have to find the way to steer the fragile craft of my life around it or be thrown into the icy waters, another victim of that hard and blinding whiteness.

But as I stood there reading those telegrams, I recognized for the first time in my life that white people were not an undifferentiated mass, an unfeeling negative Other. There were whites who cared, who did not think of segregation as a Negro problem, but who knew it for what it was—an American problem. For the first time in my life I felt that I was not alone in America.

That is why the New Community that the early Movement tried to be—had to be—Black and White together. The Old America had been one of Black and White forcibly kept apart by segregation, economics and prejudice. In 1960, most states had laws forbidding interracial marriages, and the southern states had additional laws forbidding social relationships between blacks and whites.

"Black and White together," we would sing in one of the choruses of "We Shall Overcome." What a revolutionary statement it was! Black and White together on such a scale was unprecedented in American history because Black and White together was not how the nation had ever perceived itself. It was not surprising, then, that during demonstrations, it was the whites who were singled out for the most vicious beatings. They were traitors to America's conception of itself as a white nation. William Moore, Michael Schwerner, Andrew Goodman, Jonathan Daniels, Rev. James Reeb, and Mrs. Viola Liuzzo were made to pay the ultimate price: they were murdered. Others, like James Peck, suffered for the rest of their lives from the beatings they received. Some committed suicide. Others paid and continue to pay psychically.

We did not know that America would extract such a price to maintain the status quó. We did not know that the Justice Department of Robert Kennedy would not be eager to use the power of the federal government to protect civil rights workers. We did not know that seeking the end of segregation and disenfranchisement would lead the liberal press to accuse us of wanting too much too soon. Above all, perhaps, we did not know that the values we sought to embody—the values of nonviolence and the beloved community—were not values that America wanted for itself.

One can live in the valley of the shadow of death only so long before asking, why am I doing this? I lost fifteen pounds in two weeks that summer of 1964 in Mississippi. The body is an organism with an intense awareness of itself. It knows when its existence is being threatened, even when the mind claims there is nothing to worry about. My mind thought the long and desolate highways of Mississippi beautiful; my body knew that southern trees bear a strange fruit. At night my mind would tell me that the house I was sleeping in might be bombed while I slept, but, it would add blithely, "Everybody has to die sometime." My body, trembling with incredulity, would say: "Sometime ain't this time," and refuse to fall asleep.

Faint whispers of second thoughts in voices like those of the witches in "Macbeth" disturbed a lot of us that summer of 1964. Trying to register blacks to vote was not worth risking one's life for, especially when one walked into the voting booth and had to choose between Lyndon Johnson and Barry Goldwater. And as navy men searched the swamps and countryside of Mississippi for the bodies of Chaney, Goodman and Schwerner, our own mortality stared at us with its hollow eyes and we wondered if America really cared.

In August 1964, the Mississippi Freedom Democratic party went to the Democratic Party's convention in Atlantic City and challenged the Democrats to seat it as the legitimate representative of the party in Mississippi instead of the all-white delegation led by arch-white supremacist, Senator James Eastland. The convention offered the MFD party two token seats.

Those foreboding second thoughts acquired full-bodied voices because of our feeling of having been betrayed by our country. We had offered America love; it played politics. We wanted the Constitutional ideals of equality, life, liberty and the pursuit of happiness, to stroll through the streets of cities and along country backroads with the glowing wonder of lovers discovering themselves in each other. America told us that we were young and did not understand. We understood that America's only interest was business as usual. We could not accept business as usual.

Second thoughts confront us when reality does not correspond to our expectations, when new information leads us to modify or change wholly what we had believed to be true. Second thoughts are important because they are the threshold of self-examination.

I do not remember the first time I heard of Malcolm X but I remember clearly the first time I took him seriously. During the winter of 1962 I worked for the Welfare Department in Harlem. For reasons beyond my comprehension, the month of February at the Welfare Department was devoted to raising money for the NAACP. The department was organized into units of six caseworkers, each with its own supervisor. One morning, my supervisor, who was white, informed me that our unit was to raise money for the NAACP the following day and that I was scheduled to sit at the table in the lobby from twelve to two and sell cookies, muffins or whatever it was. I told him I didn't support the N-double-A and had no intention of raising money for it. He looked at me coldly and said, "What are you? One of those followers of Malcolm X?" The way he said it told me all I needed to know about Malcolm, and I returned his cold stare and said, "Yes." Significantly, he treated me with a cool but proper respect after that, something that had been absent before. Such was the power of Malcolm X.

There were a few blacks at the Welfare Department who went to hear Malcolm at the mosque in Harlem, and on Mondays they would give me a summary of his speech. What Malcolm said was fearful to hear, even secondhand. He derided integration and mocked non-violence. He scorned love and extolled power. He had contempt for everything white and a startling love for everything black. What he preached was hard to embrace. It was even harder to deny.

We did not follow Malcolm, but what he said followed us like some nagging super-ego, especially after four little girls were murdered in the bombing of a church on a Birmingham, Alabama Sunday morning, and we began to ask ourselves whether Malcolm was right. Was violence the only appropriate response to violence?

One day in the mid-Sixties—about 1965, I think—I was in New York's Forty-second Street Library and ran into a friend whose first words were an excited, "Have you read this yet?" He thrust into my hands a book called *The Wretched of the Earth*. The author was someone named Frantz Fanon.

The Wretched of the Earth was a sophisticated reiteration of much that Malcolm had said, and reading it made our second thoughts become new convictions. Fanon gave us words through which to know ourselves anew. In his writings we found the term "Third World," and no longer would we identify ourselves as American. He told us that we were a colonized people, and that we had a political identity that aligned us with all the people of the Twentieth Century who had struggled against colonialism. Most important, Fanon told us that violence was redemptive, that it was the only means by which the colonized could cleanse themselves of the violence of the colonizers.

We did not have to wonder about the violence of the colonizers because every night on the news we watched the films of U.S. soldiers carrying out a war in a country we had never heard of, a country that none of us thought threatened America's security. The nation was at war and something happened that was perhaps unprecedented in American history: A significant number of young Americans sided openly with the enemy. Young men fled to Canada and Sweden rather than be drafted to fight an unjust war. Draft cards and American flags were burned at antiwar rallies and Phil Ochs sang "I ain't A-Marching Anymore."

At the same historical moment, the predominantly black Civil Rights Movement and the predominantly white anti-Vietnam War Movement became anti-American. Suddenly, America was the enemy. If ever there was a moment in history for second thoughts, that was one. Common sense should have told us that it is impossible to transform a nation if you hate it.

But that is one of the dangers of idealism. When it is let loose in the public arena, it is like an animal in heat and in desperate need of a sexual joining. All too quickly, unrequited idealism can become surly and aggressive. All too quickly, it becomes rage, bares the teeth that have been lurking behind the smile as pretty as a morning glory, and enraged, bites itself and never feels the pain, never knows that the blood staining its teeth is its own.

But the signs had been there almost from the beginning. I remember being at a civil rights rally in the early Sixties and hearing the chant, "Freedom Now! Freedom Now!" I muttered "Freedom any ol' time" because I was afraid of what would happen if we didn't get "Freedom Now." Later in the Sixties, Jim Morrison of the Doors shouted, "We want the world and we want it now!" We should have been frightened, and we weren't.

Freedom did not come now. We may have wanted the world, but we didn't get it, at least not warm from the oven, as light and flaky as a croissant. Because freedom did not come now, because we did not get the world, we turned against the nation we had wanted to love, a nation that did not want our love. Or so it seemed. And we turned against each other.

It is spring, 1968. I am sitting in my apartment in New York with one of my closest Movement friends. I am a very private person, and there are not many people with whom I share my home and family. This friend was one of the few who had eaten my wife's cooking and mine and had played with our children. We are alone in the apartment that afternoon chatting with an ease that is possible only with those to whom we have entrusted our souls. He and I had trusted our very lives to each other on the backroads of Alabama. Suddenly, he says, "I probably shouldn't say this, man, but I don't think you should be married to a white woman. You probably think it's none of my business." Quietly, I say, "You're right." He nods, and there is nothing more to be said— about that or anything else. After a moment of silence as long as winter, he gets up. "Take care of yourself," he says. "Yeah, you too," I respond and I close the door gently behind him. I never saw him again and a few years later he was dead, killed in a bombing.

By 1968 the Movement that had begun with the singing of "We Shall Overcome" was shouting "Black Power." I wrote a book called *Look Out, Whitey! Black Power's Gon' Get Your Mama.* It was the first book that sought to explicate Black Power, an angry book, expressing not so much personal anger as racial anger. It was also a very funny and outrageous book, which I thought would be evident from the title. Everyone took the title seriously. I will never forget the headline in a Fort Wayne, Indiana newspaper: "White Mamas In Danger, Says Black Militant Lester." I knew, however, that "white mamas" had the Army, Navy, Air Force, and Marines to protect them. I was the one in danger and in ways I had not anticipated.

I was invited to speak on college campuses and I saw the disappointment in the eyes of black students when I got off the plane and I did not have a ten-foot high Afro and was not wearing a dashiki made by Jomo Kenyatta's grandmama. I found myself being asked, angrily, to explain how I could consider myself a black activist and have a white wife. For a while, I wondered, too. But I kept remembering one close friend who had dissolved a relationship with the love of his life for no other reason than that she was white, and I remembered too, his unhappiness and shame. Having grown up in the South where whites decreed who I could and could not marry, I was not going to turn around and give blacks that power. My eventual divorce had nothing to do with my wife's race or mine but with us and who we were as persons.

Second thoughts abounded now like wildflowers. Both the Black and White movements attacked individuals within their ranks more viciously than they attacked the administration in Washington. The personal had become political, and the gray-flanneled conformity of the Fifties was replaced by a blue-jeaned and Afroed totalitarianism. A mysterious and mystical entity called The People became the standard against which everyone was measured and judged. One's actions, thoughts and life-styles had to serve the needs of The People. At one meeting, I asked a simple question: "Which people? Do you mean junkies, winos, and prostitutes? Do you mean the church-going people, the manual laborers, the unwed mothers, or the strivers?" When the meeting continued as if I had not spoken, I knew that I had committed a revolutionary *faux pas*. I also knew that I had asked a good question.

Wasn't the role of the intellectual simply that—to have second thoughts and ask good questions? But an intellectual could not do that if he or she felt guilty about being an intellectual, if she or he found virtue only in something called the "working class" or something even more amor-phous called "The People." The intellectual had to realize that to think and feel what had not yet been thought or felt was also work, though the hands remained uncalloused and the armpits were devoid of perspi-ration.

In his very fine novel, *An Admirable Woman,* the late Arthur Cohen has his heroine say:

> The mind has its work and its materials; it has no choice in this respect. It can do nothing else but work properly—balancing thrust with caution, intuition with verification, argument with detail, interpretation with groundwork, grand truth with the webbing of subtle argument. The working of the mind is a slow and patient procedure. It cannot be rushed . . . Clarity is the moral luster of the mind.

This was our birthright as intellectuals, but to possess it we needed to withstand the terror, loneliness, and isolation inherent in intellectual life. The intellectual must be an Outsider because only from the outside can one see clearly what is occurring on the inside. We succumbed to the understandable human need to be at the party, standing beside the fireplace, drinking hot cider.

Such failings were predictable because it is only a short step from idealism to ideology. Both hold out the promise of giving life meaning; both promise to shelter us from the uncertainties and anxieties of self-knowledge. Ideology does not permit second thoughts, however, because ideology is a cosmology, answering all questions, past, present, and future. Eventually, thoughts become unnecessary, even first thoughts, and the struggle to be human is scorned as individualism. The factionalism and political name-calling that had alienated so many of us from the Old Left became the language of the Black Movement and the New Left.

In the spring of 1969, SDS passed a resolution asserting that the Black Panther Party was the "vanguard" of the Black Movement, the true representative of revolutionary nationalism. In my weekly column in *The Guardian,* I objected and wrote, in part: "What is at issue here is the correct relationship a white radical organization should have to the black revolutionary movement. By presuming to know what program, ideology, military strategy, and what particular organizations best serve the interests of the black community," SDS was being "more white than revolutionary."

Two weeks later *The Guardian* published a response by Kathleen Cleaver, the Panther "Minister of Communications. Among other things, she called me a "counterrevolutionary," "a fool" peddling "madness," a "racist," and ended with these eloquent words: "Fuck Julius Lester. All power to the people!"

I did not understand. I remembered Kathleen from when she had come to work in the Atlanta SNCC office, a young woman with a big grin and a lot of enthusiasm. We were pals, in the best sense of that word, able to laugh and play together. What had happened to her? What was happening to us all? Why did Kathleen need me to agree with her? Why did blacks need me to leave my wife so they could be black? But when the personal became political, persons cease to exist. When persons cease to exist, war is imminent.

I was not surprised to hear rumors that the Panthers were going to kill me. I believed the rumors because I knew people whom the Panthers had threatened with guns because of political disagreements. But all my second thoughts crystallized into an unshakable conviction: I would choose death, because to live and not write what I believed to be true was not to live at all.

The rumors were only rumors and nothing happened, but a new round of second thoughts arose. What did it mean that I had more space and freedom to think and write in Nixon's America than in The Movement with all its revolutionary rhetoric?

In September of the same year, Ho Chi Minh died. I had been in North Vietnam for a month in 1967, and had witnessed U.S. bombing raids at a time when the government was still denying such bombing raids. Most of all, though, I remembered the lyrical beauty of that country. Perhaps that is why my response to Ho's death was to write a poem and publish it as my weekly column in *The Guardian.* This is the poem:

Half awakened by the light of morning
choking in the greyness
of a third of September Wednesday,
I reached out for the
roundness
softness
fullness
allness of her
and she, awakened,
began to move,
softly,
silently,
gently,
and my hand found that place,
that hidden place,
that secret place,
that
won-
der-
ful place
and in the quiescent light of
a third of September Wednesday morning,
I felt my penis being taken into the
salty
thick

fluidity
of her swirling movement
easily
softly
gently
(as the children were waking.)

Afterwards,
my penis, moist and warm,
resting on my thigh like some
fish washed onto the beach by full moontide,
I turned on the radio
and we heard that
Ho Chi Minh lay dying.
(The fog covered the seagulls that
sit on the rocky beach when the tide is out.)

I retreated from her,
not talking that day as the radio told me
(every hour on the hour)
that Ho Chi Minh lay dying.
Finally, when night had covered the fog,
we heard that
Ho Chi Minh was dead
and I came back to her.
Ho Chi Minh was dead.
I wanted her again.
The softness
the roundness
the fullness
the allness.

Ho Chi Minh was dead.

When the next issue of *The Guardian* came out, a poem of Ho's was in the space where my column usually appeared. Angry, I called the office wanting to know why my poem had not been published. The editor told me the staff had decided that if the poem were published the week of Ho's death, it would not be understood as the appreciation of Ho that it was. They had decided to delay publication of my poem for a week. I asked why they hadn't let me know, or discussed it with me. The editor said they had been too busy. I was not convinced.

They published the poem the following week, and the week after my final column appeared announcing my resignation from the paper. I wrote about a young black kid named George Best who used to hang around the Atlanta SNCC office. In the summer of 1967 George had gone to West Point, Mississippi to organize and had died under suspicious circumstances. The police claimed that George's car accidentally ended up in a creek, George inside. I did not learn of George's death until my return trip to Cuba. I also learned that SNCC had not sent flowers to his funeral. I was outraged and frightened and that, perhaps, was the moment when my second thoughts acquired their strongest roots. Near the end of that last column for *The Guardian,* I wrote about how instrumental SNCC's failure to send flowers to George's funeral had been in my eventually leaving the organization:

It became too much to have to fight the enemy and those with whom I was working. We had been through too much, I guess. The burdens had gotten too heavy and the frustrations had become too painful that we could no longer give each other the personal support each of us needed to do our job—make the revolution. Our love for black people was overwhelmed by our inability to do everything to make that love manifest, and after a while we could not even love each other. We got so involved in the day-to-day functioning of an organization, so enmeshed in fixing the mimeograph machine, writing leaflets, raising money, sitting in interminable meetings where we said what we were going to do and had forgotten what we were going to do by the time the meeting was over; and eventually we forget, can't even remember that the revolution is an "embryonic journey" and that we are the embryos inside society. If we cannot be human to each other, the revolution will be stillborn.

I had thought that the revolution was to create a society in which power elites did not arbitrarily determine what "the people" might and might not understand. Well, I should have known that the revolution wouldn't be erotic.

I left *The Guardian* but it was hard to leave The Movement. It had been my identity and life, my family and community. When Dave Dellinger's magazine *Liberation,* asked me to write for it, I agreed. Less than a year passed, and once again I wrote something that a Movement publication did not want to publish.

The occasion was the trial in New Haven of seven members of the Black Panther Party who had been accused of torturing and murdering Alex Rackley, another BPP member. Three party members admitted their active participation in the torture and murder of Rackley. Yet, black and white radicals were demonstrating on the New Haven Green, and many articles were published in the radical press demanding that the New Haven Seven be freed. The rationale? It was impossible for blacks to receive justice in America. White sycophancy toward the Black Movement had set a new standard for madness. I sat down to the typewriter:

> . . . we can self-righteously cite the verdict of the Nuremberg Trials when we want to condemn the military establishment and the politicians. We can say to them that you are personally responsible for what you do, that you do not have to follow orders and there are no extenuating circumstances. Yet, we can turn right around and become Adolf Eichmann's, eloquent apologists for the Movement's My Lai. . . . Our morality is used to condemn others, but it is not to be applied to ourselves. We can react with outrage when four are murdered at Kent State, but when a professor is killed in the dynamiting of the Mathematics Building at the University of

Wisconsin, we don't give it a second thought. When we kill, there are extenuating circumstances. It was an accident, we say. The blast went off too soon.

The murder of Alex Rackley was . . . the logical culmination of the politics we have been espousing, a politics of violence-for-the-sake-of-violence, a politics which too quickly and too neatly divides people into categories of "revolutionary" and "counter-revolutionary." The murder of Alex Rackley is the result of the politics which more and more begins to resemble the politics we are supposedly seeking to displace.

The editors of *Liberation* held the article for three months. Finally, I had a tense meeting with them in which they argued that the prosecution could use my article against the Panthers. Did I want that? I was asked. How many times during my years in The Movement had someone tried to control my thoughts, my words, or my deeds by saying that such-and-such would not be in the best interests of The People, that such-and-such would merely play into the hands of the "enemy," that I was being individualistic and that people in The Movement had to submit to discipline, and that their individual thoughts and lives were not as important as those of The People.

I knew only that as a writer and an intellectual, I was responsible for conveying whatever minuscule portion of the truth I could find. And as a person, my responsibility was to be as fully human as I could. Giving one's soul to ideology permitted one to rationalize murder, to attack friends, to deny the power and beauty of the erotic. Allegiance to ideology gave one permission to turn other human beings into abstractions, and as a black kid growing up under segregation in the 1940s and 1950s, I knew what being an abstraction felt like because, dear God, my soul still bled from the wounds. If I had learned nothing else, I had learned that one does not turn another human being into an abstraction without becoming an abstraction oneself, and to turn another into an abstraction is murder. I recognized, moreover, that even if murder is justified in the name of God, freedom, justice, socialism, revolution or democracy, it is still murder.

Liberation published the article, but our relationship was over. Nevertheless, among my feelings of sadness and hurt, there was a strange, new feeling. I was free. I was free to be whoever I was and would be; and slowly and painfully in the ensuing years, I came to love all the contradictions and inconsistencies inherent in being human.

Robert Frost said that he was never a radical in his youth because he didn't want to be a conservative in his old age. I was a radical in my youth, but I have not become conservative in middle age.

I am not radical or conservative because I do not see an essential difference between the two positions, despite appearances. Both are political worldviews that divide the world into an Us against a Them. Radicals and conservatives merely disagree on who is the Them. Because I am Black, because I am Jewish, I must resist the succulent temptation to define another human being as a Them, and sometimes that is very hard.

This does not mean that those responsible for the evil in South Africa should not be held accountable for their deeds. But I do not have to define another as a Them to hold him or her accountable. It is sufficient to say that they have failed, on even the most minimal level, to live humanely.

I am not politically naive about the Soviet Union, but neither do I forget that it is a nation that lost twenty million people in World War II. I cannot imagine what impact that can have on a nation's character and policies. I look at Iran and see madness, but I cannot forget the years of the Shah's reign and those of his father; and again, I cannot imagine what an impact that can have on that nation's character and policies. I am not politically naive, but I am convinced that unless I know and make a part of me the pain and suffering of another, I have no chance of comprehending his or her humanity. Trust between persons is established when each is receptive to the abiding sorrows of the other. I think that may also be true for nations.

There is a Them, but it is not out there. Them is always and eternally Me. To the extent that I take responsibility for the Them that is Me, to that extent do I free others to be persons in all their crystalline fragility. That is the vision with which The Movement began, and it is a vision many of us are still trying to live.

The Movement disappointed us and we disappointed ourselves. Perhaps, then, it is important to remember these words of Bertolt Brecht:

> You, who shall emerge from the flood
> In which we are sinking,
> Think—
> When you speak of our weaknesses,
> Also of the dark time
> That brought them forth . . .
>
> Even the hatred of squalor
> Makes the brow grow stern.
> Even anger against injustice

Makes the voice grow harsh. Alas, we
Who wished to lay the foundations of kindness
Could not ourselves be kind.

But you, when at last it comes to pass
That man can help his fellow man,
Do not judge us
Too harshly.

I sincerely hope that, in our second thoughts, we will judge ourselves, but not too harshly. Judging ourselves too harshly is to think that the proper expiation for radicalism is conservativism. Having attempted to balance ourselves by standing on our left legs, we must not shift all our weight to our right legs.

Standing on both legs, the weight distributed evenly throughout the body, is an intricate and demanding task. It means being neither radical nor conservative. It means examining issues and recognizing that in certain cases a radical methodology is wisest. In others, a conservative methodology will bring us closer to realizing the ideals of freedom and justice and economic equity. Though both theories present themselves as if they are truth incarnate, they are not. But each does carry a truth, and each must be listened to for its truth.

Radicalism and conservativism are merely two ways that one attempts to make sense of the world. We delude ourselves when we use them to seek our identities, when we wear them and think we know who we are. Identity cannot be resolved so easily.

Ultimately, the task is to be utterly human. Only to the extent that I know and accept my humanity will I be able to see others as they are, as nothing more and nothing less than utterly human. When we are able to do this, we will have moved beyond ideology into terror and then, only then, will we be free.

CHAPTER 3

WHAT IS TO BE DONE?: AN ANTI-COMMUNIST MANIFESTO

Joshua Muravchik

In the first sentence of "What is to be done?", Lenin speaks of the conflict between "socialists and democrats." And that exactly is the great political question of our epoch, bearing in mind that what Lenin meant by "socialist," we mean by the term "Communist."

In 1776 the first modern democracy was created. It was one of the most successful political experiments ever, perhaps the most successful. It pushed back the frontiers of human freedom, inventiveness and productiveness. American democracy was of course not perfect. It contained many imperfections and one monstrous flaw—slavery, which after 90 years and a terrible war gave way to the somewhat lesser shame of Jim Crow, which in turn endured another 100 years, until it was vanquished by the civil rights movement.

This is one of the keys to understanding the agonies of the 1960s. They were, we might say, in part the penalty America paid for the sin of slavery and racism. For many of us who came to political consciousness during the 1960s, the civil rights movement's struggle against Jim Crow was our formative experience, and that experience gave us a distorted view of our country, predisposing us to believe ill of it. Because it was the first issue on which we focused, we tended to assume that it was characteristic of the state of justice in America when in fact it was anomalous.

Riveted as we were by the cruelties of racism, we did not appreciate the extraordinary nature of the victory of the civil rights movement even as it unfolded before us, surely one of history's great episodes of constructive social reform. It should have told us more about America than racism did. Sad to say, the existence of racism, discrimination, and

227

even slavery did not distinguish America from a thousand other societies. What did distinguish America was the victory over racism, an act of collective conscience so intensely felt that we have since gone on to the era of affirmative action. Where in history can you find the precedent for *that*? Where else can you imagine that a minority race, economically impoverished and politically weak, is given preferential treatment by the dominant majority in order to atone for past injustice?

In 1917, another political experiment was begun, perhaps the most catastrophic in history. The only frontiers that it pushed back were the frontiers of tyranny, cruelty, and mass murder.

It has, however, been at least as successful as the democratic experiment in one respect—reproducing itself. The democratic experiment has reproduced itself primarily by inspiring emulation around the world. The Communist experiment has reproduced itself by means of imperialism and by inspiring emulation, too, among bands of would-be tyrants whose blood is stirred at the thought of ruling their own utopia. Both systems claim universal validity, and both have some supporting evidence. A little more than 200 years ago there was no democracy on earth. Seventy years ago there was no Communism. Today more than one-third of the world's population lives under each of these systems.

The contest between them constitutes the overriding political question of our epoch. It is a stark choice between a system as humane as man has ever constructed and a system as cruel as man has ever constructed. When I said just that in a debate with Frances FitzGerald once, she accused me of holding a Manichean point of view. My answer can only be that this is a Manichean reality.

So, what is to be done?

First, we must resurrect the term "Communist" as a category in our political discourse, both about the domestic political scene and the international scene. Domestically, we have been unable to speak about Communism for nearly 35 years. That is the crippling legacy of McCarthyism. Membership in the Communist Party is kept secret. Although the Party itself is small, there are a number of Communists and Communist front groups that play important political roles. But the unwritten rule of our public discourse is that no one may be called a Communist unless he has been the Communist Party's candidate for President. Vice President will not suffice. Thus the party's national ticket in 1984 was Gus Hall for President and Angela Davis for Vice President. The newspapers do identify Gus Hall often as a Communist; but Angela Davis is almost always identified as a "black activist".

You might say that this is trivial, because Communists are few, but the problem does not concern only Communists. It is also not considered proper to call someone pro-Communist, and the ranks of pro-Communists—those who express support for Communist rulers or insurgencies—are not so small. The category includes groups like the Institute for Policy Studies and the Committee in Solidarity with the People of El Salvador (CISPES); it includes several members of Congress and one of the leading contenders for the Democratic Party's presidential nomination.

The ability to apply terms like Communist or pro-Communist is not something to be desired for the purpose of launching congressional investigations or police actions against these people. The purpose is to be able to stigmatize them. Not to stigmatize them as subversives, but as people whose political perceptions or moral values are so deeply flawed that their counsels deserve no weight. When Jesse Jackson embraces Castro and Ortega he has told us all we need to know about his qualifications for the presidency: so what if he has interesting ideas for, say, improving the quality of inner city education. It is as if, suffering from emotional distress, I sought out a therapist and there in his waiting room found a wall bedecked with portraits of his heroes—Charles Manson, the Marquis de Sade, Madame de Farge, and Torquemada. I don't think I'd stay around for the appointment.

This kind of stigmatization is used with great effect in the opposite direction. People are often called fascist, although fascism does not exist and has not for more than 40 years. But anyone who can credibly be described as a supporter of such Rightist governments as Somoza's or Pinochet's is read out of political discourse. Much the same happens when people are identified as ultra-conservative or far-Right.

The New York Times, yesterday, reported on the possibility that Jeane Kirkpatrick might run for president and referred to one of her leading supporters in New Hampshire, former Governor Meldrim Thompson, as follows: "Mr. Thompson, a one-time member of the John Birch Society, served three terms as governor." I wait for the New York Times to write of, say, Congressman George Crockett, "Mr. Crockett, long-time adherent of Communist Party causes, served three terms in Congress."

In the 1940s Mr. Crockett was part of the Communist faction expelled from the UAW and a member of the Communist-dominated National Lawyers Guild; in the 1950s he was a leader of the support campaign for the Rosenberg atomic spies and Communist Party Smith Act defendants; in the 1960s he was a Vice President of the National Lawyers Guild; and in the 1980s he sponsored the World Congress of the Soviet front World

Peace Council, spoke at the annual banquet for the Communist Party newspaper, *The People's World,* and abstained when Congress voted by 416 to 0 to condemn the shooting down of the Korean airliner by the Soviet Union.

Congressman Crockett, as you know, is the Chairman of the House Subcommittee on Hemispheric Affairs, that is the subcommittee with jurisdiction over Latin America. He succeeded Michael Barnes in that post. It is worth recalling the recent history of that subcommittee. For four years the Chairman had been Congressman Gus Yatron of Pennsylvania, a Democrat and no conservative. Last year Mr. Yatron earned a 65 percent correct voting record in the eyes of ADA and an 82 percent rating by the AFL-CIO. But in a rare act, the Democratic members of the Foreign Affairs Committee voted to override Yatron's seniority and to strip him of his chairmanship in favor of Barnes because they believed, in the words of the Almanac of American Politics, that "Barnes would be a more articulate and more dependable critic of the Reagan policy in Central America." When Barnes gave up his seat, the next Democrat in the subcommittee's seniority line was Dan Mica of Florida, who last year had a 55 percent ADA rating and a 56 percent AFL-CIO rating. He was deemed unacceptable by his colleagues and was passed over in favor of the less senior Mr. Crockett. Note that Yatron and Mica were stigmatized by their fellow Democrats for insufficient anti-Reaganism although Yatron was not even a supporter of aid to the Contras. But nothing in Crockett's record which I have just described to you made him anathema to the Democrats.

Not only has the term Communist disappeared from discourse about domestic issues, it has, at least since Vietnam, gone into eclipse in our discourse about foreign political movements as well. For example, throughout the last years of its struggle for power and even to this day it is rare indeed to see the Sandinista National Liberation Front described in the major news outlets as Communist. The same could be said about the FMLN in El Salvador and numerous other guerrilla movements or parties including the People's Democratic Party of Afghanistan which seized power in 1978 and was identified by the *Washington Post,* in one article, as "agrarian reformers." Ever since the dissolution of the Comintern, there is no official list of Communist parties and movements, and many do not go by the name Communist. Of the 18 ruling Communist Parties, not counting Nicaragua, only 8 call themselves Communist (including that of Yugoslavia which does not call itself a party, but rather a "League"). The others go by such names as the Polish United Workers Party, the E. German Socialist Unity Party, the Kampuchean People's

Revolutionary Party, the Korean Workers Party, the Hungarian Socialist Workers Party, and the like. Communism, in short, is the future that dares not speak its name.

But we will be handicapped in our battles against it unless we dare speak its name, for it is the only name that accurately describes the reality itself, and a thousand other euphemisms, like Marxist or Leftist and even unfriendly ones like totalitarian or Stalinist, too often serve only to blunt the issues at hand.

In addition to restoring to our discourse the name of what it is we are against—Communism—we need to bring new determination and new elan to speaking about what we are for—namely democracy. There are no cultural taboos, akin to the legacy of McCarthyism, that inhibit our speaking about democracy, but still we speak about it too little and with insufficient excitement in part because we take it for granted; in part because it seems too limited or mundane an ideal for passionate devotion and we yearn for something more perfect or more utopian; in part because cultural relativism makes us reluctant to say that our ways are best; in part because we have yielded to cynicism about what less developed countries are capable of.

But we ought not to take democracy for granted because it is precious and can be destroyed. We ought not to view it as insufficient a goal because democracy is the only true utopia. All other utopias that promise perfection or bliss, promise what cannot be delivered. What democracy promises and delivers is to put people's fate in their own hands: it gives them a chance for success and a chance for happiness. And that is about all you can ask of a political system.

And we ought not to be reluctant to say that our way—democracy—is indeed best. This is not arrogance because we are not the ones who created American democracy, we are merely its beneficiaries—and it is not arrogance to wish similar blessings upon other peoples. And we ought not to be cynical about democracy's prospects both because democracy has in fact spread, albeit gradually, to an ever wider area and because our own democracy rests on the premise that all men are endowed with rights that can only be fulfilled through democracy.

Finally, I urge maximum tolerance and fraternity within the democratic camp. There are a range of views and legitimate disagreements, but the differences between liberals and conservatives, between free marketeers, welfare staters and social democrats are all very small gauge compared to the titanic struggle—yes, the Manichean struggle—between democracy and Communism, and these disagreements ought to be debated in a manner that is mindful of that sense of scale.

This stricture applies not only to debates about domestic issues, but also to foreign affairs, which is the realm in which we confront our Communist foe. Combatting this foe is a long and difficult task which must naturally give rise to innumerable debates about strategy and tactics. I, myself, am generally a "hard-liner" on foreign and defense issues, but I do not suppose that recognition of the huge moral distinction between democracy and Communism makes it axiomatic that a tough policy is the right answer to every question.

We hard-liners must bear in mind that it is quite possible for others to favor different policies or tactics without any less patriotism, less love of democracy, less abhorrence of Communism than we feel. Conversely, soft-liners must remember that differences within the democratic camp are far smaller than those between it and the Communist camp, that they, themselves, are infinitely closer to the views and values of Ronald Reagan than those of, say, Daniel Ortega. To castigate Reagan and Ortega equally, or worse, to address Ortega as a fellow opponent of Reagan's policies, is to risk wandering outside the democratic camp.

In urging constructive good spirit in discourse among democrats, do I contradict my own appeal for blunt condemnation of Communism and pro-Communism? No, I merely urge recognition that Lenin was right. The issue of our epoch is the conflict between socialists and democrats. It is a struggle worthy of all the energy and idealism that we can summon.

CHAPTER 4

A "HUMBLE WISDOM"

Michael Novak

It's so odd to talk to a group of people who have gone through the same experiences and the same intellectual journey as I have. I speak almost always to hostile audiences who regard this journey as an apostasy, treason, and all the rest. But I do on such occasions remind myself how big the world really is. My favorite story in this regard is a story I heard in Bern, Switzerland, from someone high in the Foreign Ministry. The story is presumably about the provincialism of the Swiss, but I took it to be about the provincialism of intellectuals. Three years ago, Soviet officials recognizing that the 70th anniversary was coming up (the 70th anniversary of a spate of bad weather) sent a delegation to interview people that might have known Lenin, for the official biography to be issued on the occasion. Remembering a phrase somewhere in Lenin's works about a housekeeper, they went looking all over Europe interviewing older people who might have known someone who had been there. They finally found a man in Bern who had been a housekeeper and perhaps the one mentioned by Lenin. They talked to one man in particular who couldn't quite remember. They showed him pictures of Lenin—with the beard and all the rest—and then mentioned something about a gift of chocolates. And he remembered. "What a nice man he was," he said. "I wonder whatever became of him?"

There is a world saved from things that worry us. The only pessimistic fact to draw from that is that in the world of television such people are going to be harder and harder to find. And the sources of immunity in our society from the general cultural sickness are going to be more difficult to find. As many of you know I studied at one time to be a priest and I remember discussions in theology about whether the priests found hearing confessions interesting. The word among the old veterans was quite the opposite: nothing more boring in the world. The parade of the same fundamental human weaknesses—the lusts, the desires, the prides—and the details no longer matter very much. The sinner believes he has done something extraordinary, exciting, original, only to be repeating an ancient pattern codified even outside of religious terms: human it is to err. There is nothing more common in the world than to sin. Alas, that doesn't give us any excuse either. Because there is also nothing more common and necessary than after a sin or an error, to strive to see more clearly, to do some penance. Repentance is the perennial need of the human race.

But there is another ritual form very active in American politics that I would like only partially to recall, namely, the form of an evangelical meeting, which I think was the ritual form of the New Left, and is often the basic ritual form of much in American life. I bet all of you can remember the moment of your radicalization. The moment of confessing another set of errors in renouncing imperialism or whatever it was that we were then renouncing. And it often occurred in a sort of saw-dust—floor meetinghall in which people confessed publicly how they had suddenly come to have their consciousness raised and now rejected the works and pomps of their previous existence. Recalling both the benefits and dangers of that ritual form, I do now sometimes recall with horror the image of all of those Vietnamese, with whom all of us protesting the war said we were so concerned struggling, a million and a half to two million, to push off by small boat from Vietnam knowing how many would perish in the sea. I can't help feeling that if that ideas have consequences—and those *were* some of the consequences of what we said, wrote, and did—we have blood on our hands. For myself, I also have some sorrow and shame that we took those actions not considering with sufficient clarity what would happen after the war. Some sorrow and shame because by those actions we increased the power of the Soviet Union in the South Pacific.

I have to ask: what is it in myself, what is it in our culture that makes it such a regular occurrence that we come to regret our political actions and political interpretations, and that we particularly embrace a certain, form of utopianism again and again? C.S. Lewis once remarked, rather in the area of love than of politics, that the rise of a rebellious form of love—romantic love, falling in love with love, not with another person—is an oceanic current of Western history that goes back at least to the Crusades. It was a revolt against monogamy, compared to which the Protestant Reformation was like a ripple on an ocean. Arguing in effect less about its political consequences than about its personal consequences, he maintained that there is a distorting virus in Christianity and also in Judaism that leads to a form of rebellion, a premature messianism. I'd like to talk about that disease for a few moments.

One thing that has been overlooked in the rise of the neoconservatives, and the rise of the generation of second thoughts, is that this political rethinking has been followed by a religious rethinking. A reattachment to a certain traditional wisdom, carried by both Christianity and Judaism. Thus when some people are able to say "My Kronstadt was Kronstadt", for many of us we want at a certain point to say something like: I *have* a religion; I don't need politics to be my religion. I have a reference point to something transcendent; my politics don't have to be transcendent. I want my politics judged by its effects, by its real effects in the real world. As for nourishing the needs that I have to belong to the human community and for reference to something that gives meaning to life, beyond the pragmatic, I have Judaism or Christianity. And this distinction is every bit as important as the distinction between church and state in politics, this distinction between utopian and realistic politics.

Now, it's not an accident, I think, that the framers of this most successful of revolutions, in this country, exactly two hundred years ago, made so many references to Judaism and Christianity in justifying their realism. Theirs was the first realistic revolution, which took into full account the vast extent of the power of human sin and human error, and they put on the seal of the United States and on our coinage "In God We Trust," to mean: "Nobody else."

A few words are needed on the image of God on that seal. Remember the pyramid, which at the peak had an eye looking right at you, firm and resolute? No doubt, it is an invocation of providence, of conscience, of God, and a rather bold statement to make for a political experiment. But they were using it as a word of judgment. Hamilton wrote in first *Federalist* that it would be given to his generation to make in this place a decision crucial for all humanity. Given all the blessings of this continent, the possibility of a fresh start, we have the opportunity to decide whether human beings will ever be able to form a government by *reflection* and *choice,* or only by accident and force. They were favored by Providence in getting a new beginning, but they were filled with the sense that they had already botched it. In 1776, had declared their principles, and they had gone on to win the revolutionary war and after they had won the war rebellion and riot had broken out and New York, calling itself the Empire State, had designs on Western Pennsylvania and the rest of the country. The states were in grave danger of falling into war with one another and imposing tariffs on one another. And they felt the humiliation of this great failure. Among a people that could not govern itself, they met again in 1787 to try to constitute a government. It's not enough to make glorious declarations about rights. One must also establish realistic institutions secure to those rights. And in the eyes of the Providence that smiled on their beginnings, they had been humiliated.

Now behind that eye of Providence, there are two features. First, the God of Israel and Christianity. This is a God with such names as Truth, The Way, Judge, and Creator. When the framers spoke of "natural liberty," they spoke not of American liberty but a liberty natural to all of God's created men and women. There's a universalism in the Jewish and Christian "God of Israel." And that God's proper name is Providence, the God of particulars. Of a particular people, of a particular land, and (by the way) a very poor land. Mainly desert. And yet this is the land, this is the people, that the universal God, the Creator, chose. This was very important to the framers. It taught what they called the "humble wisdom." The modest wisdom of Judaism and Christianity. The Creator God, this great God, works through ordinary, humble, and particular things, with all their embarrassments, with all their non-idealistic features.

At the same time, because this God is transcendent he also awakens in some a false idealism—and this is a disease accompanying Judaism and Christianity—it awakens in us a false idealism that goes beyond the flesh, and beyond particular institutions, and makes us ashamed of who we are. It calls us to compare ourselves to some great utopian vision of compassion, of caring, of great oneness. And of course that false ideal is so out of keeping with the real world that the vision can only be achieved by a kind of "consciousness-raising." You have to get out of the real world. And of course it springs out of a sort of hatred of the real world, so it always ends in violence. As soon as you hear people talking about a certain vision of compassion, you should start counting the silverware and preparing to flee. There is a kind of gnosticism, a feeling that a select few will be saved, by a superior knowledge and by simply having superior opinions. You don't have to do anything, only have the right opinions. Gnosticism is a sub–theme in thousands of years of Jewish and Christian history. It's no wonder it should come back in our age.

The hardest lesson to learn in life, it seems to me, is to be reconciled with who we are, and to accept the conditions of human life in their frailty and fragility, and in their sinfulness. Both Judaism and Christianity teach us that the proper name for God is not Justice, but Mercy.

Justice would be too cruel, because if we were held up to this standard, none of us would pass.

But in the same instant that Judaism and Christianity carry this utopian virus by lifting our sights so high, so too we are given a remedy for it. As Madison argued in *Federalist* papers ten and fifty-one, the trick for the Framers was to build institutions for a democratic-republic as remedies for the diseases that are always carried in democratic-republics. They knew well, every republic in history had failed after a few years. The *Federalist* papers are studded with examples of them. Democratic-republics had never succeeded. That's why the Framers called their republic the *Novus Ordo,* the new order, because they thought that they had discovered some new remedies. For the diseases carried by republics and democracies there are three remedies that do help us deal with the dangerous, murderous and utopic drive in all our hearts.

The first remedy is to identify the true God: "Thou shalt not have others before Me." Why not seek God in politics? Politics is much messier, much more imperfect. If you are going to build a new republic, like the Framers, you might as well build it for sinners. The only moral majority there is are sinners. Don't try building your new republic for saints. There are too few of them, and the ones there are are impossible to live with. You've got to build it for people as we are.

Second, Judaism and Christianity intend to defend the concrete, the limited, that's all we are, and we have to learn to defeat our own weaknesses, and make something good out of what there is. The proper name for God then, and the proper aspiration in our own lives, is mercy rather than justice.

Finally, like many of you, my roots are in Eastern Europe, where not much good has happened in a thousand years. The one advantage of having roots there is that pessimism is native to our minds. When things look good we get uneasy. When things look bleak our spirits lift a little. And when things look desperate, the adrenaline is really up. The pessimism so often voiced in *Federalist* suits as perfectly.

We live in a period where we will likely see "P. J. O'Rourke's return of the Balto Cong." AIDS is only a metaphor. The immune deficiency is in our spiritual lives and is deeply damaging. With television there's no place to hide. There are so many people who live in that valley and don't know what happened to Lenin. Living there infuses many with visionary gnosticism. So I think we are heading into a dark future, which is why so many feel so lighthearted and alive, ready for the struggle to come.

AFTERWORD

A NEW LEFT BALANCE SHEET

K.L. Billingsley

> *Whoever controls the past controls the future.*
>
> —George Orwell

> *The struggle of man against power is the struggle of memory against forgetting.*
>
> —Milan Kundera

THE OLD LEFT

> *I'm always thinking about Russia*
> *I can't get her out of my head*
> *I don't give a damn for Uncle Sham*
> *I'm a left-wing radical Red*
>
> —H.H. Lewis

In the eyes of the Old Left, the United States represented the past and its chronicle of oppression. As Carey McWilliams of *The Nation* put it, "America is not only eternally judged but eternally condemned."[1] The Soviet Union, on the other hand, represented a new human dawn, the wave of the Future. Even when it was wrong, Soviet Communism was the hope of the world. Even when it was right, anti-Communism was arrayed on the side of war, exploitation, and man's inhumanity to man.

Such was the Old Left's faith in the new socialist society and its Great Leader, Joseph Stalin, that it was ready to deny or defend the purges and the Terror, the cynically induced famine in the Ukraine, the Nazi-Soviet alliance, and the Moscow show trials, which Owen Lattimore—speaking for most progressives— called a "stroke for democracy."[2] Though the USSR´ violated all the human rights they claimed to hold sacred, the partisans of the Old Left glossed over these crimes in the interests of the Cause, which to them was more important than justice or truth. To acknowledge the truth about the Soviet Union was to play into the hands of the Dark Forces of World Reaction, headquartered in the democratic USA.

The peacetime victims of Soviet Communism ran into the tens of millions, but the Old Left viewed those "liquidations" as necessary to historical progress. As the progressive slogan had it, you can't make an omelet without breaking eggs.

The tide of Soviet atrocities might have been perpetually denied but for the CIA operative who leaked the secret Khruschev Report to the Western press. After reading the Report, some Old Left stalwarts such as Lillian Hellman sneered that Khruschev had "stabbed Stalin in the back."[3] They continued to make excuses for the greatest mass murderer of all time while perceiving themselves and being perceived as enlightened progressives and brave reformers.

Khruschev had actually revealed nothing new. Disillusioned leftists such as Max Eastman, Trotsky and Arthur Koestler had reported these facts and were called renegades and liars and fascists by the Old Left for their trouble. It took some fifty years—half a century—plus an official confession to force the "progressive" faithful to acknowledge the facts. But by then they had moved on to new areas of strategic deception.

At the beginning of the Cold War, publications such as the *Nation* and *Monthly Review* denied that the USSR was expansionist and contended that the Soviet occupation of Eastern Europe was a fully justified defensive measure and progressive to boot. The newly proliferating police states were really "people's democracies," beacons of a new socialist world order.

Forty years later only the most dedicated can deny that the occupation of Eastern Europe was neither defensive nor liberating but aggressive and imperialistic—not a temporary expedient but a permanent occupation. In nearly half a century, the Soviets have not relinquished one inch of seized territory and have brutally crushed democratic reform movements in Hungary, Czechoslovakia, and Poland. *Monthly Review* sanctioned these repressions as a kind of "radicalism of the blackjack."[4]

Far from evolving into a new species of "democracy," the USSR's Eastern European colonies continue as police states and prison camps. Like their Soviet master, the Eastern Bloc regimes are all social and economic failures. As Romanian novelist Panait Istrati observed, "I can see the broken eggs, but where is this omelet of yours?"[5]

In view of what was fully known by the early 1960s, it would not have seemed possible for the New Left to continue the patterns of the Old and call it "idealism." But while the new, post-Stalin Left in America professed to reject the Soviet model, it managed to keep the faith just the same.

THE NEW LEFT

The triumph of the Cuban Revolution in 1959 was the first international cause of the New Left. New Leftists became Fidel Castro's American mouthpieces, blaming pre-revolutionary Cuba's social and economic problems on U.S. imperialism. What Cuba needed was a revolutionary social transformation that would end its dependence on U.S. corporations.

The liberation of Vietnam was the New Left's second and most important international cause. The victory of the National Liberation Front and a U.S. defeat would pave the way for national independence for all of Indo-China, economic well-being, social justice, and, above all, peace.

In China, the New Left welcomed the Cultural Revolution and hailed its leader Mao Tse-Tung as a national savior and a hero for the age.

Twenty years have passed and the New Left, like the regimes it has supported, now possesses not only a Glorious Future, but also a recoverable past, open to scrutiny and judgement like any other. Nonetheless, the record of the New Left remains for the most part stuffed down the public memory hole, where many doubtless would like it to remain. Those with corpses in their closet tend to view any probing of their political past as a kind of necrophilia. Or better still, *McCarthyism.*

Employing idealistic phrases like "social liberation" and "social justice," the New Left has enjoyed a kind of innocence by association. But after a quarter of a century, the statute of limitations on such immunity has run out. It is time to examine the New Left's balance sheet on Cuba, Vietnam, and other "liberated zones," and set the record straight.

THE NEW LEFT AND CUBA

With the ideological capital of the USSR used up, the New Left began to transfer the hagiographical fantasies once inspired by Stalin to Fidel

Castro. As Dennis Wrong has observed, Castro was, "a natural hero for the New Left from the first."[6] Castro presented himself to the world as a democrat. His revolution, he said, was not red nor red, white and blue, but Cuban olive green. To Norman Mailer, "it was as if the ghost of Cortez had appeared in our century riding Zapata's white horse. The first and greatest hero to appear in the world since the second War." Castro further gave "a bit of life to the best and most passionate men and women all over the earth" and was "the best answer to the argument of the Commissars and Statesmen that revolutions cannot last, that they turn corrupt or total or eat their own."[7] Dave Dellinger saw in the Castro regime "the possibility of a genuine libertarian communism."[8] Elizabeth Sutherland assured *Nation* readers that Castro was "first of all, utterly devoted to the welfare of his people."[9] Paul Sweezy and Leo Huberman insisted that "first and foremost, Fidel is a passionate humanitarian."[10] To Saul Landau, Castro was "a man who has been steeped in democracy . . . a humble man."[11]

Yippee leader Abbie Hoffman liked Fidel's macho political style. Wrote Hoffman: "Fidel sits on the side of a tank rumbling into Havana on New Year's Day . . . girls throw flowers at the tank and rush to tug playfully at his black beard. He laughs joyously and pinches a few rumps . . .the tank stops in the city square. Fidel lets the gun drop to the ground, slaps his thigh and stands erect. He is like a mighty penis coming to life, and when he is tall and straight, the crowd immediately is transformed."[12]

Julius Lester summed up the New Left's position by stating, accurately, that "Fidel is Cuba . . .Cuba is Fidel."[13]

The fact that, like Stalin, Castro had killed, jailed or exiled many of his revolutionary colleagues did not affect this tide of adulation. Nor, for the most part, did his subsequent denunciation by Jean-Paul Sartre. Few on the American left were bothered by Castro's approval of the Soviet invasion of Czechoslovakia in 1968. Other New Leftists, like Saul Landau, even survived Nat Hentoff's searing portrait of Castro's crimes, "The Revolutionary As Sadist," when it appeared in the *Village Voice* twenty years later. In May 1987, Landau wrote that "under Fidel, the Cubans have done an admirable job," and that Castro was "the greatest figure in Latin American history since Bolivar."[14] Landau described Cuba as "the first purposeful society that we have had in the Western Hemisphere for many years—its the first society where human beings are treated as human beings, where men have a certain dignity, and where this is guaranteed to them."[15]

And the reality? Where the Batista regime had controlled Cuban politics, the Castro regime controls everything; it is the first totalitarian state in the Americas. Staple foods are rationed and in short supply. Block committees and a secret police force keep watch on everyone and everything. Cuban life is effectively nationalized on the Eastern European model. Here is the way former Fidelista and editor of *Revolucion* Carlos Franqui sums up the results: "We used to have one main prison, now we have many. We used to have a few barracks; now we have many. We used to have many plantations; now we have only one, and it belongs to Fidel. Who enjoys the fruits of the revolution, the houses of the rich, the luxuries of the rich? The *comandante* and his court."[16]

Socialist food shortages do not bother Castro's American apologists. Jonathan Kozol writes that "the long lines . . . the ration cards, and other forms of deprivation do not seem to dampen the high spirits of most people."[17] Similiarly, in the 1960s over a million Cubans fled, sometimes making a getaway on pieces of wood or inner tubes. The mass exodus, however, did not trouble the New Left, which considered them the remnants of a capitalist past unable to adapt to the new society. Their departure only confirmed the radical nature of the changes that the revolution had wrought.

In the Spring of 1980 some 120,000 more Cubans fled through the port of Mariel. Although most of these had grown up under Castro and were fleeing poverty and repression, Philip Brenner of the Institute for Policy Studies described them as "animated by nostaligia for the Batista regime."[18] Johnetta Cole (now President of Spelman College) chastised the refugees as people "who have been unwilling to work and would want to live off crime and prostitution."[19]

Though pre-Castro Cuba had the highest standard of living in Latin America, the New Left charged that US imperialism kept it from fulfilling its potential. But twenty-eight years of Castro dictatorship have transformed Cuba into one of the poorest nations in the Americas, with an annual growth rate of *minus* 1.2 percent and a per capita national income of $810, worse than Jamaica and the Dominican Republic.[20] At a time when Eastern Bloc countries like Hungary are successfully experimenting with the free market, Cuba has banned the classified ads section of newspapers on the grounds that they "encouraged capitalist ideas."[21]

Another common charge of the New Left in the Sixties was that the U.S. purposely kept Cuba a one-crop economy, a crime for a land blessed with good soil and a pleasant climate. U.S. imperialism forced Cubans to grow sugar for the international market rather than food for the people themselves. But, after three decades of revolution, Cuba remains a one crop economy more dependent on its new Soviet market than it ever was on the United States.

Even those favorably disposed toward the regime note that the Cuban Revolution is "at a dead end," and a "failure." A quarter-century under Castro has produced a "bored and fatigued nation" in which "no decision can be made unless Fidel signs it."[22]

The obvious economic and social failure of the Cuban Revolution has illicited few apologies or changes of mind on the Left; silence is the preferred response.

The New Left was fond of decrying what it perceived as excessive American influence or "imperialism" in Cuba. However, soon after Castro's takeover the island became a *de facto* Soviet colony and military base.

Not only has Cuba become an outpost of Soviet imperialism, but an aggressive agent of its expansion. It is likely that Cuba now has more men under arms on a *per capita* basis than any country in the world. Except for Brazil, with many times the population, Cuba has the largest military in Latin America.[23] A large portion of these forces serve as a mercenary army for the Soviet Union in Angola, Ethiopia, and Nicaragua. There are some 37,000 Cuban troops in Angola alone, and it is estimated that over 10,000 Cubans have perished there since 1976 (in American terms, more soldiers than died in World War II).[24] In addition to its African interventionism, Castro trains and equips revolutionary guerrillas throughout Latin America, in the hopes that they will establish other Cubas.

In 1969, Susan Sontag claimed that no Cuban writer "has been or is in jail or is failing to get his works published."[25] According to Amnesty International and other sources: the poet Miguel Salas was given a twenty-five year sentence for preparing to flee Cuba. Angel Cuadra, another poet, was sentenced to fifteen years. Tomas Travieso was imprisoned after his play was produced in Miami. Amaro Gomez was sentenced to eight years for possessing a copy of *The Gulag Archipelago*. Heberto Padilla was arrested, jailed, and forced to recite a bogus "confession." Rene Ariza, winner of the 1967 Cuban Writer's Union Award, was locked up for eight years for "defaming the Revolution." When guards found unorthodox poetry in the cell of Raul Martinez, he was given an *additional* sentence of fifteen years.[26] While some denied these repressions, others justified them. Joseph Kahl wrote that "the independent intellectual, the critic of all societies and all beliefs, is a luxury that [the Cuban regime] cannot afford."[27]

"The chief difference between Batista and Castro," writes historian

Hugh Thomas, "was not that the first was ruthless and the second just; on the contrary, Batista's tyranny seems, from the angle of the present, a mild and indolent undertaking, an insult to responsible citizens, no doubt, but far removed from the iron certainties imposed by Castro."[28]

Cuba holds more long term political prisoners than any country in the world. The sentences of these prisoners are the longest in the Communist Bloc and many inmates are kept long after their sentences have expired. The captives may be described as Fidel's personal prisoners, since he frees them at whim, often as a gesture of good faith for foreign admirers of himself and his regime such as Jesse Jackson.[29]

The poet Armando Valladares was the best known of Amnesty International's adopted prisoners of conscience, and was released after twenty-two years at the behest of French President Francois Mitterand. Alexander Cockburn of *The Nation* criticized not the jailer but the prisoner, condemning the "propaganda campaign against Cuba" and the "commotion over Valladares."[30]

Pierre Charette, a *Quebecois* revolutionary who spent ten years in Havana, described the entire island of Cuba as a "concentration camp, where the prisons served as dungeons for those with the hardest heads."[31] Those who refuse political indoctrination are brutalized, beaten, and denied medical treatment.[32] There is substantial evidence that Cuban prisoners are subjected to biological experiments.[33]

The religious Left was an important component of the New Left in the 1960s and 1970s. Armando Valladares has revealed how some American religious Leftists actually contributed to the misery of Cuban prisoners. A delegation of American churchmen visited Cuba in 1977, well after many of the regimes human rights' abuses had been publicized. Robert McAfee Brown and James Armstrong, the former president of the National Council of Churches, issued no moral condemnations of Cuba, but were "profoundly impressed and humbled by a secular government that is carrying out the gospel demand to feed the hungry." The visitors were so fond of standards that they had two of them: "There is a significant difference between situations where people are imprisoned for opposing regimes designed to *perpetuate* inequities (as in Chile and Brazil, for example) and situations in which people are imprisoned for opposing regimes designed to *remove* inequities (as in Cuba)." [Emphasis added, parentheses theirs].[34]

Valladares writes that "every time a clergyman would write an article in support of Fidel Castro's dictatorship, a translation would reach us, and that was worse for the Christian political prisoners than the beatings or the hunger."[35] Defense of his regime by prominent foreigners only helped convince Castro that he could repress and jail with impunity. In similar fashion, the Old Left's defense of Stalin only increased the misery of his victims.

THE NEW LEFT AND VIETNAM

> *And before I'll be fenced in*
> *I'll vote for Ho Chi Minh*
> *and go back to the North and be free*

—song mailed from the SDS national office[36]

For the New Left, the Vietnam War was an ongoing dramatization of the Cause, a political morality play about good and evil in which the American Goliath confronted the Vietnamese David, who, though small and weak, had History on his side. Stokely Carmichael insisted that the "real reason" the U.S. was in Vietnam was to "serve the economic interests of American businessmen who are in Vietnam solely to exploit the tungsten, tin and oil."[37] Susan Sontag wrote that Vietnam was "stationed inside my conscience as a quintessential image of the suffering and heroism of the weak."[38] For Noam Chomsky, Vietnam was "the cause of humanity as it moves forward toward liberty and justice, toward the socialist society in which free, creative men control their own destiny."[39]

The reality was somewhat different. The partitioning of Vietnam in 1954 had left the North under a group of Stalinists who in 1956 forcibly collectivized the country's agriculture. As in the Soviet Union and China, the collectivization process was accompanied by massive terror, with entire segments of the population "liquidated" for being on the wrong side of the Marxist political equation.

New Left stalwarts Tom Hayden and Staughton Lynd travelled to North Vietnam and returned to explain that "the events of 1956" were "part of the struggle against the French" and that the violence, "should be assessed in the same context as the terror of the resistance itself."[40] Nearly a million refugees made a different assessment and fled to the South.

From 1959 to 1961, the number of South Vietnamese officials assassinated by the Vietcong rose from 1,200 a year to nearly 4,000.[41] Away from the roving eye of U.S. TV crews, the Vietcong conducted a terror campaign for the duration of the war. Eighty percent of their victims were ordinary civilians, peasants, and teachers. As witnessed by Austrian journalist Bruno Knoebl, the Vietcong sometimes executed their victims by disembowelment, with villagers forced to attend.[42] The Northern forces and insurgents sowed terror with mines designed to blow up only the most heavily loaded busses. They thus proved to the people that the South Vietnamese government was unable to protect them.[43]

Like most New Leftists, Princeton University Law Professor Richard Falk justified these war crimes, writing that "the insurgent faction in an underdeveloped country has, at the beginning of its struggle for power, *no alternative other than terror* to mobilize an effective operation." [emphasis added][44] Falk later hailed the advent of the Ayatollah Khomeni as a triumph for the oppressed people of Iran.

Brigades of New Left worthies journeyed to North Vietnam to report that the insurgents were gentle, peaceful people attempting to build a "rice-roots" democracy. The Stalinist dictator, Ho Chi Minh, even reminded Father Daniel Berrigan of Jesus Christ.[45] Other North Vietnamese commissars, like the saints and martyrs of the Church according to Berrigan possessed "great reserves of compassion."[46]

When American forces took the fight to the North in bombing campaigns, Berrigan charged that "a monstrous and intentionally genocidal air war" was being carried out.[47] Susan Sontag said that it was "self evident" that an "organic connection" existed between "the *Reader's Digest,* Lawrence Welk, Hilton Hotels, and napalming."[48] The International War Crimes Tribunal, composed of such North Vietnamese partisans as Dave Dellinger, Simone de Beauvoir, and Stokely Carmichael, charged that the U.S. was "waging a war like that waged by fascist Japan and Nazi Germany."[49] The evidence for these charges seemed to be provided by on-the-spot reporting by *New York Times* reporter Harrison Salisbury, whose dispatches from Hanoi created the impression that the U.S. was deliberately bombing civilian targets. It was subsequently revealed, however, that Salisbury's reports were taken directly from North Vietnamese propaganda. Though Salisbury was later denied a Pulitzer prize because of his faulty sources, the damage had been done.[50] The truth, as reported by neutral observers such as English journalist James Cameron, as well as outside military specialists, was that U.S. attacks were exclusively against military targets, and that civilian damage was accidental, not intentional.[51]

Jean-Paul Sartre, Theodore Draper, Daniel Berrigan, Frances FitzGerald, Richard Falk, and others charged that the U.S. deliberately conducted a policy of genocide against the people of Vietnam.[52] These inflammatory charges ignored the fact of steady population *increase* in Vietnam during the war years. At the height of the bombing, and when

South Vietnamese youths were being conscripted for combat by the Saigon dictatorship, there was no stream of "boat people" fleeing their country with tales of genocide. That would only happen *after* U.S. withdrawal and defeat. Even Daniel Ellsberg was forced to admit that the Vietnam War was "no more brutal than other wars in the past."[53]

The death of several hundred civilians at the hands of American troops at My Lai became a *cause celebre* for the New Left, but atrocities of far greater magnitude by the North caused no stir at all. During the occupation of Hue, North Vietnamese regulars murdered some 3,000–5000 civilians; many were shot and buried in mass graves after having their hands chopped off. Others were tortured or buried alive.[54] As confirmed by Vietnamese documents, these atrocities were not an aberration but a calculated policy for which no one was court martialed or sentenced, as was the case with many American soldiers guilty of war crimes.

Mary McCarthy summed up the New Left attitude with her disbelief that the Communists could do such things. "There is no way of knowing what really happened," she wrote, "I prefer to think that it was the Americans" who had done it.[55]

Ninety-five of the American military men taken prisoner by the North Vietnamese were tortured to extract propaganda statements or military information. Twenty percent of the American prisoners died in captivity, with most of the deaths avoidable.[56] French journalist Olivier Todd, a man of the Left disillusioned by what he had discovered, wrote that in a Communist regime there can be no torture "by accident." The fact that uniformed officers carried out the torture was conclusive evidence that it was official policy.

In an article entitled "How I let Myself be Deceived by Hanoi," Todd wrote that the torture "exposes the true nature of the Hanoi regime."[57] No such honesty was forthcoming from the New Left partisans of the North in America, whose actions and words only worsened the prisoners' plight. When Jane Fonda, William Sloane Coffin, Cora Weiss, Noam Chomsky and others visited the North, they denied that prisoners were mistreated. Some harangued American troops over Radio Hanoi. Coffin and Weiss participated in a prisoner release staged for publicity. Richard Falk, Richard Barnet, Dave Dellinger, Seymour Hersh, Ramsey Clark and others downplayed reports of torture or dismissed them as myths and hoaxes.[58]

During this sorry episode, the New Left resurrected the career of the Communist "journalist" Wilfred Burchett, an old Stalinist who had participated in the interrogation of American prisoners in Korea as a KGB agent and invented tales of germ warfare during that conflict and now was a propagandist for the Hanoi regime.[59] Alexander Cockburn, whose father had been a flack for Stalin's secret police in the Thirties, celebrated Burchett as his journalistic hero. For many news services Burchett became an authoritative but often unidentified "source." As an example of the sinister fatuity of which the New Left was capable, some even claimed that the injuries of the U.S. prisoners had been inflicted by American doctors on their return.[60]

The New Left did more than help topple the "essential domino" of public opinion. Through such groups as the Coalition for a New Foreign and Military Policy, they did everything possible to precipitate the withdrawal of U.S. forces. They were rewarded with such measures as the Case-Church and McGovern-Hatfield amendments, which cut off military aid to South Vietnam and sealed its fate. After the Paris Peace Accords were signed, the North's "final offensive" began; without U.S. military support, Saigon quickly fell on April 30, 1975. The liberation hailed by the New Left had finally arrived.

Contrary to New Left propaganda, American withdrawal brought neither peace nor social justice to Vietnam. In 1976, French journalist Jean Lacouture wrote that "never before have we had such proof of so many detained after a war."[61] The Vietnamese Communists herded hundreds of thousands into "re-education centers" and executed tens of thousands more. The Reverend William Sloane Coffin (now head of SANE), Richard Barnet, Cora Weiss, Corliss Lamont, Richard Falk, Paul Sweezy, among others, took out a newspaper ad defending the Vietnamese regime as an example of "moderation" and blaming the United States for any problems that might exist.[62] The National Lawyers Guild stated that the "re-education program" was "absolutely necessary," and that it was being carried out in a "remarkable spirit of moderation."[63]

As they had done in Cuba, personnel from the National Council of Churches sprang to the defense of the regime. In testimony before Congress, they compared the re-education camps to "tropical resorts" and referred to the inmates not as prisoners but as "camp members" engaged in a "work/study experience."[64]

But the hundreds of thousands who fled—the "boat people"—gave the lie to such apologists. Not only did they fail to blame the U.S. for their plight, but it was their most desperate hope to gain admission to reach its shores, or to any non-Communist country that would accept them. Jim Wallis, a Leftist pastor, activist, and editor of *Sojourner* magazine, wrote that the boat people were those who had been "intoxicated with a taste for Western lifestyle during the war years" and were "fleeing to support their consumer habit in other lands."[65]

Those who remained had to cope as best they might with a Stalinist police state that accepted less dissent than the Kremlin, and whose economic policies were unable to provide the basic necessities of life to its inmates. To pay off its debt to its Soviet masters, Vietnam's Communist regime began shipping "labor brigades" to the USSR and the Socialist Bloc to perform menial tasks. Estimates are that 200,000 Vietnamese work abroad, in such extreme and unfamiliar climates as Siberia. Work "terms" are four to seven years; families must be left behind; the work is never chosen but rather assigned. While abroad the "guest workers" are housed in crude hostels and kept under constant surveillance.[66] The plight of these twentieth-century slaves is totally ignored by the Left.

As the record shows, the New Left managed to get it all wrong: the Vietnamese Communists were aggressors, not victims; brutal, not gentle; imperialistic and pro-Soviet, not nationalistic. Vietnam's army, the fourth largest in the world, has invaded and occupied Cambodia and Laos, and now threatens Thailand. The Soviet military has set up shop at Da Nang and Cam Ranh Bay and is reaching out into the Pacific. With help from the Left, millions of people are now guaranteed a life of repression, poverty and abject servitude. Douglas Pike's 1970 prediction of what would take place after a Communist victory has been uncannily fulfilled: "All foreigners would be cleared out, especially the hundreds of newsmen . . . a curtain of ignorance would descend. Then would begin a night of the long knives . . . but little of this would be known abroad. The communists in Vietnam would create a silence. The world would call it peace."[67]

SIDESHOW: THE NEW LEFT AND CAMBODIA

> The red, red blood splatters the cities and plains
> Of the Cambodian fatherland
> The sublime blood of the worker and peasants,
> The blood of revolutionary combatants of both sexes
>
> —the national anthem of "Democratic Kampuchea"

The capital city of Cambodia, Phnompenh, fell to the Khmer Rouge forces on April 17, 1975. Noam Chomsky had predicted that, after such a takeover, "a new era of economic development and social justice" would lie ahead, once the progressives he admired and supported were at the helm.[68] But the Khmer Rouge leader, Pol Pot, proclaiming "Year Zero", proceeded to forcibly evacuate the city of several million people;

the old, the infirm, those in hospitals, were marched into the countryside. On April 18, 1975, Fernand Scheller, a United Nations Official, warned that "what the Khmer Rouge is doing is pure genocide. They will kill more people this way than if there had been fighting in the city."[69] Like the doctrinaire Marxist-Leninists that they were, the Khmer Rouge killed on the basis of class, for offenses as minor as wearing glasses and speaking foreign languages, both indicative of a "bourgeois" origin. Families were tortured and murdered together.[70] Two common forms of execution were cudgeling and suffocation with plastic bags, both apparently used to save ammunition.[71] It is estimated that out of a population of seven million, nearly two million perished. The bloodbath that conservative anti-Communists predicted in the wake of American withdrawal did take place and could not be denied by any honest observer.

Yet New Left veteran, Daniel Schecter, now a $100,000 a year producer with ABC-TV's 20/20, returned from Indochina after the massacres raving about the revolutionary achievements of Pol Pot and sporting a t-shirt that boasted: "We Won in Cambodia." Nor was Schechter alone. Noam Chomsky and Edward Herman dismissed the reports of genocide as mere "tales" designed to resurrect America's "imperial ideology." Gareth Porter, whose book on Cambodia Chomsky praised, testified to Congress that the reports of genocide were "totally baseless" and a "fantasy." The regime was merely implementing a policy of "self-reliance" and there had been "mistakes." If there had been any real suffering, the U.S. was to blame. (Congressman Stephen Solarz called Porter's testimony contemptible and compared him to those who deny Hitler's atrocities against Jews).[72] Nor did the Left remain content with defending a genocidal regime; they promoted it as well. Another contingent of credulous apologists went to Cambodia and returned with glowing reports. ("U.S. Leftist Editor Says Cambodians are Thriving" NY Times, 5/12/78)[73]

Not even a genocide proved sufficient to disturb the political dogmas of the hard-core American Left.

THE NEW LEFT AND CHAIRMAN MAO

Political power is the power to oppress others.

—Mao Tse-tung

"Traditional China, based on institutions and ideas developed over 2,000 years ago, did not die a clean and quiet death," wrote Michael Chinoy (now a correspondent for Cable News Network) in 1975; "a violent revolution and bitter civil war were necessary to sweep away the decay, exploitation and backwardness of old China."

In a society more secretive than the Soviet Union, there is no way of knowing how many victims this revolution claimed. There were death sentences for a wide variety of crimes. Every day the papers published lists of those who had been executed. The revolutionary government stated in 1951 that 800,000 cases had been "dealt with" in the first six months of the year, and Chou En Lai later admitted that 16.8 percent had received death sentences, which works out to 22,500 executions a month. Other estimates of the total number killed in the early days of the regime run to 15 million, far outpacing the National Socialist regime in Germany.[74] Efforts to collectivize agriculture caused massive famine, as they did before in the Soviet Union and later in Ethiopia. But these facts did not enter the picture created by the American Left.

"In China," wrote Corliss Lamont, "even though it remains a dictatorship, they don't shoot their dissenters; they re-educate' them."[75] Harvard Professor, John K. Fairbank reported that "the people seem healthy, well fed and articulate about their role as citizens of Chairman Mao's New China . . .the change in the countryside is miraculous. . . . The Maoist revolution is on the whole the best thing that happened to the Chinese people in centuries. . . . Maoism has got results." Hans Konigsberger described "a country which had become almost as painstakingly careful about human lives as New Zealand."[76] Ramparts editor, David Kolodny, wrote that "at the same time that we adopted the Chinese model of revolutionary purity as political touchstone . . . we drew upon it as a source of energy and hope. China served as proof that the revolutionary process can make a difference, that it can realize a vision of fundamental social change . . . China's intransigence gave us hope . . .the real importance of the Chinese revolution to the American Left was . . . in the widely held conviction that this revolution was really revolutionary."[77] Tom Hayden and Staughton Lynd found a "different world" in Peking. "We could feel the West was behind us . . . everyone has the pulse of purposeful activity."[78]

The American Left did not protest when the Chinese revolutionaries invaded, crushed, and annexed Tibet. Nor when the Communists slaughtered one million Tibetans and destroyed 6,000 monasteries and a 2,500-year-old culture in the decade that followed. In 1979, China invaded Vietnam, but Cora Weiss and other New Leftists found a way to blame even this invasion on the United States.[79]

When the Great Leap Forward and the eight "antis" campaign did not get the job done to Mao's satisfaction, the Chairman concluded that a "cultural revolution" was needed and launched the greatest witch-hunt in human history. Michael Chinoy saw such a cultural revolution as necessary because "traditional values still exist in China, even as the Chinese attempt to eliminate them." The proven way to accomplish this was by murdering those who held them. The most reliable estimates of those killed by the Red Guards during the Cultural Revolution is 4,000,000. With complete impunity the Red Guards persecuted teachers, religious believers, and scientists, burned books and shut down theaters. Homosexuality became a capital crime.[80] At a point of maximum chaos, Mao declared: "let the students fight for another ten years. The earth will revolve as usual. Heaven is not going to fall."[81]

In a book published by the National Council of Churches, Stuart Dowty wrote that "while Liberation turned the whole society toward socialism, the Cultural Revolution deepened and continues that process. Mutant social growths were identified and unceremoniously uprooted."[82] Hitler's apologists could not have expressed it better.

In writing of Mao's China Rev. Eugene Stockwell of the National Council of Churches stumbled onto an early formulation of liberation theology, stating that "the vast social improvements in China are the work of the Holy Spirit" and the "part of God's work in China may be to challenge us in the West to re-look at our own social system where injustice or repression is institutionalized or condoned."[83]

It escapes the Left's notice that tiny, capitalistic Taiwan, with a population of 17 million, *1.6 percent* of Mainland China's has a per capita GNP *six times* that of the Communist regime. Life expectancy in Taiwan rose from 58.6 years in 1952 to 70.7 years in 1979 and Third World-style poverty has been eliminated. (By contrast, life expectancy and the pace of economic growth have declined in Cuba since the revolution).[84] Nor is Taiwan the only such example of capitalist success. In Singapore, Hong Kong and South Korea, economic growth, life expectancy and annual income far outstrip that of comparable states in the socialist bloc.[85] Moreover, while these states are not democracies in the Western sense, they provide many more freedoms than the regimes in Cuba, North Korea and mainland China—like the freedom to organize trade unions, strike and vote in multi-party elections.

The man of the future is the one who will have the longest memory.

—Nietzsche

Don't imagine that for years on end you can make yourself the bootlicking propagandist of the Soviet regime or of any other regime and then suddenly return to mental decency.

—Orwell

In seventy years, Marxist-Leninist totalitarianism has killed and enslaved more people, created more refugees, caused more human misery and suffering, and destroyed more of the past's heritage than all previous tyrannies since the dawn of time. In view of this record, it takes a special kind of moral blindness to maintain the apologetic patterns of the Left. So rigid is the Left's scenario of who are the carriers of good and evil in our time that Leftists are able to believe that some of the most brutal and obscurantist tyrannies are models of social justice and equality, and that these tyrannies must be defended in the name of human progress. At the same time they are also able to believe that the freest, most productive, most tolerant societies in history—particularly the USA—are actually the most oppressive regimes, and that these societies are to be disparaged and attacked at every opportunity.

The Left—the *internacionalistas*—do not live in the gulags they defend; those are for other people—mainly Third World people—clearly of less importance than themselves. These Leftists maintain a hypocritical and elitist posture, availing themselves of the freedoms, privileges, and material advantages of the very societies they despise. They use the privileges of freedom and democracy to undermine the foundations of freedom and democracy.

Like the Old Left before them, New Left radicals have, in Frances FitzGerald's words, "performed a kind of surgery on their critical faculties."[86] In most cases, such surgery appears to be irreversible: "As I am writing this, more than twenty years later," Arthur Koestler lamented in the 1950s, "the storm is still on. The well meaning 'progressives of the Left' persist in following their old, outworn concepts. As if under the spell of a destructive compulsion, they must repeat every single error of the past, draw the same faulty conclusions a second time, re-live the same situations, perform the same suicidal gestures. One can only watch in horror and despair, for this time, there will be no pardon."

NOTES

1. Quoted in William O'Neill, *A Better World*, NY Simon and Schuster, 1982, 285

2. Ibid. p. 276

3. Quoted in Arthur Eckstein, "Lillian Hellman, True and False" *Chronicles* September, 1987, p. 38

4. O'Neill, op. cit. p. 211

5. Quoted in Heller and Nekrich, *Utopia in Power,* Summit 1986 p. 259

6. Quoted in Paul Hollander, *Political Pilgrims,* p. 243

7. Hollander, ibid. p. 236

8. Ibid. p. 244

9. Ibid. p. 238

10. Ibid. p. 239

11. Ibid.

12. Ibid. p. 238

13. Ibid. p. 239

14. *Monthly Review,* May 1987

15. Ibid.p.223

16. Carlos Franqui, *Family Portrait With Fidel.*

17. Hollander, p. 254

18. Hollander, p.233

19. "Scholars Here Assess the Exodus from Cuba," *Daily Hampshire Gazette* May 13, 1980

20. Paul Johnson, *Modern Times,* NY 1983 p.628

21. San Diego Union, 9/14/86

22. Tad Szulc, *Fidel A Critical Portrait,* 1987

23. Johnson, op cit

24. *LA Times* 6/16/87

25. Hollander, p. 266

26. Ibid.

27. Ibid.

28. Hugh Thomas, "Castro Plus Twenty," *Encounter* October 1978

29. Aryeh Neier, "20 Years in Jail for Insulting Fidel" *USA Today* 6/28/84. See also the Cuban section in the *Amnesty International Report* for 1984–1986. A collection of human rights data on Cuba is available from "On Human Rights," Georgetown University, Box 2160 Hoya Stn. Washington DC 20057

30. *The Nation* 9/20/86

31. Quote in Lloyd Billingsley, *The Generation That Knew Not Josef,* Portland Multnomoah Press, 1985 p. 126

32. See Cuba entry in Amnesty International's *Torture in the Eighties,* 1984.

33. Jose Goig, "Cuban Captives Describe Brutality" *San Diego Union,* 3/35/87)

34. Statements of Church Leaders After Visiting Cuba, June 19–28 1977, quoted in *A Time For Candor* Washington, Institute for Religion and Democracy, 1983, 81

35. Quoted in Humberto Belli, *Breaking Faith* Westchester, Crossway Books, 1986, 247)

36. Quoted in Paul Berman, "Don't Follow Leaders," *The New Republic,* August 10, 1987

37. *NY Times* 3/30/67

38. Hollander, p. 267

39. Quoted in Sidney Hook, *Out of Step* Harper and Row, 1987, 594

40. Hollander, p. 424
41. Stanley Karnow, *Vietnam: A History* NY 1984, p. 238
42. Bruno Knoebl, *Victor Charlie: The Face of War in Viet-Nam* NY, 1967, 95–96
43. Guenter Lewy, *America in Vietnam* NY 1978, pp.272–273
44. Lewy, p. 271
45. Hollander, p. 374
46. Ibid. p. 273
47. Lewy, p. 400
48. Hollander, p. 414
49. Lewy, p. 312
50. Lewy, p. 401
51. Lewy, pp. 304, 405–6
52. Ibid. pp. 299–304
53. Lewy, p. 300
54. Karnow, p. 530
55. Hollander, p. 67
56. Lewy, pp.333–340
57. Lewy, p. 338
58. Lewy, pp.334–342
59. Lewy, pp. 340, 342, 344
60. Joan Colebrook, "Prisoners of War," *Commentary*, January 1974
61. Peter Collier and David Horowitz, "Lefties for Reagan," *Washington Post* March 17, 1985.
62. Ibid.
63. Hollander, p. 270
64. See joint statement of Rev. Paul McCleary and Midge Austin Meinertz of the NCC's Church World Service, *Human Rights in Vietnam,* June 21, 1977
65. Jim Wallis, "Compassion, Not Politics for Refugees, *Sojourners,* September 1979.
66. Maxine Pollack, Thousands of Citizens Sent to Uncertain East Bloc Future," *Insight,* 7/27/87
67. Lewy, p. 278
68. Collier & Horowitz, op cit
69. Quoted in John Barron and Anthony Paul, *Murder of Gentle Land,* NY Reader's Digest Press, 1977 p. 203. Though denounced as a cold war tract when released, this volume has stood the test of time. See Arch Puddington, "Pol Pot in Retrospect" *Commentary,* May 1987.
70. Karnow, p. 45
71. David Miller, "The Continuing Conflict in Southeast Asia" in Rays Bonds, ed. *The Vietnam War: The Illustrated History of the Conflict in South East Asia* NY Crown, 1979.
72. See Porter's statement in *Human Right in Cambodia.* Subcommittee on International Organization of the Committee on International Relations, House of Representatives, 1977. See also Hollander, p. 447.
73. Hollander, p. 448
74. Johnson, op. cit. p.548
75. Hollander, p. 339
76. Ibid. p.283

77. Ibid. p.282
78. Ibid. p.293
79. Hollander, p.69
80. Fox Butterfield, *China, Alive in the Bitter Sea,* NY New York Times 1982, p. 145.
81. Johnson, op. cit. p. 566–561
82. Stuart Dowty, "Work China" in *China: People-Questions,* p. 22. Dowty also authored *Huan-Ying: Workers' China,* published by Monthly Review Press
83. Quoted in Raymond and Rhea Whithead, *China: Search for Community* NY Friendship Press, 1978, 61.
84. Peter L. Berger, *The Capitalist Revolution,* NY Basic Books, 1986, 147.
85. Ibid. pp. 140–171
86. Hollander, p. 231

THE SECOND THOUGHTS CONFERENCE
Sponsored by
The National Forum Foundation
Washington, D.C. October 17–18, 1987
Co-chairs: Peter Collier & David Horowitz

Saturday Morning 9–12:00
Welcome: Peter Collier

I. Second Thoughts on a Political Decade
Chair: David Horowitz

1. Richard Neuhaus
2. David Hawk
3. David Ifshin
4. Doan Van Toai
5. Jeff Herf

Interlocutor: Sam Leiken

Lunch 12:00–1:30
Speakers: Fanor Avendano, Fausto Amador, Anthony Ibarra-Rojas

Saturday Afternoon 1:30–4:30
II. Second Thoughts on Revolution: The Case of Nicaragua
Chair: Peter Collier

1. Ron Radosh
2. Robert Leiken
3. Arturo Cruz
4. Xavier Arguello
5. Fausto Amador
6. Bruce Cameron

Interlocutor: K.L. Billingsley

Saturday Evening 6:00–10:00
III. Dinner & Program "Generational Perspectives"
M.C. P. J. O'Rourke

Panel Chair: Martin Peretz

1. Hilton Kramer
2. William Phillips
3. Irving Kristol
4. Norman Podhoretz
5. Nathan Glazer

Sunday Morning 9–12:00

    IV. Second Thoughts on a Political Culture

       Chair: Peter Collier

       1. Michael Medved
       2. Carol Iannone
       3. Stephen Schwartz
       4. Glenn Loury
       5. Michael Novak

       Interlocutor: K.L. Billingsley

Lunch   12:00–1:30

    V. Speaker Julius Lester

       The New Left's Legacy: What is to Be Done?

Sunday Afternoon 1:30–4

    VI. The New Left's Legacy: What is to Be Done?

       Chair: Peter Collier

       1. Barry Rubin
       2. Sam Leiken
       3. Stanley Crouch
       4. Josh Muravchik
       5. David Horowitz

SELECTED BIBLIOGRAPHY

The following is a list of books that reflect second thoughts or that we have found useful in developing our own second thoughts.

Peter Collier & David Horowitz

Peter Berger, *The Capitalist Revolution*, Basic Books, NY 1987

Vladimir Bukovsky, *To Choose Freedom*, Hoover Stanford, 1987

John H. Bunzel, ed. *Political Passages*, NY Free Press 1988

Whittaker Chambers, *Witness*, Regnery Gateway, Wash. DC 1980

Shirley Christian, *Nicaragua: Revolution in the Family*, Random House NY 1988

Doan Van Toai and David Chanoff, *The Vietnamese Gulag*, Simon & Schuster, NY 1986

Carlos Franqui, *Family Portrait with Fidel*, Vintage, NY 1984

M. Heller and A. Nekrich, *Utopia in Power*, Summit Books, NY 1987

Sidney Hook, *Out of Step*, Harper & Row, NY 1987

Paul Johnson, *Modern Times*, Harper Colophon, NY 1983

Jean Kirkpatrick, *Dictatorships & Double Standards*, Simon & Schuster, NY 1982

Leszek Kolakowsi, *Main Currents in Marxism*, 3 vols. Oxford University Press, NY 1981

Irving Kristol, *Reflections of a Neo-Conservative*, Basic Books, NY 1983

Milan Kundera, *The Book of Laughter and Forgetting*, Penguin, NY 1981

Guenter Lewy, *America in Vietnam*, Oxford Univ. Press, NY 1978

Jose Luis Llovio-Menendez, *Insider: My Hidden Life As a Revolutionary in Cuba*, NY Bantam Books 1988

Charles Murray, *Losing Ground*, Basic Books, NY 1984

Richard Neuhaus, *Dispensations: The Future of South Africa As South Africans See It*, Erdman's Grand Rapids, Michigan 1986

Gerhart Niemeyer, *Aftersight and Foresight*, University Press, Lanham Md. 1988

Michael Novak, *Will It Liberate?* Paulist Press, NY 1986

Norman Podhoretz, *Why We Were In Vietnam*, Simon & Schuster, NY 1982

Jean-François Revel, *How Democracies Perish*, Doubleday, Garden City 1984

Thomas Sowell, *Civil Rights: Rhetoric or Reality?* Wm. Morrow, NY 1985

Armando Valladares, *Against All Hope*, Knopf, NY 1986

Ludwig Von Mises, *Socialism*, Liberty Classics, Indianapolis 1981

261

For more information about the Second Thoughts Project contact:

The National Forum Foundation
214 Massachusetts Ave NE
Washington, DC 20002

Tel. 1–800–622–3388

CONTRIBUTORS

FAUSTO AMADOR was a founder, along with his brother Carlos Fonseca, of the FSLN (Sandinista Party) in Nicaragua. He is presently the Executive Director of COPAN in Costa Rica.

XAVIER ARGUELLO is a former columnist with *La Prensa* and anti-Somoza organizer during the 1970s, and former General Secretary of the Sandinista Ministry of Culture. He is currently a member of the Nicaraguan Resistance.

FANOR AVENDANO was an anti-Somoza activist who now heads the youth movement of the Social Christian Party.

K. L. BILLINGSLEY is a writer based in California. Raised in Canada, Billingsley came to the United States in the late 1960s and was active in the anti-war movement in Berkeley. His works have appeared in the *Wall Street Journal, The San Diego Union,* and *National Review.* He is the author of four books including *The Generation That Knew Not Josef.*

BRUCE CAMERON is a lobbyist for the governments of Guatemala and Mozambique. In the 1970s he was a member of the Coalition for a New Foreign Policy and a lobbyist for Americans for Democratic Action.

PETER COLLIER is co-director of the Second Thoughts Project at the National Forum Foundation. During the 1960s he was an editor of *Ramparts* and active in the anti-war movement at Berkeley. His books include the novel *Downriver* and *The Kennedys: An American Drama; The Rockefellers: An American Dynasty;* and *The Fords: An American Epic.* His articles have appeared in *The Washington Post, Commentary* and other magazines.

263

ARTURO CRUZ JR. is the former Washington representative of the Sandinista Party and Chief Advisor of the Sandinista Ministries of Economic Planning and Foreign Affairs. He is currently an advisor to the Nicaraguan Resistance Directorate. His articles have appeared in *The New Republic*.

DOAN VAN TOAI is the director of The Institute for Democracy in Vietnam. A native of Vietnam, Doan was Vice-President of the Saigon Students Association during the 1960s, leading demonstrations, sit-ins against the South Vietnamese Government. From 1969–1972 he served as an editor of the radical *Tu Quyet* (Self-Determination). He was also a frequent visitor to the United States, speaking at U.S. college campuses against the war. In 1978 Doan left his native Vietnam for the West. He is the author of *The Vietnamese Gulag,* and co-author of *Portrait of the Enemy,* and *A Vietcong Memoir.* His articles have appeared in the *New York Times Magazine,* the *Washington Post,* and the *Wall Street Journal.*

NATHAN GLAZER is a Professor at Harvard University. He is the author of *Remembering the Answers* and co-author of *Beyond the Melting Pot.*

DAVID HAWK was active during the 1960s in the National Student Association, the Vietnam Moratorium Committee and the Dump Johnson Movement. He is currently an Associate at the Center for the Study of Human Rights, Columbia University.

JEFFREY HERF is a Professor at the Department of Strategy at the Naval War College and a Research Associate at the Center for European Studies, Harvard University. In the 1960s he was a member of the RYM II faction of SDS. He is the author of *Reactionary Modernism: Technology, Culture, and Politics of Weimar Germany and the Third Reich.*

DAVID HOROWITZ is co-director of the Second Thoughts Project of the National Forum Foundation. During the late 1960s he was an editor of *Ramparts* Magazine. He also authored one of the earliest books on New Left activism *Student* and a number of New Left books on U.S. foreign policy including *The Free World Colossus,* and *Empire and Revolution.* Since that time he has co-authored numerous books with Peter Collier.

CAROL IANNONE is on the faculty of the Gallatin Division of New York University and an editor of *Academic Questions*. She has written for *Commentary* and other publications.

DAVID IFSHIN is a Washington lawyer. During the early 1970s Ifshin served as the President of the U.S. National Student Association, and as Political Director for the National Welfare Rights Organization. His work has appeared in the *Stanford Law Review, University of Chicago Law Review* and other professional journals.

HILTON KRAMER is the editor of *The New Criterion* and the author of *Revenge of the Philistines*.

IRVING KRISTOL is the editor of *The Public Interest* and *The National Interest* and the author of *Two Cheers for Capitalism* and *Reflections of a Neo-Conservative*.

ROBERT LEIKEN is currently at the Center for International Affairs at Harvard University. During the 1960s Leiken organized and spoke at anti-war teach-ins and was a member of the New University Conference (the faculty counterpart of the SDS). His books include *Central America: Anatomy of Conflict*, and *Soviet Strategy in Latin America*. His articles have appeared in *Political Science Quarterly, The New York Review of Books*, and the *New York Times*.

SAMUEL LEIKEN is writer, former machinist and current President of the Massachusetts Product Development Corporation. In 1960's he worked for the Northern Student Movement, a black counterpart of the Students for a Democratic Society (SDS), and was publisher of *Freedom North*. His articles have appeared in *The New Republic & The Boston Globe*.

JULIUS LESTER was a SNCC organizer in the 1960s and the author of *Look Out Whitey! Black Power's Gon' Get Your Mama*. He is now a professor at the University of Massachusetts, Amherst and has written for numerous magazines including *Liberation*, the *Guardian* and *The New Republic*. His most recent book is *Lovesong*.

GLENN LOURY is a former civil rights activist, currently a professor at the Kennedy School of Government at Harvard and author of *Free at Last? Racial Advocacy in the Post-Civil Rights Era*.

SCOTT MCCONNELL was active in a number of anti-war causes during the 1960s, including his work with Dispatch News Service in Saigon from 1970–1. He is the author of the forthcoming book *Leftward Journey: The Education of Vietnamese Students in France, 1919–1939*. His articles have appeared in *Commentary*, *The New York Times*, and *The New Criterion*.

MICHAEL MEDVED is a TV film critic, co-host of PBS' "Sneak Previews." In the 1960s he led the drive at Yale to terminate the ROTC program and served as chairman of the Vietnam Moratorium in Connecticut. He is the author of numerous books including *What Really Happened to the Class of '65?; The Shadow Presidents*, and *Hospital: The Hidden Lives of a Medical Center Staff*.

JOSHUA MURAVCHIK is currently a resident scholar at the American Enterprise Institute. From 1968 to 1973 Muravchik served as the National Chairman of the Young People's Socialist League. From 1977 to 1979 Muravchik served as the Executive Director of the Coalition for a Democratic Majority. He is the author of *The Uncertain Crusade: Jimmy Carter and the Dilemmas of Human Rights Policy*.

RICHARD NEUHAUS is a former activist in the civil rights movement, and founding member of Clergy and Laity Concerned. He is the author of *The Naked Public Square* and is currently the Director of the Rockford Institute Center on Religion and Society.

MICHAEL NOVAK holds the Jewett Chair at the American Enterprise Institute and is the author of *The Spirit of Democratic Capitalism, Freedom With Justice* and *Will It Liberate?*

P.J. O'ROURKE is a humorist, journalist, author and poet, and the former Editor-in-Chief of *National Lampoon* magazine, and is currently a Foreign Correspondent for *Rolling Stone*. During the 1960s, Mr. O'Rourke took a lot of drugs, although he maintains this did not cause any permanent mental damage. He edited an underground, anti-war newspaper and was generally active in the end-the-war-and -pester-the-hell-out-of-the-college-administration movement. He participated in a number of very violent confrontations at the dinner table and several lesser riots involving the police. He listened to loud music and did the sort of thing that got Gary Hart kicked out of the presidential race. Mr. O'Rourke also wrote poetry that could not be read because words didn't mean anything anymore. He wrecked two motorcycles, and flunked his draft physical by acting psychotic. He met Abbie Hoffman once. His books include *Republican Party Reptile* and *The Bachelor Home Companion*.

MARTIN PERETZ is the editor of *The New Republic*.

WILLIAM PHILLIPS is the editor of *Partisan Review* and the author of *A Partisan View: Five Decades of the Literary Life*.

NORMAN PODHORETZ is the editor of *Commentary* Magazine and the author of *Breaking Ranks, Why We Were in Vietnam* and *The Bloody Crossroads*.

BARRY RUBIN is a Fellow at the John Hopkins School of Advanced and International Studies. During the 1960s Rubin served as the Foreign Editor of the radical newsweekly *The Guardian*. His books include *Paved with Good Intentions, Secrets of State* and *Modern Dictators*. He is co-editor of *The Central American Crisis Reader*.

INDEX